Autobiographical
Reflections
on Southern
Religious History

Frederick A. Bode

John B. Boles

Thomas E. Buckley

Robert M. Calhoon

Wayne Flynt

Jean E. Friedman

David Edwin Harrell Jr.

Samuel S. Hill

E. Brooks Holifield

Lynn Lyerly

Andrew M. Manis

Donald G. Mathews

Albert J. Raboteau

John Shelton Reed

Mitchell Snay

Charles Reagan Wilson

Autobiographical Reflections on Southern Religious History

Edited by John B. Boles

THE UNIVERSITY OF GEORGIA PRESS

ATHENS AND LONDON

© 2001 by the University of Georgia Press
Athens, Georgia 30602
All rights reserved
Designed by Betty Palmer McDaniel
Set in 10/13 Electra
Printed and bound by Thomson-Shore
The paper in this book meets the guidelines for
permanence and durability of the Committee on
Production Guidelines for Book Longevity of the
Council on Library Resources.

Printed in the United States of America
05   04   03   02   01   C   5   4   3   2   1

Library of Congress Cataloging-in-Publication Data
Autobiographical reflections on southern religious
history / edited by John B. Boles.
p. cm.
Includes bibliographical references.
ISBN 0-8203-2297-0 (alk. paper)
1. Southern States—Church history. 2. Church
historians—Southern States—Biography.
I. Boles, John B.
BR535 .A88 2001
277.58'0092'2—dc21
[B]   00-068274

British Library Cataloging-in-Publication Data available

Contents

Preface

On Saturday morning, 8 November 1997, a group of scholars whose research interests focused on the history of religion in the South—most of whom were in Atlanta attending the annual meeting of the Southern Historical Association—gathered at the Candler School of Theology at Emory University for a mini-symposium on southern religion. Wayne Flynt of Auburn University and Charles H. Lippy of the University of Tennessee at Chattanooga had invited the group to meet and talk about their scholarship. After leaving that stimulating meeting, I suddenly realized that in the discussions in which we had all participated, several who spoke made autobiographical references when analyzing their work. Out of that realization came the idea for this book. Upon returning to my home institution I thought some more about the topic and then wrote letters to a representative group of scholars of southern religion. I hoped to identify scholars who helped shape the field from its beginning, and of course I wanted to find a diversity of voices. Practically every person I originally asked to consider submitting an essay agreed, and the resulting collection indicates the variety of paths people followed in pursuit of their scholarly calling.

My invitation letter asked each person to write an essay "that discusses your scholarly work in the context of your background, the social conditions during which you completed your work. . . . How did growing up in the Bible Belt, or not doing so, affect your choice of topics? How did your experiencing of southern racial relations, or being a religious outsider (or insider) in the South, or in the North, affect your choices? Did your own religious background, or absence thereof, help shape your research interests? What was the influence of your graduate mentors? What was the motivation or inspiration for your work? In other words," I suggested, "these are meant to be quite personal essays that help to situate the field as it has emerged in the individual background of the scholars themselves and in the social-intellectual-racial context of the time."

When the solicited essays began arriving in the mail, I was immensely gratified by how thoughtfully and gracefully the authors addressed the questions posed. I offer the essays here in the hope that they allow readers, as it were, to look over the shoulders of one group of historians doing their work. To change the metaphor slightly, the essays provide a window into the minds and motivations of sixteen scholars who have been active participants in the discovery of southern religious history over the last generation. Thanks to the pioneering work of people like Sam Hill, building on that of such scholars as Walter B. Posey, Rufus B. Spain, Kenneth K. Bailey, and others, the contributors to this volume have all been privileged to help create a vital new subfield, southern religious history. I regret that considerations of time and space did not allow me to expand the list of contributors, because the published and ongoing work of a cadre of young scholars is enhancing and complexifying the field in exciting ways. Perhaps in a decade or so a successor volume can tell their stories. Jeremy D. Popkin's 1999 article in the *American Historical Review*, "Historians on the Autobiographical Frontier," and Fred Hobson's book on one genre of southern autobiography, *But Now I See: The White Southern Racial Conversion Narrative* (Louisiana State University Press, 1999), suggest that more attention will be paid in the future to this kind of self-discovery and self-revelation. Jacquelyn Dowd Hall has also shown in her 1998 article in the *Journal of American History*, "'You Must Remember This': Autobiography as Social Critique," how autobiography can reveal much about human motivation. We can hope that more autobiographies will be written and studied in the future. There is no better window on the past.

Note

I would like to thank my graduate assistant Charles A. Israel for checking the citations and quotations in the essays.

Autobiographical
Reflections
on Southern
Religious History

Southern Religion and the Southern Religious

Samuel S. Hill

I may be clearer on what factors were not present when I began to work on southern religious history than on those that were. At any rate, I can declare that a developed, well-established, and formulated field did not exist when my composing began about 1963. Setting sail on this particular sea was my own doing. I simply did not test to see if the wind was at my back.

In the late 1960s, Thomas J. J. Altizer, religion professor at Emory University, was making the rounds as an exponent of death-of-God theology. Speaking without a hint of a southern accent, he repeatedly told audiences that the American South was the best place anywhere for doing theology, because there "people know what you are talking about." He was implying further that they regarded what theologians were saying as important, a subject altogether worthy of consideration.

There is no mistaking that he had been seeing what was there. Doubtless he had observed that religion is *not* one of the two topics people avoid in polite conversation. Just any old exchange among southerners might get around to the subject. Moreover, the expression could be quite explicit, even confessional, evangelistic.

But the lot about whom he spoke did not include professional historians practicing their craft on the same society that was palpably forthright about personal religion. More accurately, in those years only a few had begun to address a dimension of the historical culture that had long been prominent and, surely, influential.

It took the emergence of a new generation of historians to consider such study legitimate and elemental. A seminar at Vanderbilt about 1958 led by Henry L. Swint provided an early boost to the new inquiry. Out of it came some southern denominational histories that were of admirable quality partly because of their avoidance of any tendency toward hagiography. David Edwin Harrell Jr., Milton L. Baughn, and Rufus B. Spain were three of those people—and Harrell was soon to widen his net to include many aspects of southern (and American) religious history. (Harrell credits Walter B. Posey with mentorship; Posey looms as a kind of protofounder of the field.)

Kenneth K. Bailey published in the field in 1964, soon followed by Donald G. Mathews and also this writer—although in my case the field of training and orientation was religion (religious studies). This is not the place for tracking the field's progress, but I will mention two other names that became associated with studying southern religious history during the early 1970s: John B. Boles and E. Brooks Holifield. From then on the enterprise took off. Today its expanse is vast and its importance simply taken for granted.

When I published *Southern Churches in Crisis* in 1966 I was "winging it." Not quite excessive, that way of saying it points out that I had received no training at all, not a course, not a list of books. Indeed, I had scarcely heard a scholarly conversation on the topic in advance of composing that book. Some would want to say that that fact is amply apparent, yet the book hardly went unnoted or undiscussed, it is fair to observe with more than thirty years' perspective. It has been "cussed" as well as discussed.[1]

There were no tradition of scholarship, no seminars, and few studies in print to get me started down this track. Something did, of course; namely, it was my own existential involvement in the "southern church" in interaction with my professional vocation in the academy. A third factor is evident: the social crisis embroiling the South in the 1960s.

An autobiographical essay does not offend by making personal references, it should be superfluous to note. The pertinent features of my family and personal life begin with the notation that my father was a Southern Baptist minister. On his side, and my mother's, there had been several ministers and numerous devout people. It is hardly strange that from my earliest years we all were in church all Sunday morning, all Sunday evening, and at "prayer meeting" on Wednesday evenings. The rest of the week was about church and faith explicitly or as the primary datum of our existence.

On me all of this "took." That I knew no other way is irrelevant. I was a child of the church, finding a home there. Our genuineness is not an evaluation we can make. But my participation and enthusiastic responses are not in doubt. By my teenage years I was exhibiting a "call to the ministry," perhaps even as a foreign missionary.

Just as I had been about to enter the second grade, we moved from Richmond, Virginia, to Louisville, Kentucky. That relocation turned out to have great significance for one who seems to have been born thinking comparatively and observing sociologically. The distance between those two cities was greater than the 581 miles on U.S. Route 60. Virginia Baptist life included many "Baptist bourbons"; they were among my father's most admired mentors and fellow professionals. In Kentucky there were some individuals so oriented, but no tradition of any such sort infused itself into the denomination's life. One way of describing the difference is that the Virginia Baptists were rendered "liberal" by the subjects with which they did not concern themselves, such as "hell fire," liquor as the ultimate abomination, and denominational superiority, even the assumption that only the Baptists were faithful Bible believers. The Baptists of our new home state were not "liberal." (Here I have generalized but not overstated.)

By the time I became reflective I had accumulated a large supply of intra-Baptist encounters, illustrated by the family's westward move and my meeting ministers from different constituencies. Some wrestling with the data I was amassing and what they might mean was a part of me in the college and seminary years. Naturally both institutions were Southern Baptist (both in Kentucky). But for some reason I decided to undertake a master's program in English at a secular university (Vanderbilt, once Methodist) between the second and final years of seminary. Thinking to consider and do that strikes me now as quite unpredictable. The academic year I spent in that program at that place was a season of real growth—toward what I could not then have said. In actuality I was already being lured to the study of religion in southern culture. Doing so was instinctual, of course, rather than formal and deliberate.

In the course of a beneficial thirty-one-month pastorate in northern Kentucky, for some reason, I decided to attend the 1954 World Council of Churches General Assembly in Evanston, Illinois, and a summer pastors' school at Union Theological Seminary in New York. (The company of Southern Baptists at the former was tiny, their representation of slightly larger proportion at the latter.) Comparative reflection was proceeding apace.

A successful application for a Rotary International Fellowship to spend a year in study at Cambridge University only intensified the process that by now was manifestly of four or five years' duration. Having arrived at the conclusion that my vocation was to teach at the college level, I returned to enroll in the graduate program in religion at Duke. The cliché seems to apply: the rest is history.

Well, not exactly. To repeat myself, no courses in the study of religion in the South were offered at Duke or anywhere else—"religion in America" was taught there and at some other institutions, but not "religion in the South." But most of my fellow graduate students in religion were southerners, and the setting of the university then was the regional culture. Quite naturally I was searching, in my own mind asking questions and raising issues about the connection, or lack of it, between the classical Protestant tradition in thought and practice that formed the core of the curriculum and, on the other side, what was within me and around me.

A crucial focus had to do with Assurance, a theological matter that was so central in my background but totally lacking from any treatment in the curriculum, readings, or discussion. This term and concept refer to confidence that the person has been saved, forgiven by God through one's acceptance of Christ as Savior. When evangelism is the central activity of the church because personal salvation is Christianity's central teaching, inner knowledge, Assurance, that you have claimed this salvation is all-important.

Nor was this omission from consideration in the curriculum something entirely new. At Cambridge I had tried to engage a major theologian on the subject. Plenty pious and authentically Calvinist, he sought to respect my interest but had virtually nothing to say about Assurance. (Calvinism's position on Assurance is tantalizing enough that it helped generate Max Weber's "the rise of Protestantism and the spirit of capitalism." That doctrine became an existential concern among many Calvinists. So Assurance is hardly absent from that classic Protestant tradition; it is only supposed to be transcended, ideally, for a people who are meant to put absolute trust in God and not place much stock in personal experience.)

At Duke my Methodist mentor responded similarly. I sensed that in both cases the general subject was present but was folded into a larger framework, probably outflanked without being ignored.

So the issue gestated for some time, as one element in the larger consideration of religion in the South. In 1960, after one year of teaching at Stetson, a Baptist-affiliated university in Florida, I was invited to join the still young Department of Religion at the University of North Carolina. To my great surprise, the stated reason for their selection of me was the desire to acquaint the North Carolina students with their culture's religious heritage in its social setting. That the faculty wanted a colleague who would regard that as his field of study and teaching was altogether admirable; why they chose me was a mystery. That I was an ordained Southern Baptist minister whose graduate work had been undertaken in a major university with an ecumenical faculty seems to have qualified me. Again, no courses, no research, no program of study, leaped off the couple of pages that made up my dossier. Providence, I suppose, or somebody's hunch or gamble.

In any event I soon realized that my new colleagues included many of the primary scholars of the study of the American South. The Chapel Hill setting was conducive, indeed persuasive. Within three years I was fashioning ideas and topics within the not-yet-quite-existent field that is the incentive for the essays in this book.

Later dubbed one of the founders of the field, I can only respond by expressing my gratitude and declaring that I was an "accidental pioneer." That is quite literally the truth. (I suspect it is rare for anyone to set out to found a field of study.) Not many years later Don Mathews, a "fellow founder," put it just right when he noted that he was working on religion in the South "because it is there." Can one think of a culture more influenced by religion than the South? It seems to be more "there" there than most places. To examine the life of that society demands giving attention to that dimension of its life.

In 1964 a colleague from the northern Baptist setting, church historian Robert G. Torbet, and I published a small study, *Baptists North and South*, to coincide with the unprecedented joint meeting of the two major regional white Baptist conventions.[2] Emboldened by that "going public," I suppose, I soon signed a contract with Holt, Rinehart and Winston to write (what became) *Southern Churches in Crisis*.

A postdoctoral year at Harvard University provided more than just time to complete the book and inexhaustible library resources. What deserves mention is the quality and frequency of "interregional contacts." The new book appeared in early 1967, greeted by a Kenneth Woodward review in *Newsweek* and numerous newspaper columns. Mostly the study was praised, but what is significant is how many invitations I received over the next few years to lecture on campuses and to speak to church groups. What I learned in preparation, presentation, and responses was very great. Perhaps it is fair to state that I could not, after all that, have extricated myself from this area of study if I had wanted to. I had a mission, a field of work, and a reputation (some of which I could have done without).

Ken Bailey had published *Southern White Protestantism in the Twentieth Century* three years earlier. Don Mathews had brought out *Slavery and Methodism* in 1965, and John Boles was underway on a dissertation dealing with the Great Revival in Kentucky.[3] Ed Harrell had contributed mightily with his research on the Stone-Campbell movement, as had Rufus Spain on the Southern Baptists and social ministries. Wayne Flynt was thrusting his strong oar into these waters. There were signs that a field was forming. No time to weary or slack.

Repeating, we do not necessarily see with great clarity why we attend to one area rather than others. Don Mathews recently helped me see, thirty years after my launching, why I had felt compelled to investigate "religion in the South." By perceiving that it took someone theologically trained to give an early impetus to the young field of study, I realized that I was grappling with Christian claims of meaning as I witnessed the performance of the southern churches (and not just in the 1960s). Before that observation I had not realized how theological my book was. While not an instance of raw advocacy, *Southern Churches in Crisis* had a point of view, embodied some moral concerns, and, most of all, framed its interpretation in theological terms just as integrally as it did in historical and sociological terms.

As best I can tell, the broadest use of that book has resulted from its effort to describe and categorize the popular theological positions of the most influential churches. My goal was to delineate the reigning popular belief-action system that pervaded the largest number of churches, led by the Southern Baptists, in the region. In the process of making the description simple I did some simplifying, no doubt. But the pictorial attempt to capture the driving force in southern evangelicalism was a virtual first. That is to say, no theology books laid out the animating beliefs of these churches, what had become the standard fare of generalized regional Christianity. Tracts and brief denominational "study course" booklets were nearly the sole source of this single-issue program. Not only could you not find southern evangelistic Evangelicalism described anywhere else in its full import, but you looked in vain to find its lineaments detailed in wider evangelical textbooks.

Obviously, this meant that I first had to figure out what that belief-action system was and then identify ways to communicate clearly the "southern accent in religion." Reckoning with the doctrine of Assurance afforded the key. The pervasive theme, evangelism—the mandate to convert the lost, the unsaved, to faith in Christ—is seen best by taking the next step, that is, toward verification of salvation. If we have been saved, we want to know it. More, it is imperative that we know with certainty that this gift and condition have come into our lives. To be unsure, to entertain any doubt that "I am saved," is to acknowledge that life's greatest event has not occurred. Assurance! This conviction of certainty is sometimes expressed this way: "I was there when it happened." That circular reasoning, far from defective or merely self-reflexive, stands as the ultimate logic in this way of understanding the Christian faith, what we may properly call revivalistic or evangelistic Evangelicalism.

While Calvinism stood in the historical background of much of the South's religious development, that classic approach had been modified significantly. Now instead of focusing on the truth of God revealed, on trusting God for our salvation, and that constituting our Assurance, we may and must know in our hearts, through personal experience, that we have been given that new and eternal standing.

I had begun to grasp why my two respected theology professors were puzzled by my insistent questioning on the issue of Assurance. One trusts rather than knows. Besides, there is something amiss about concentrating on "its" happening to me. The message is what really matters; one's preoccupation is rightly placed there. The authority of the Bible outranks the authority of personal experience and alone is to be trusted.

My mind kept drifting back to an event during college years when, at the end of a sermon in a "youth revival," I realized that what I was urging my listeners to feel and do, to be sure of the authenticity of their experiencing salvation, had never really happened to me in that captious way. The fruitage of those moments of concern (almost panic) was to consummate a dozen years later.

Any persons of this evangelistic persuasion reading this account may argue that I have oversimplified and overstated—a point altogether worth making inasmuch as much else is taught, many other doctrinal positions held. Yet this one matter of experiencing conversion and knowing for sure that it has occurred has been the animating force of so much that is distinguishing about the southern accent in religion.

Was, or is, this a matter of establishing priority? Well, yes and no. I began to reflect on what lay beneath the disposition to rank convictions and claims. I judge that the foundation of such thinking is serial reasoning: there is a number one teaching, a number two, a number three, and so on, in order of importance. In contrast, what I had begun learning about the classic Christian tradition was that it engaged in dialectical and correlative ways of thinking. There are many basic Christian doctrines; there are multiple imperatives. None of them is subject to ranking; rather, they are to be held comprehensively.

I suppose that this progression of thinking impelled my existential quest that doubled as my continuing effort to examine the South's popular theology. So theology did have much to do with my determination to understand. When this is added to a natural sociological interest and an enlarging historical understanding, the incentive to work away at this nascent field was compelling.

When we ponder the emergence of the study of religion in the South, we have to note that an often-stated reason for *not* including it in regional study is the paucity or shallowness of the theology present in that tradition. Presumably, historians and scholars generally are drawn to concept-rich resources. Yet here I am contending that a doctrine, Assurance, that turns out to be many doctrines mutually implicated is fundamental to the heritage and its powerful hold on the southern mind. Now I want to add that this one teaching with many tendrils and tentacles is not so shallow, that what distinguishes "popular southern theology" is pretty solid and firm. The real "culprit" in this case is the elevation of serial thinking over correlative or systematic thinking.

Thus there is some impressive intellectual history to be mined here. Sophisticated Calvinism or Wesleyanism it is not (nor the labors of mind of "the gentlemen theologians" of whom Brooks Holifield has written in his book by that title), but a creative departure from each and both it is. Perhaps the historians' problem with facing and seeing this is not only the apparent simplicity of Assurance and its supporting field of concepts but also southern confessionalism's high degree of explicitness and personal piety (sometimes treated as piosity). There is little doubting that it is safer and more stimulating to wrestle with Calvinist predestinarianism and Wesleyan sanctification than with "I have been saved, and here's how I know that this is true."

By now all historians in our field acknowledge that the development of events and the social-cultural context do not disclose enough of the story of southern religion. Ideas, concepts, and lines of reasoning are present, too, and must be incorporated into our telling the story. Various kinds of historians — social, cultural, institutional, and intellectual — are now demonstrating this in their work.

It has become quite clear that we need to know what the southern faithful believe as well as what are the surrounding social, cultural, economic, demographic, and political factors.

When I am thinking along these lines, I trace back to the pastoral days of my college and seminary years when I served rural churches on weekends, and for the thirty-one months of my single postseminary assignment. Early on I began to wonder what these loyal people were hearing when they listened to a sermon or a Sunday school lesson. I knew their thoughts were not simple acquiescence to the words spoken from pulpit or lectern. They often surprised me with their insights. In a recent essay I had occasion to make this point; here I will repeat or paraphrase what I wrote then.

"People of the church often transcend the popular interpretations of its teachings, or alternatively . . . they reconfigure the standard elements within what is, after all, a several-part body of teaching." If these interpretations were subjected to scrutiny by the stoutest orthodox defenders, they might be branded as some kind of heresy. But these people are hardly heretics. "What marks off their positioning may be a judgment that the whole is greater than the parts, or that a dialectical, not serial, manner of treating the correlated teachings is more authentic. Or still again, they may demonstrate an ironic view of truth and truths; in so doing they affirm that truth, notably truth that is not 'of this world,' is fraught with mystery, has many surprising twists and turns, that it is greater than our logic, and that it may be expressible only as paradox. . . . I have observed many occasions on which the faithful saw quite beyond what they had been taught and heard (even that they did not hold precisely to what they had been taught). A quiet sophistication abounds among the southern faithful, a sensitivity that reveals 20/20 penetration of the message."[4]

Divining what people really believe is finally impossible. But it is not unfair to judge them by their actions. In my lifetime of being one of them, culturally or institutionally or both, I have seen some unexpected behavior. In the ethical area, for example, among them are pacifists, radical communitarians, courageous defenders of civil rights, advocates of the right to life and the right to choose (when abortion was not a subject focused on), and followers who rejected the almost universally accepted middle-class values of earning and spending money. Theologically, some of them are genuinely radical in their suspicion of all human institutions, including the denomination to which they belong, whose leaders all but certify that the body closely resembles the Kingdom of God.

Very impressive to me has been the sensitivity of many who have wanted to bring every person into the Christian fold but who have seen this as one of multiple imperatives, not the only one or even the greatest among the few at the top of the list. This, too, being a subject that I have addressed before, I paraphrase or repeat words written earlier. In the ranks of the faithful are numbers who are "censorious of guilt-based religion"; people who are "particularists without being exclusivists"; some who are "dedicated Christians but without a conversion experience." I was pointing in the same direction when I wrote that there are many "who are not 'in this thing' either for what they could get out of it or because they felt obligated to be." Specifically, that reference is to people whose motives are removed from personal destiny issues—that is, whether one is going to heaven or hell after death—and who being impelled by the divine message of love pay scant attention to the cultural desirability or theological necessity of being among the saved.

Nor are they governed by the assumption that "southern religion" is the purest form of Christianity anywhere or that their evangelical perspective is the sole legitimate description of the high road in faith. More than a few are "fundamentally ecumenical," are "critical of much in the southern EP (evangelical Protestant) tradition," are "incipiently sacramental," are "affirmative toward Jews and their religious identity," are "appreciative of the Roman Catholic tradition."[5] Even in the denominations that have denied the authenticity of other faith perspectives or stood aloof from cooperation with other Christian people, many have quietly yearned to learn about them and happily collaborated with them in joint efforts of service and even dialogue.

Facile assumptions about the universal hold of accepted positions are no more valid among the southern faithful than among any other human groups in free societies. Perhaps I began to perceive this within congregations of which my father was pastor when I was quite young. But I learned it emphatically from those rural people whom I served as pastor on college and seminary weekends. They were far ahead of me in practicing the conviction that God's spirit moves in wondrous ways in disclosing truth and in calling church men and women to relationships that the society did not readily approve. Later, in my early years as a professional intellectual, I often wished that I had been listening to other preachers and teachers every Sunday when I was in the age range of eighteen to twenty-four rather than serving those roles myself (when minimally prepared). But also I came to see how much those "simple" friends had taught me and how much they contributed to my growth. A recent visit to one of those communities sealed this conclusion; a "love feast" greeted our reunion after nearly a half century of absence. They and I had been through some powerful, if quiet, experiences together, some of them in the area of belief in what the Bible teaches.

Turning now from those formative periods to the early years of analyzing religion in the South, I realize how extensive has been my own evolution as a scholar in the field. My readers and I both knew that words written in the 1960s and early 1970s were existentially acute. There was indeed a crisis in the southern churches; within the sensitivity of the young author there were also some stirrings that upset and called for resolution. The 1966 book that seemed authentic to many readers displayed some passion. The printed fruit of those stirrings was not tamped down enough to be "a lover's quarrel," but it was clearly an expression of an insider's response to social conditions. Nor was it always 100 percent fair. More accurately, it got stuck on certain issues and certain manifest opinions at the expense of other positions and practices.

That social crisis brought out some anger and highlighted some aspects of the theology and ethics on which I had been nurtured. Probably I and everyone else could have done without the former, and I do regret some excessive reactions that were not precisely justified and certainly were not constructive. But it does seem accurate to note that these were excessive reactions and not misguided charges hurled at the positions and practices of the southern church. Over time the reactive elements became recessive or even, as I hope, vanished. I believe that some advance is reflected in the transition between my 1966 book and an essay written some six years later, "Toward a Charter for a Southern Theology."[6]

Small signs of growth may have been appearing in the next phase of my work in this still small and young field. They are bound up with my realizing that even the dominant tradition, southern evangelistic Evangelicalism, was anything but monolithic. There were "varieties of southern Evangelicalism."[7] Alongside the "conversion party," embodied by the Southern Baptists, there were at least three other parties, the "truth," the "devotional," and the "service." In the "truth party," what really matters, what denotes authenticity, is correct belief, sound doctrine defined and held to absolutely. The "devotional party" feels its religion, is keenly aware of the Divine Spirit's stirring within, and does not measure genuineness in faith either as converting the world or insisting that there is truth with a capital "T." The "service party" interprets Christian meaning and responsibility as loving concern for the neighbor, all neighbors, in personal and social settings. On this viewing the evangelistic outreach and doctrinal, biblical absolutism are superseded and their significance altered by the call of Christ to "love one another as I have loved you."

Concretely, each person in the four parties almost certainly holds to more than one of the defining emphases. That is to say, most people are truth-minded as well as conversionist, or devotional as well as service-oriented, for example. Hardly any individual concentrates on one to the exclusion of all the others. But there have always been some who have practiced all four, or three at any rate, and who do so without ranking them by priority. We may refer to this cluster of Christians as belonging to the "progressive party" because of their comprehensive approach. When this spirit has appeared in the South, the resulting configuration has resembled classical Evangelicalism, an embodiment that is fairly common among Protestants in the upper Midwest and New England.

Imperfect as this typological formulation is, it does highlight the real diversity within southern Evangelicalism, a condition that was overlooked in my earliest work.

As I was recognizing this condition, and partly because of doing so, I began to address the vast number of component parts that comprise this southern evangelical phenomenon. The original impetus for citing and describing the many parts that make up this whole came from a press editor who discerned that the field was far enough advanced for a reference book (indeed two). Accordingly, I set myself to the task of preparing an encyclopedia. In a labor that was "years in the making," I was forced to think about the "phenomenology" of religion in the South. Two hundred or so fellow scholars joined me in the task; together we developed an inventory of hundreds of aspects of the subject. They had to include historical topics, institutional, doctrinal, and biographical subjects, special regional features, and several other categories. A king-sized product issued from those labors.[8] Imagine what any of us who are among the accidental pioneers learned from this undertaking. My scope enlarged exponentially. One has to judge that the field prospered because so many scholars conceived and described these varied assignments. The volume made its appearance in 1984 and may have signaled the arrival of a new stage in the evolution of the field.[9]

The autobiography of this student of southern religious history and life contains numerous other chapters; attending to them took some maturing over a period of time. I will mention three. One is the comparison of religious developments in the South with those that have occurred in the rest of the country, "the North." This, of course, has been mainly a historical investigation. Tackling the work of the young field from this perspective has proved illuminating. To cite an instance, I gained greatly from realizing how little the demographic factor of immigration affected southern religious patterns, by contrast with its pervasive influence in the North. A second instance was the dominance of the particular biracial nature of southern culture and society. And one more: at about the same time that evangelistic Evangelicalism receded from prominence elsewhere, it became the most popular form in the South, in many respects the regional norm, to remain so for a long time.[10]

The second subject that captured my attention was consideration of the religious life of the plain folk, most obviously in the mountain areas and in rural communities but also in towns and cities. Doing so drew me away from the quasi-official institutions and practices and toward improvisations and new forms. Thus my recent work has taken into account Holiness and Pentecostal people, also independent churches, and modes of expression deemed (or branded) as more "simple" or "primitive."[11] Although others have devoted more work to these forms than I have, I can report how richly my understanding of the entire scene has expanded because of this recognition that came after several years of immersion in the field.

The third fresh angle was implemented in my case by a single invitation: the request that I write for and help plan the Religion section of the *Encyclopedia of Southern Culture*. Without that assignment, for example, it might never have occurred to me that the American South is probably the only locus in Christendom to have placed the sacrament or ordinance of Baptism ahead of the Lord's Supper (Holy Communion) in importance. Seeing that in the South the rite of initiation has outranked the central act of worship for the historic church virtually everywhere else came as a great revelation to me. Methodologically it meant that ritual practice may be as significant as history, demography, and social-cultural phenomena, indeed that ritual practice is itself a cultural force and factor, what might be called a "sacred independent variable." At least one constant characterizes my work all the way through from the early 1960s; namely, that I have been concerned to examine and interpret the religion of the southern religious *on its* (and their) *own terms*. Thus more than most of my colleagues, I have asked about the intentions of the faithful, what they actually say they believe and mean to practice. There are limitations inherent in such an approach. It does risk a parochialism of perspective. It may also skirt the edge of being church history for the churches, devoid of general cultural inquiry and significance. I hope that those extremes have been averted. In any event, there surely is a place for asking who these people are and what they and their institutions stand for.

The central goal of these essays, I take it, is to identify and describe the reasons for which we scholars of religion in the American South began to work on the topic; a second goal is how and why we have continued to do so, with some evolution in interest and a degree of deepened understanding. Much of what has preceded in this essay is my personal reckoning with the route by which I was steered (and steered myself) into the analysis of this dimension of the region's history and life. Beyond any doubt, major incentive arose from the conditions of my childhood and early adult years and from the compelling need to understand the religious heritage and particular religious sensibilities that constituted my being so vitally. Increasing exposure to people from other regional and national forms of Christianity, Evangelical Protestantism especially, played a huge role in my insistence on achieving some grasp of the phenomena. In turn, that prompted areas and venues of study that facilitated the gradual dispelling of provincialism in favor of a wider perspective. It was thus rather predictable that I would investigate historical data and intellectual issues, an activity that led to research and publication. This development generated many interchanges with people both in and outside the region. One thing led to another, and another, and on and on. The whole cloth really is of a single piece.

What effect did all this have upon the autobiography of my personal life? Much, obviously. It has shaped my career, as teacher, lecturer, author, and social commentator. But it also produced a heavy impact on my religious life. This is seen most sharply in the necessity to locate my religious setting somewhere other than the Southern Baptist framework of my rearing. When I was confirmed into membership in the Episcopal Church in 1973 (as a layman), I had no sense of rejecting anything, only of settling into a context of worship, belief, and practice that, I hoped, enlarged and sensitized the faith life that had always been part of me. I really did not change much, either as a person or as a representative of the Protestant tradition. By intention, at any rate, the aim was to foster a richer grounding in classical Christianity. More than a few times my friends and hearers have concluded that I am a "Southern Baptist Episcopalian." I suppose that gets it about right.

For many decades now I have been a professor of religion in both senses of the term. Perhaps it is also fair to say that I am a southern religionist in more ways than one. I confess to liking the complementarities and mutual interaction of my vocation and my personal religious life.

Notes

1. Samuel S. Hill Jr., *Southern Churches in Crisis* (New York: Holt, Rinehart and Winston, 1966).

2. Samuel S. Hill Jr. and Robert G. Torbet, *Baptists North and South* (Valley Forge, Pa.: Judson Press, 1964).

3. Kenneth K. Bailey, *Southern White Protestantism in the Twentieth Century* (New York: Harper and Row, 1964); Donald G. Mathews, *Slavery and Methodism: A Chapter in American Morality* (Princeton, N.J.: Princeton University Press, 1965). Boles's study was later published as John B. Boles, *The Great Revival, 1787–1805: The Origin of the Southern Evangelical Mind* (Lexington: University Press of Kentucky, 1972).

4. Samuel S. Hill, *Southern Churches in Crisis Revisited* (Tuscaloosa: University of Alabama Press, 1999), 6.

5. Samuel S. Hill Jr., "The Shape and Shapes of Popular Southern Piety," in David

Edwin Harrell Jr., ed., *Varieties of Southern Evangelicalism* (Macon, Ga.: Mercer University Press, 1981), 95, see also 89–114.

6. Samuel S. Hill Jr., "Toward a Charter for a Southern Theology," in Hill, ed., *Religion and the Solid South* (Nashville: Abingdon Press, 1972).

7. The title refers to Harrell, *Varieties of Southern Evangelicalism*.

8. Samuel S. Hill, ed., *Encyclopedia of Religion in the South* (Macon, Ga.: Mercer University Press, 1984).

9. For evidence of growth in the field, see John B. Boles, "The Discovery of Southern Religious History," in Boles and Evelyn Thomas Nolen, eds., *Interpreting Southern History: Historiographical Essays in Honor of Sanford W. Higginbotham* (Baton Rouge: Louisiana State University Press, 1987), 510–48.

10. Samuel S. Hill Jr., *The South and the North in American Religion* (Athens: University of Georgia Press, 1980).

11. Samuel S. Hill, *One Name but Several Faces: Variety in Popular Christian Denominations in Southern History* (Athens: University of Georgia Press, 1996).

Crucifixion—Faith in the Christian South

Donald G. Mathews

nswering the altar call of southern history was a gift of grace. Being born in southwestern Idaho among people whose ancestors—some of them abolitionist perfectionists—lie in New Jersey graveyards would not have driven me to study religious life in Dixie. That special commitment came through a long process sustained by a hidden logic based on Christian theology and transformed by study and experience into an attempt to engage the meaning of religion in social life. In this process, the possible meaning of Christ's Crucifixion for interpreting religious creativity among people across racial and gendered lines was transformed into a partially conscious, unexamined principle of judgment that shaped my understanding of Christianity in the Old South. That the powerful and powerless, white and black, invaders and native, high and low, could share a religion preached originally to "liberate" the "captives" and later to shackle them was not a surprise, but what the sharing meant remained elusive. That such sharing meant a "cross," that is, suffering, victimization, and death was clear; that it meant the ability to endure that suffering in victory (resurrection) seemed a fair inference. That the inversion of power and value in crucifixion privileged black Christians over white also seemed plausible. In continuing research on religion in the South since emancipation, I began to realize that the Crucifixion of the Christ and its place in Christian culture demanded greater attention. The reason is sobering, for as the white South became more "Christian" in the late nineteenth century, it also became more dramatically and publicly violent as the high priests of southern white culture sacrificed blacks on the cross of white supremacy. While becoming oriented to issues inherent in studying white violence and punitiveness in the

South as well as in the religious consciousness itself, I was asked to write about why I came to study religion in the South. It was then I realized that it was because my grandfather had been lynched.

That event was one of the most traumatic events of my father's life. He remembered its effects upon him until the day he disappeared into an Alzheimerian mist, asking over and over again, "Why? Why? Why?" No one had to ask "Why—what?" The "what" had for years afflicted my own life as well as that of my mother and sister. The story was an essential part of familial lore; my father told it over and over in various ways whenever he began to agonize over his tortured psychological inheritance in a narrative that always began with the first of two terrible nights in Oklahoma almost ninety years ago. The story was about John Demerest Mathews, a man who believed friendship to be sacred and the need for social approval to be contemptible. He planted cotton outside Chandler, Oklahoma, at the beginning of the twentieth century and married a preacher's daughter with whom he settled down to create the family life of which he had been deprived in his youth. Lula Waltman Mathews had birthed three sons and a daughter before the night with which the family myth began. There had been rumors of race riots in faraway cities—my father could remember that; but he was told such things would not happen "here," and he usually included in his story the fact that he had played with African American children when very young.

The narrative would gather momentum as he recalled the night when a black father fled with wife and child to John Mathews's house in terror. He ran through the kitchen door screaming, "John, they burned me out and they'll kill me." "No," replied John Mathews, "they won't. Git out a' here an' don't look back." Then he parceled out the guns—one each to Lula, and two sons, Bill and Leo (Arthur was too small), and maybe one to his daughter, too (this part of the story was vague); he herded his little band out into the yard and turned over the grain wagon behind which to protect them from the mob he knew were coming. And they did. "We want the nigger!" someone had shouted. Silence. "Who wants to die first?" John Mathews had supposedly called out. No one volunteered.

The night became the longest of my father's life. The mob—sentimentalized by social historians who never faced one—shouted insults. From behind the wagon, Lula was probably praying; John was probably cursing, which is the same thing, his second son would later say. By first light the standoff was over; the trespassers had slipped away; but John Mathews was not popular with his neighbors for having made them cowards over a "nigger." Someone took a shot at him, and a braver man tried to knife him; once a plug of poison fell out of an apple he was peeling for his children. The mob was still convened in their own collective mind and bided their time; when Lula finally got the nonreligious John to go to prayer meeting, they abducted him as he left the church. They unhitched singletrees from wagon tongues and beat him, as they thought, lifeless. They left his body beneath a tree beyond the church. "Nigger lover!"

John Mathews did not die, but he was changed: broken and with a profound fury that would erupt as if he were possessed. (At this point someone will insist that since Mathews did not die, he had not been lynched; there is a special place in Hell for those enamored of such nicety.) The trauma that damaged John Mathews's brain and mind and body and family unto the third generation was deep and broad and long lasting. Into his nineties, John's second son, Leo, would scream in terror during a fitful sleep as in his dreams his father raised a chair to crush him as he had tried to do in real life. A gentle father who had never struck his children before punishment by the mob now seemed compelled to express himself in a violence that increased the trauma of the original violation with every reenactment inflicted upon his family. The fury in John's battered self erupted all too often upon his second son until at last he fled to the home of a minister of the gospel whose name was Cloud. The dignified little man was one of the Native people who had been settled in Indian Territory; he was one of the wise—both a judge and spiritual leader. In Cloud's home and under his care the boy found safety, and when, almost fifty years later, I was graduated from Yale University Divinity School, Leo brought me to Cloud for a blessing. It was a liminal moment; Cloud witnessed to the power of the Holy Spirit; all we could say was "Amen."

John Mathews's son had come to religion out of violence and terror. Religion had given him the resources to contend with the demons unleashed by a lynch mob robbed of its African American prey. John Mathews, crippled in body and soul, lost his farm even as he was losing his family—he could no longer work as he had. As many others had done before him, he decided to find a new life in the West. His son, having been nurtured among holiness Methodists in

Oklahoma and Kentucky, now returned to help the family farm in Idaho. The fear of violence—his father's, his own—never left Leo; the raised chair seemed ever to be raised over his head like a guillotine as the symbol of betrayal, lost innocence, unjust punishment, and perpetual danger. It is not surprising that his view of salvation was in the suffering love of Crucifixion as he and his family wrestled with the trauma bequeathed them by the mob.

John Mathews's son raised his children within the church and under the threat of his own violence; his daughter-in-law reared them in gentleness. She remained sanctuary against the rage and anguish of her tortured husband. Himself the victim of physical violence, Leo tried to restrain his own capacity for it; he never struck his daughter, he struck his son only once, and he threw his wife to the floor twice—three blows that came at the end of such fury that every storm within the family thereafter sobered, frightened, and disciplined them all. Given the epidemic of domestic abuse in this country and the millions of bruises, wounds, and terrors inflicted upon women and children, these three blows by comparison were infinitesimal. But John Mathews's son lived in fear that the rage he felt so very often in his depression and after disappointment would explode into the physical violence that throughout life afflicted his dreams. He did abuse his family with threats and emotional blackmail; he did leave scars seared into his children's consciousness with their own dreams and fears; but he was a good man, and he found healing in the love of a forgiving Christ. His family, too, found redemption in the same love—though experienced in varied ways. The family was united in nausea at any expressions of anger, including their own, and an almost automatic revulsion at the ease with which it was possible to scapegoat classes of people in American culture. This political leap no doubt came from seeing oneself as a potential victim of unreasoning and potentially violent anger. This self-consciousness would never prevent harming other people in fractured relationships, but it would perpetuate feelings of sorrow, shame, and guilt. That the son should have felt compelled to study religion and that the daughter should have expressed her religion in a gentle but tough-minded and loving feminism are not surprising.

Discovering religion within a family mythos makes sense; but how does one discover the South in Idaho? The region somehow became in my father's imagination an abstraction for where he had lived in innocence before the savage fall; the presence of African Americans in his valued past seemed to symbolize the capacity of humans to reach across boundaries to live in harmony—at least that was the way he told it. He had somehow decided—possibly during his years at a holiness academy in Kentucky to which Cloud had sent him—that he was a southerner; the many displaced southerners around his father's home in Oklahoma may have reinforced the view as well. For whatever reasons, Leo would bristle at discussions scapegoating the South for racial hatred even as he warned his children that they were never to take their cues as to how to behave or whom to value from "the crowd." The majority, John Mathews's son would say, are always suspect: beware their hysteria, hatred, and treasured beliefs; beware especially their tendency to punish others for their own failures and fears. John Mathews's son thus aroused in his own son and daughter an interest in a region where they had never lived and a curiosity about the contradictions in their father's attachment to Dixie, which their mother—a commonsense Presbyterian through her Scottish ancestors—often observed had achieved its identity through lynching black men. An antisocial suspicion of stereotype, the "crowd," and "popularity" was mixed with curiosity about the South and racism and was eventually interpreted through a neo-orthodox Christian identity. An abstraction of the "South" and a family myth of violence identified with that abstraction somehow became real for me in graduate school at Duke University, although the "reality" was and remains filtered through the eloquently expressed imaginations of valued "in-laws," the works of W. J. Cash and Lillian Smith and the gospel of Martin Luther King Jr.

Studying religion in southern history can thus begin with the idiosyncratic, which is not exactly an innovative theoretical insight, but the idiosyncratic may nonetheless have substance. My original commitment to studying history was part of a religious commitment, a statement conducive to such perverse misinterpretation that a wiser person would immediately delete it. There is far too much tasteless and self-important posturing about "Christian" conviction in the public forum now to make the confession entirely felicitous; but history seemed to come alive only after reflecting on a theologian's observation that the first inquiry of ethics is always "what is happening," and because the theologian was also a historian, the question became "what was happening?" A neo-orthodox understanding that Christianity is one of many religions under suspicion of idolatry before judgment of the Cross made all historical judgments as relative as a postmodern mystic could wish and revealed most pretense to purity as delusional; it also sustained a curiosity as to the Word in historical experience. "Religious" commitment became the study of ordinary believers wrestling with ethical problems, fully cognizant that ethical issues often contain within themselves the contradictions (judgments) that reveal the nature of human pretensions. Thus slaveholding may be understood as "Christian" because Christians said it was, but with the necessary understanding that all parties to a relationship must be polled, including slaves (well, most especially slaves), and that all moral judgments in history are so relative to position and knowledge that they must be understood before the Cross—that is, in such suffering as that of the God of victims. This last phrase is, of course, scandalous; why conceive of the past in moral terms that privilege sacrifice?

The response can be complex, but the short answer is because religion is about the textured relationships of community in which identity, obligation, connection, and destiny are learned and projected back into collective life. Religion calls attention to the ethos and action of people within the webs of meaning that they themselves (as Max Weber pointed out) have spun. Economy, polity, class, gender, and race all impinge, and they help us understand "what was happening"; but religious historians study moral beings who value the sacred as well as food, drink, and raiment. To be sure, studying theologians or ecclesiastical publicists can distort our understanding of the past as well as of religion, and fascination with perceived exoterica such as devils, witches, spirits, and "wonders" can deflect attention from the presence behind such things as are invisible to modernists who sometimes fondle too intimately the mysteries that others have regarded with awe. Religious life is the portal to an imagined sacred and moral reality that historians distort if they nurture an aloof and naive incredulity when approaching it; we await others who can learn from the brilliant insights of David Hall.[1] The moral engagement that seems inherent in past human (religious) encounters with evil—naming it, understanding it, escaping it—does not require that we be executioners or partisans, to be sure, but it should imply an openness to the moral dimensions, especially in suffering. The suggestion is "openness" and an approach to our subjects through the "prayer of humble access."

Reference to the God of victims, of course, privileges a theological construction in historical understanding; and while this may be permitted in the pulpit and at the mass, it is absolutely forbidden in writing history. Demythologized, the Crucifixion, as the symbol before which the believer is awestruck at the revelation of what Transcendence "endures" and thus transforms in the worst experiences of human life, effected an awareness both of "victims" and the possibility of their salvation (being unvictimized) through identifying with the Transcendent. The crucified sensibility was subconscious and incomplete. Not until confronting the meaning with which African American writers freighted lynching in the New South and rereading with greater understanding the role of scapegoating in religious ritual as explained by René Girard was it possible to become conscious of the early bias favoring "victims": those punished by the mob, that is, "society." Antislavery romantics, abolitionists, slaves, slave preachers, missionaries to slaves, and women unconsciously became surrogates for the profane, stubborn, and cruelly punished John Mathews because they, like him, were perceived by the scholar as positively working out their lives contrary to the ordinary rules of the world.

This vicarious substitution was made quite unconsciously even though studying a "Methodism" that had been created by the preaching of "Christ and him crucified," a phrase that became the shibboleth of Wesleyan preachers. This crucified sensibility, encouraged by alienation among circuit riders from family, power, and ease, made them liminal enough to see what responsibilities enforced by marriage and ownership would later conceal: that ownership of human beings "in Christ" was a very strange kind of discipleship. A crucified sensibility must have been essential to the attraction of the Wesleyan message for both women and slaves, to whom the preachers for a time appeared to be especially sensitive. The ferocious chant of James Meacham when contemplating slavery was, after all, "Blood, blood, blood, blood, blood."[2] And Francis Asbury, when especially depressed by combating the Devil and Virginians, could seek out women as media of God's grace precisely because they were not men— that is, they were not considered authoritative by the world—thus revealing the power of the crucified sensibility.[3]

Some time ago, I was criticized on the Internet for believing that slaveholding was un-Christian. This occurred a short while after I had attacked (with more sarcasm than *caritas* and decorum condoned) the self-congratulatory proposition that "Christianity" had abolished slavery. Observing, on the contrary, that the conjunction of Union armies, absconding slaves, opportunistic radicals, political calculation, Abraham Lincoln, and a Republican Congress should receive credit, I recalled that slaveholders had, after all, defended their position by pleading Christian stewardship; their "Christianity" had not made them abolitionists. This position was dismissed as an example of secular humanism, almost as insipid a comment as the original homily on the abolitionist effect of Christianity. The exchange was not very profound—the Internet is more conducive to "gunfights at the OK corral" than to effective engagement—and my resident conscience (my wife) ordered me back to research and writing. The knee-jerk contempt for "Christian" claims of moral superiority is based on historical observation and the prayer of confession—"we have done . . . we have left undone." Any value system professing the highest ideals may be evaluated according to those ideals; the historian knows that Christians enslaved people and created rules to govern them accordingly in various cultures, all of which claimed to be part of Christendom. Professing, "spirit-filled," pious, and self-righteous Christians sustained slavery in such a way as to justify arguing that it was a Christian institution. Arguing that slaveholders, however, were "less" Christian than abolitionists makes no more sense than arguing that they were "more" Christian. The standard of judgment is not "Christianity," but the Cross. Raising this standard is a faith commitment, to be sure, but not rigidly sectarian. H. Richard Niebuhr once observed in class that the crucified sensibility lay indeed in responding to the Cross, but that in the 1950s (when he said it) perhaps a more appropriate way of conveying the message was to understand it through the sinister shadow and terrible stench of the Gas Oven. If the crucified sensibility attempts to evaluate institutions and relationships from the standpoints of those least benefited by them and is therefore a continuing moral commitment, it spares no one—including the self and nothing—certainly not the American Holocaust.

This faith commitment distorted southern history but did not make me hate the South. My parents and sister lie in southern graves, and I have too many friends, former students, respected associates, and loved ones living here to hate it. To be sure, I cannot elevate the South as an idolatrous standard of judgment on American culture; but since all scapegoating is tinged with evil I am dismayed at the self-righteous bigotry of nonsoutherners. (Slavery was an American [human] institution; racism is an American [human] disease.) My distortion, such as it was, lay in abstraction, which I learned partially in my father's stories, partially in the pulpit, and partially in W. J. Cash's and Lillian Smith's eloquent meditations on the South.[4] In these arresting texts lay the "lessons" that prepared me to hear the Word from the Preacher King so that the "South" became the chancel within which to receive the fusion of religion and history. Doing history became "doing" religion, too, possibly to compensate for the pulpit and vestments I had given up, but certainly to understand the ironies of moral conflict and the inversion of value and the valuable that lay within both history and religion.

To be sure, I read concrete church records of blacks and whites in conversation together about their different as well as similar experiences of the Word. I read concrete diaries, journals, periodicals, letters, hymns, theology, sermons, prayers—even census returns (the essence of concreteness), all the things that students of religion in history read. I gagged at the sin of abstraction and then committed it myself. After partially engaging the dramas within one denomination relative to slavery and expanding my view to include all denominations, I attempted next to understand the creative dynamic (and irony) of evangelical innovation in the Old South as captured in Isaiah's phrase to preach "liberty to the captives." The change in focus within the book from white to black—from antislavery fantasy to proslavery rationalization to African American "salvation"—should have suggested a crucified sensibility and at the same time should not have distorted what had happened because I thought that that was what "had happened" in the Old South. I thought African American spirituality did convey—ironically to be sure—the plenitude of Christianity when masters failed to live up to their own best understanding of Christian stewardship, frozen as it was in a self-congratulatory literalism and self-serving imperviousness to the Spirit. But by editorial decision, my "Liberty to the Captives" became *Religion in the Old South*—identified not with the descent from the Cross of a black Christ painted by a black artist, as I had requested, but by a white preacher preaching to white people.[5] So much for authorial intent!

My abstraction of the South also included an abstraction of "evangelicalism." For this sin I hope someday to atone. My goal, as I understood it when I first conceived of attempting to convey the dynamic that drove religion in the South to the Civil War, was to address not the entire religious spectrum—the manuscript was, after all, to be only 310 pages—but the triumphal mood that characterized the churches and the expectancy of African American Christianity before Deliverance. That mood I understood as evangelical because the adjective characterized the kind of preaching that elicited the experientially legitimized New Birth and launched a sanctified life authenticated by an authoritative Bible. Subjective confirmation, aggressive expansion, expressiveness, and openness to witnessing by charismatically chosen preachers meant that women and blacks assumed spiritual responsibilities that later were partially and formally rescinded (thus ending genuine "evangelicalism"). The adjective was natural for Protestantism in early-nineteenth-century America; Timothy Smith used it in 1957, and so had Robert Baird in 1856.[6] The word *evangelical*, however, conveys a greater agreement than existed, as more than one—but especially one, thank you—of my students has pointed out. And, truth to tell, the word later became so catholic that many Presbyterians were inappropriately included. Putting Robert Lewis Dabney, for example, in the same category with John Jasper, Toney Stevens, Frances Bumpass, and Francis Asbury is absurd.[7] Indeed, during the nineteenth century in the South, the word *evangelical* lost specific meaning. Religious contentiousness in the South at the end of the nineteenth century, together with changes wrought by Sunday school materials and fundamentalist controversies (which some historians deny even existed in the South), changed whatever evangelical consensus prevailed in 1860. Even then, the ecumenism inferred from the term was never very strong, which was why each denomination published its own tracts and periodicals during the Civil War.

If we have too readily accepted an evangelical ecumenism, we have ignored something else that almost all southern Protestant Christians did share. That common feature has been called "otherworldliness"; orthodox Christians called it "salvation"; folk dialecticians expressed it in the simple choice between Heaven and Hell. The word *otherworldliness* was frequently used in the late nineteenth and early twentieth centuries as a pejorative description of religion that focused not on worldly service to Christ but on an imagined heavenly home in which one who had accepted Christ as savior would spend eternity. Requirements became ambiguous as loved ones were allowed in with such forgiving regularity as to make eternity (for better or worse) one long family reunion. Yet in most ways, religion in the South has been decidedly "this-worldly." The culture is, after all, not conducive to the contemplative life, and worship here is more expressive of communal solidarity than an overwhelming awe of Creation or breathless wonder at Redemption. Baptist church records recount over 175 years of disciplining members for this-worldly actions such as "fornicating," fighting, or walking in ways other than those of the Lord. When the forum for settling such things became public instead of congregational policy, this world was the field, not Heaven. Most churches were very fastidious about behavior; historians studying it have avoided "otherworldly topics" as if they were unusual indeed.

Decidedly not unusual was discourse about whether or not one was "saved." Although this theological concern became an ecclesiological one—whether or not one had joined the church—salvation remained such an issue that a few dissenters complained of a pervasive antinomianism. Antinomianism insists that the right kinds of religious "experience," "doctrine," or "mood," as opposed to right action or conduct, characterize people who are "saved." The mood privileges subjective orientation or "spirituality" over ethical or moral action; it explains salvation as a privileged state rather than an agonistic process and may appear to be heedless of social realities such as power and injustice. This privileged status, although theoretically received as a divine gift, is nonetheless achieved—one of the many contradictions that infused salvation in the South. The antinomian mood was continually challenged, however, by the demands of Christian discipline. Early evangelical preaching in the region had attacked Unitarianism and Deism as mere moralism but then had proceeded to emphasize morality enforced by mechanisms that revealed shame and induced guilt. Here was religion working very much through mundane dramas of punishment and probation to remind Christians of the cosmic drama of Crucifixion. This mystery, which took place simultaneously in history on Golgotha and in eternity before divine justice, was essential to Christians' self-understanding, but historians have failed to discuss it, possibly because it was, well, too *other*worldly.

The Bible, the New Birth, the power of the Holy Spirit, and the Atonement were the four manifestations of divine action that suffused religion in the Christian South. Of these, the Bible was the most palpable among both whites (as a book) and blacks (as a history, as an experience, and then as a book). The New Birth and the power of the Holy Spirit were capable of being experienced by both races, but believers were accepted as Christian only if they accepted salvation through the most mysterious of God's works. The Atonement was elusive to understanding because it could not be sensed; it had happened to the Christ in substitution for what should—but could not—have happened to humans. The distance between God and humans resulting from the Fall became ever greater as they struggled in the quicksand of their own sinfulness. Because their sin was against Infinite Being, an infinite penalty was demanded, so God Himself substituted for humanity and satisfied justice by Christ's sacrifice on the Cross. The Christian paradigm of salvation rested on an act of violence in which efficacious action was divine. Theologically literate people in the South argued about the Atonement, to be sure. Strict Calvinists and Arminians disagreed on whether Christ had died to save the elect or (potentially) all who called upon His name. They and others argued about the nature and degree of sinfulness for which humanity was condemned, the nature of innocence imputed to the saved, and the security of salvation once received; but a rough consensus among whites was achieved on one thing. Salvation lay in the "substitutionary" satisfaction paid by the Son. Such a drama seemingly based on the ancient sacrifices of a barbarian people made absolutely no sense to Unitarians such as Thomas Jefferson, who much preferred to base their Christianity upon the life, philosophy, and "morals" of Jesus. In this alternative understanding, emphasis was on the efficacious action of human beings. There were vast differences between Savior and Teacher.

Those differences and their implications sustain my continuing interest in southern religion because they reveal the importance of violence and punitiveness in white southern religions. I have taught courses on women and religion and on public religion in American life, as well as on the religious lives of southerners, and although I am interested in the ideology of fundamental Christians and how women stretch the theological boundaries of male "orthodoxy," I remain "in the South." If the original source of my interest in southern religion lay beyond consciousness in the responses of my grandfather and father to acts of violence resolved in religion, my continuing curiosity focuses on the relation between religion and southern society at the intersection of salvation, violence, and popular culture. I have begun to think about the implications of the punitive ambience of soteriological dramas. The substitutionary sacrifice was, of course, not imprinted upon the imaginations of all believers in the same way; anyone who understands theological discourse knows that even for dogmatists it is pliable to the moods and situations of those for whom it is meaningful. The standard sermonic emphasis in salvation—for all whites but Quakers—would have been the substitutionary Atonement with its emphasis on blood and penalty. The focus on penalty would have come naturally to the continuous insistence on sin and guilt that drove the disciplinary dramas of the local church; Lillian Smith in her brilliant *Killers of the Dream* reminded her readers that children in the South knew that the lesson of Christian culture was that Someone had the right to punish you. Punishment pervaded the South in ways that did not infuse the North. The social system was based upon it. We do not have to believe all Theodore Dwight Weld told us in *American Slavery as It Is* to contemplate the meanings of scars on the bodies of slaves; we do not have to believe that masters lashed their servants every month to understand slavery as driven not only by paternalistic negotiation but also patriarchal discipline. The penalty, if not always physical, nonetheless had to be sure and memorable; the only good master was one whose rule was enforced with certain punishment.

Punishment was essential to the rules of life beyond slavery. Bertram Wyatt-Brown among others has reminded us that local opinion defined justice, and justice emphasized appropriate retributive reaction on the part of individual men as well as the community to every action that betokened challenge to the moral economy. Balance was maintained by personal as well as collective violence, informal as well as formal force. The honor that Wyatt-Brown has shown suffused southern culture rested on a broad understanding among men of personal boundaries, self-respect, public esteem, personal integrity, and the implied threat of violence against anyone who impugned or violated any of these aspects of a man's self-worth. Penalty was to be sure and visible for those who breached the rules of honor. Punishment was inherent in all associations where authority was exercised: whites should punish blacks; fathers should punish wives and children; and if the self-esteem of the patriarch were involved, punishment seemed all the more appropriate beyond that justified by the offenses themselves. To be sure, communities could moderate punishments assigned by law, but punishments there would be—and as direct, immediate, and sure as the punitive could make them. Southern whites were convinced that somehow someone should "pay" for all offenses; it was a widespread assumption about the moral orderliness of life. If legal punishment seemed to languish, dawdle, or fade, the community could always impose it illegally. Wyatt-Brown believes that lynchings such as that of Leo Frank by a mob in 1915 demonstrated "the power that common folk held" in such matters; he notes that the man who tried to save Frank's life, Governor John Slaton, "was disgraced," at least by the mob.[8] So was John Mathews.

If Christianity had once seemed to erode honor among the patriarchy by appealing to slaves and women and disciplining men for violence, it also buttressed honor with its own punitiveness. As the *Southern Presbyterian Review* insisted in 1847, the "primary and chief end of punishment is to vindicate the right."[9] That on this point duelists and theologians could agree was not surprising. The theory of atonement that made salvation credible in the South had originally been fabricated in a culture of honor at the beginning of the twelfth century by the chief theologian of the Norman conquest. Southerners claimed that the theory was biblical: the proof texts were of course piled high and deep. The problem was that before Anselm became archbishop of Canterbury in 1093 and wrote *Cur Deus Homo?* (Why the God-Man?), those texts had not been interpreted as southerners would later interpret them. Anselm was an Italian thoroughly versed in the legal systems of the West from Lombardy through Rome and Normandy to England, a background that shaped a theology of satisfaction. His society was an "honor society" of which the most historically minded of southern patriarchs would have been proud, one in which a clear hierarchy assigned to each person a place in which he or she was to be rendered what was due him or her according to rank. Anselm's view of the universe was imagined according to the same structure and values so that it was logical for the lawyer in him to understand sin as the infringement of God's honor. "Whoever violates another's honor," Anselm wrote, must "make restoration in some way satisfactory to the person they have dishonoured." With God's honor breached, cosmic orderliness was disturbed, and justice—God's justice—required either satisfaction or punishment. Since only Infinite Being could pay satisfaction sufficient to substitute for the penalty of dishonoring God, only the God-man (Deus Homo) could do so. God's mercy or love did not effect salvation but, rather, Christ's satisfaction. This explanation survived the Reformation in Calvinism, Methodism, and radical Dissent into the nineteenth century.[10] That it lasted longer among believers in the South than in the North was partially the result of experience within a system structured on punishment. Penalty through pain not only sent a Pavlovian signal to effect action but also functioned to "vindicate the right"; this meant that both individual masters and the ruling class as a whole would be "vindicated." As the historical process continued, vindicating the "right" eventually meant vindicating white supremacy.

The violence at the crux of Christian salvation would be remembered in images of hell and damnation. The flagellant tongues of angry preachers who mistook their own passionate hatreds for divine wrath could move imaginations already trained by parents to believe in their own culpability. Forbidden thoughts, shameful fantasies, half-understood references, and careless disappointments inflicted upon fondly remembered parents could become fuel for the furnaces of Hell. The petty failures of adolescence could become sins, and broken promises in once brightly envisioned relationships could become crimes against the holiness and honor of God. Or, as every scholar of southern religion knows from reading the astonished confessions of the past, one could be taken unawares by what were at first perceived as banal, formulaic, unctuous performances and sent reeling in such inner confusion as later to confess "conversion." Or one could simply move through the conversional process in lock step with cousins, siblings, or acquaintances as befit someone in his or her late teens and move into adulthood through a fairly prosaic experience of grace. The standard confession, whatever the actual internal state of the soul, was of sin for which one deserved death; hope lay in satisfaction paid by Christ ("He died for me") and acceptance into the company of "faithful people." Whatever the intensity of faith, the formula was clear: punishment and satisfaction were at the very center of what it meant to be sensible to the moral universe. In the South, the moral economy was affected by the need to control not only the self but also others; if even God paid "the price," so must those others.

Students of southern culture and theorists of "satisfaction" both agree that "vindicating the right" demanded "blood." Although a few scholars seem to believe that the conflict between honor and Christianity was resolved before the Civil War by a slaveholding ethic and the masculinization of faith, it is more likely that whatever resolution was achieved came much later through a more traumatic process is which large numbers of young men as well as "society" learned the meaning of sacrifice. Experiences in warfare made the blood sacrifice at Golgotha more accessible than all the theology of divine retribution that ever urged conversion before the war. The sacrifices at Antietam, Gettysburg, and Petersburg left stigmata on both body and soul that could never be erased.

Whether or not the widespread activity of lay preachers, missionaries, and chaplains in Confederate armies actually converted enough men to have masculinized southern Christianity by the 1880s, some of us—especially Kurt Berends, who has studied the matter more efficaciously than anyone else[11]—believe that the wartime experience was crucial in making the South a more pervasively religious region by making men "more religious." Salvation through sacrifice was the message; the sacrifice of comrades to the Lost Cause—as some came to think of it—could enable survivors to understand both "sacrifice" and "vicariousness." The punishment endured as a penalty for defending home and family and the shame inflicted by having lost, perhaps, as Christ had "lost"— for the "salvation" of others—could all have the cumulative effect of enabling an almost unconscious receptivity to Christian salvation. The culture itself, quite beyond the chastened and chastening tone of insistent preachers, many of whom had themselves shouldered arms for the Confederacy, seemed to endure a Golgotha that politicians could transcend through their own understanding of the Redemption that came after the hated Yankee attempt at "reconstruction." Christian and white southern myths coalesced.

That violence lay at the center of southern white salvation is obvious. A sacrificial death that resets the moral balance of the universe sanctifies violence. Crucifixion that thus dramatized the seriousness of sin, as Anselm and his heirs intended, also justified the death of the victim. This theological sleight of hand placed the believer in the ironic situation of shouting with the mob at Pilate's court, "Crucify him!" and in the blasphemous position of identifying oneself in the Crucifixion paradigm with the wrath of God. The gospel teachings that one was never to avenge oneself, never to do violence, and always to overcome evil with good were, of course, completely at odds with the theology of violence. Jesus' message that God's power is disclosed in weakness and His act of obedience in bearing the Cross both call attention to victims of violence—what our violence does to victims—in such a way as to change those to whom God is disclosed by grace. Thus changed, the believer identifies not with wrath but with those victimized, as was the Christ by the violence of humanity, and in the process realizes the love of God in the transformation of self. Sensing the love of God, she or he is freed from the need to seek those upon whom the wrath of God must fall (scapegoating) and, instead, seeks those to whom the love of God is revealed in healing.[12] In this rendition, the Crucifixion remains essential to understanding the restored relationship with God and focuses not on the necessity of punishment but on salvation from violence in the love of God. This view has been understood as a "way of the Cross" historically alternative to that of Anselm, and it is a view associated with African American Christians among many others. God's identification with the victims of violence was clear in the prominence of Exodus in African American Christianity; Moses, who could not enter the promised land, was a type of the Christ whose death was entry into it. That the Christ's sufferings redeemed their own and infused them with theological meaning was essential to African American Christians; it was natural during the white terror of lynching for them to imagine a black Christ upon the Cross.

Religion pervaded culture more completely in the New South than ever before. Economic growth, lynching, and religion waxed in strength over the region at the same time. If connections among the three remain elusive at present, it is nonetheless clear that the punitive theology of white Christians supported a scapegoating mentality that moved beyond laws governing work and political relationships into the realm of the sacred. For historical reasons as well as social-psychological motives, whites needed to control a dependent black labor force as completely as possible and eventually to remove blacks from the political process. "Scapegoating" refers to the attribution by whites of responsibility for any failure in interracial relationships, public safety, and civil policy to black people. By virtue of their difference and social status, African Americans were always available for whites to blame. Scapegoating African Americans was nurtured by military defeat in a culture of honor where failure elicited shame, an emotion that rewards those who feel it with a conviction of their own innocence. When honor was offended by blacks' stepping out of traditional place, southern whites responded with individual, collective, legal, or illegal violence "appropriate" to the offense inferred. That whites could punish African Americans more or less with impunity meant that punishment acted not only to vindicate the "right" but also to assign guilt—African Americans were guilty because they were punished. In any adversarial traffic between whites and blacks, being "black" always made a person "wrong" by definition.

This assumption eventually sustained a movement that fused racism, anxiety, sexuality, and religion into systems of racial segregation. The goal was social purity and control achieved by establishing boundaries, etiquette, taste, values, and sacred (white) space into which it was forbidden that the "other"— the designated incessant alien in a "white" land—should venture. Systems varied in detail throughout the South, something that always kept traveling blacks on their guard, but they all distanced African Americans from whites and established boundaries to fabricate a cherished whiteness (purity) in which African Americans by definition could not share. Any breach of boundary or closing of distance by blacks violated not only human but also divine law. Originally based on a sexual fascination with the "other" expressed in "anti-miscegenation" laws and segregated school systems immediately after the Civil War, segregation was given impetus by the economic progress of African Americans during the waning years of the nineteenth century. Economic competition was not the only source of conflict; another lay in the presence of African Americans as a class of permanent "victims" perpetually available in the whites' worldview. This racist understanding was religious in the sense that it established sacred standards of purity sustained by complex systems of symbols, signs, and values. These were understood to reflect a moral reality that motivated actions and dictated moods believed to be absolutely legitimate. Violating taboo meant that something sacred had been violated. To be sure, there were political and economic motives behind segregation, but the energy that sustained the system was commitment to purity. This commitment could interpret any contact, gaze, comment, or act that reflected ambiguity, confusion, or challenge with regard to race as sin that demanded punishment.

The religion of segregation was but one expression of a general cultural concern with purity and authenticity. Holiness movements sought to separate true from false Christians. Purifying Baptists continued to insist on adherence to landmarks that established their authenticity as the only true Christians. Charismatics of both races sought new openness to gifts of the Spirit that attested to the power of God far better than did choirs and organs. Behind these impulses was the suspicion that certain people, especially members of the elite, were not always the faithful believers that they professed themselves to be. Demands for receiving a second blessing (holiness) after the first (conversion), or celebrating spiritual gifts, or scrutinizing seminary professors, or reaffirming covenants, or recommitting self in revival, or resisting corrupt reunion with Yankee co-religionists all reflected a widespread fear of pollution. A sense of danger was amplified by alarmist newspapers that "reported" an African American crime wave. The danger was more clearly focused by the broadly shared image of the "black beast rapist" that threatened the very source of white purity. This pervasive cultural commotion was magnified and focused by campaigns to disfranchise African Americans as the "source" of danger and pollution in the political process. With *segregation* sacralizing a culture already anxious about authenticity, and with *honor* sustaining the obligation to punish those who broke taboo, the history of brutality against African Americans seemed to justify further violence against a class that was by definition to be victimized.

Moving the narrative from atonement to the culture of lynching continues my original motivation for studying southern religion. Since ambivalence is natural whenever I use the words "southern religion," I need to explain why I did not write "religion(s) in the South," because doing so will help begin to explain why the intersection of atonement, violence, lynching, and "South" has become so important. Ambivalence is natural because there is not yet a very good historical understanding of the rich variety of ways in which religion has been lived in the southern United States. Religious studies scholars are, to be sure, engaging the ethnographic realities that will eventually allow further historical studies rooted in place and developed over time. Students should be encouraged to study the broad range in experiences of religion in the South to challenge the assumptions of a monolithic, possibly abstract, South. Understanding the flaws in doing so, however, I must persist in studying "southern religion" because the religious meaning of the historical experience of the "South" is so important for addressing current issues of race, violence, and religion in the United States. By "southern religion" I mean the assumptions and discourses of people living in the South relating to their ultimate concerns about morality, holiness, "salvation," and the sacred that distinguish them as a people from other regions of the country. Such a study is not to elevate the "nation" as a standard of evaluation, but to see something of the "American" in the "southern" experience and the other way around. That at the present time the subject is "the Southern Rite of Human Sacrifice," a study of religion in lynching, is not surprising given the religious violence in the world beyond as well as in the bombing of women's health centers. I hope to clarify the religious supports of the punitive mentality that not only justified lynching black men but continues to justify the death penalty and takes more pride in prisons that make humans "pay" than in mental health facilities that heal. A culture of vengeance persists.

Lynching and religion belonged together in ritual, sacrifice, celebration, and the feelings of justification associated with shed blood. There were, to be sure, those among the "religious" who also opposed and resisted violence; one understanding of crucifixion—of Holocaust—is that human violence will end only when humans are repelled by the violence in themselves. Many southern white Christians, when confronted with the loathsome cruelties of lynching mobs, were absolutely nauseated at the ghastly horrors that could occur in their society. Offended though they were, they often believed, however, that what had happened had been a perversion of justice and not a revelation of what white justice meant for black people. They still identified African Americans as those deserving of punishment as a class because they continued to believe that the source of lynching lay not in the false assumptions of white innocence and the morality of punitive violence, but in the equally false assumption of a criminal ethos in African American culture. They did not understand the violence that lay at the core of their own best understanding of God. This is not to say that Anselm's theory of atonement made southern white Christians lynch black people. Anselm is not the culprit; he was merely trying to answer his question—*Why the God-Man?*—in ways his own society could believe. What he did, and what his unknowing southern disciples did after him, was to sanctify rather than heal violence. That African Americans—from their own experience with white punitiveness—could understand the appropriate Crucifix as one in which the Christ is black was consistent with a crucified sensibility revealed in the Gospels as well as Resurrection.

The impetus for continuing to study southern religious history thus comes from the broken bodies and souls of historical and familial records; it comes from theology and revulsion at racism and violence. The theology is driven neither by the elaborated structures of scholasticism nor a precious obsession with orthodoxy but by an Incarnational faith ever in process as befits the genre and is ever shaped by historical evidence. I am not a historical theologian—I lack the requisite gifts; I work with historical actors and ideas. The hurt I myself have inflicted prevents satisfaction at displaying the evil that pervades some of our best human aspirations; but the evil is there, and since it is there, historical actors will themselves reveal it. That the South is a credible site of historical inquiry is validated by the many excellent historians who study it. That religion sets the region off from the rest of the country as a credible site for study salvages most projects from antiquarianism. That the sacred in a culture transcends religious institutions is a reality that has finally pushed me outside the familiar surroundings of the churches and into the culture they helped to shape. This expulsion is a relief even though I have yet to publish its results.[13]

The opportunity to think autobiographically about choosing to write on religion and the South has revealed the theological ground of my continuing work, and this is a source of some surprise. I have always been aware of a homiletic tendency because I have always been impressed by the Word inherent in the crucified sensibility. Trying to explain my calling has made me more aware of the connection between subject matter and theological bias. Those who have borne the burdens of racism, sexism, and violence have been crucifers—cross bearers after Simon of Cyrene—who have broken the power of violence to dictate completely the meaning and achievements of their lives. Bearing violence as if crucified, many have also been "resurrected." Writing history may help understand why and how both conditions occurred—questions for the stubborn John Mathews, such men as laid him low, and the countless millions subjected to the fury and vengeance of the powerful. Maybe then we can entertain the meaning of such punitiveness for understanding the American present as well as the southern past.

Notes

1. David Hall, *Worlds of Wonder, Days of Judgment: Popular Religious Belief in Early New England* (New York: Knopf, 1989).

2. James Meacham in William K. Boyd, ed., "A Journal and Travels of James Meacham, Part 1, May 19–August 31, 1789," *Historical Papers* (Trinity College Historical Society) 9 (1912): 94.

3. Donald G. Mathews, "Francis Asbury in Conference: Women and the Spirit," unpublished paper being revised for publication by the author.

4. Wilbur J. Cash, *The Mind of the South* (New York: Knopf, 1941); Lillian Smith, *Killers of the Dream* (New York: Norton, 1949).

5. Donald G. Mathews, *Religion in the Old South* (Chicago: University of Chicago Press, 1977).

6. Timothy L. Smith, *Revivalism and Social Reform in Mid-Nineteenth-Century*

America (New York: Abingdon Press, 1957); Robert Baird, *Religion in American; Or, An Account of the Origin, Relation to the State, and Present Condition of the Evangelical Churches in the United States* (New York: Harper and Brothers, 1856).

7. John Jasper was a famed African American Baptist preacher in Richmond before and after the Civil War; Toney Stevens was the African American leader who baptized and buried Charles Colcock Jones, who was famous for his championing of missions to the plantation slaves of low-country Georgia; Frances Bumpass was the holiness editor of *The Weekly Message* of Greensboro, N.C., before, during, and after the Civil War; and Francis Asbury was the founding bishop of the Methodist Episcopal Church in the United States of America. Robert Lewis Dabney was a Presbyterian theologian who mistook his own punitive Calvinism as gospel, railed against the barbarian hordes of northern abolitionists for despoiling his homeland of Virginia, and screamed at his Presbyterian colleagues for daring to consider the training and ordination of African American presbyters. For the latter, see Hilrie Shelton Smith, *In His Image, but . . .: Racism in Southern Religion, 1780–1910* (Durham: Duke University Press, 1972), 239–40.

8. Bertram Wyatt-Brown, *Southern Honor: Ethics and Behavior in the Old South* (New York: Oxford University Press, 1982), 369, 371, 380–91, 397, but especially 440.

9. Edward Ayers quotes this statement in *Vengeance and Justice: Crime and Punishment in the Nineteenth-Century South* (New York: Oxford University Press, 1984), 54.

10. As translated in Timothy Gorringe, *God's Just Vengeance: Crime, Violence, and the Rhetoric of Salvation* (Cambridge: Cambridge University Press, 1996), 93, but see also 85–103, 169.

11. Kurt O. Berends, "'Thus Saith the Lord': The Use of the Bible by Southern Evangelicals in the Era of the American Civil War" (Ph.D. diss., Oxford University [St. Catherine's College], 1997).

12. René Girard, *Job: The Victim of His People* (Stanford: Stanford University Press, 1987), 34, 122, 140, 159; Gorringe, *God's Just Vengeance*, 213–15; Robert Hamerton-Kelly, *Sacred Violence: Paul's Hermeneutic of the Cross* (Minneapolis: Fortress Press, 1992), 15, 21, 25, 27, 28; Richard B. Hays, *The Moral Vision of the New Testament: A Contemporary Introduction to New Testament Ethics* (San Francisco: HarperSan Francisco, 1996), 317–46.

13. But see Donald G. Mathews, "The Southern Rite of Human Sacrifice," *Journal of Southern Religion* 3, http://jsr.as.wvu.edu (23 Aug. 2000).

Recovering the Underside of Southern Religion

David Edwin Harrell Jr.

I was born in Jacksonville, Florida, the son of a physician and the grandson of a sharecropper from Coffee County, Georgia. My father was caught between two worlds, a transitional figure who through chance and hard work escaped the farm, graduated from medical school at the Medical College of Georgia, and attained respectability and modest wealth as physician. Nonetheless, he remained a South Georgia cracker, steeped in populist values and prejudices. By the time I was a teenager, my father owned a substantial amount of farmland in South Georgia, which was worked by about a dozen poor black and white families. Each summer my sisters spent their vacations at Ponte Vedra Beach getting a tan, but I was shipped off to the farm to labor in the fields, live with sharecroppers, and experience the world that had shaped my father. There was nothing contrived about the decision to send me to the fields; it was not part of a grand scheme to teach me some higher moral lesson. Rather, from my father's point of view, the farm defined who we were—and I was cheap labor. I think that my career as a historian was shaped largely by the insights I gained before I was twenty years old. Among other things, I never imagined that the sweaty, arduous world of the tobacco field was less real, nor its people less estimable, than were the country club at the beach and the kids in the pool.

My family became members of the Churches of Christ when I was a youngster—my oldest sister first, I at age twelve, and my father last. Ours was a classic conversion story that started when my sister began attending Sunday school with an aunt and ended in long, home study sessions between the amiable local preacher Gilbert Shaffer and my father. Earlier, we had been a typical religious, but unchurched, southern family. My mother's background was

Methodist; my father's parents had been Free Will Baptists, and most of his nine siblings were Pentecostals. Once converted, my father was devout and committed. Encouraged by the doting elderly sisters in the congregation, I soon began making talks around town. By the time I was fifteen, I had preached in a variety of little churches, both white and black, and though my choosing to preach was a rational decision rather than a calling in the Churches of Christ, many felt that I was destined to be a notable preacher.

Athletics and other matters received most of my attention during my high school years—not academics. Like many staunchly religious southerners, I balanced a rambunctious flirtation with the world with a genuine religious commitment. A bit of carousing and a fairly serious case of adolescent rebellion ended with my expulsion from two public high schools in Jacksonville, and I was shipped off to Abilene, Texas, where Abilene Christian College operated a small private school for the children of devout members of the Churches of Christ in the area and for seemingly incorrigible cases from elsewhere. My heartening graduation from high school was followed by short tenures at a junior college in South Georgia (where I was scheduled to play basketball) and at Abilene Christian College. In both schools I flunked most of the courses I attempted, and I returned to Jacksonville to await directions from my father. Assuming that my forte would not be in the academic world, I spent two years as the manager of my father's Ford agency in the small South Georgia town of Alma, where I partied, played poker, dated a robust Bacon County lass who was Miss Georgia in 1950, and preached. In 1950 I received greetings from Selective Service in Jacksonville expressing an interest in sending me to Korea; my father, desperate to protect his only son, persuaded the local congressman in South Georgia to offer me a congressional appointment to the Naval Academy. No one, including me, had high hopes that I would be able to pass the entrance exam to the Naval Academy, but after a year of prepping at Marion Institute in Alabama, I did pass and was admitted to the academy. During my junior year at the academy, my father, fearing that I was about to be overcome by the world, persuaded me to offer a letter of resignation on the grounds that I had decided to enter the ministry and to enroll at David Lipscomb College in Nashville. I arrived in Nashville in the fall of 1953, entered school, and began preaching in the rural churches around Nashville. I graduated from Lipscomb after one year, majoring in history largely because it was the shortest route to satisfying the graduation requirements.

With no pressing career options appearing on the horizon, I applied for admission to the graduate school at Vanderbilt University, where I had taken a few undergraduate courses during my senior year as an exchange student, to pursue a master's degree in history. My highly suspect undergraduate record (though I had been a decent student at the academy and had a good record at Lipscomb) was partly compensated for by a good GRE score, and Vanderbilt admitted me on probation. Soon off of probation and the recipient of a teaching fellowship, I was quickly drawn toward a study of my own religious roots. My master's thesis was entitled "A Decade of Disciples of Christ Social Thought" (1958), and my Ph.D. dissertation was "A Social History of the Disciples of Christ, 1800–1866" (1962).

My interest in the history of the American restoration movement was entirely predictable; I continued to live in the dormitory at David Lipscomb College while a graduate student at Vanderbilt, married a Lipscomb coed, and preached in the beautiful village of Kingston Springs. Other factors combined, however, to encourage me to write about the Disciples of Christ. First, the Disciples of Christ Historical Society was located just one block off the campus of Vanderbilt, providing me with nearly all of the primary materials used in my dissertation. Second, Professor Henry Lee Swint, probably the most popular director of graduate students during my years in the history department at Vanderbilt, taught an early version of social history that emphasized the nonpolitical dimensions of the past and stressed the importance of religion. Professor Swint's social history emphasis, and his meticulous editorial temperament, influenced a generation of students. Third, a number of Vanderbilt students who either graduated shortly before I did or were my contemporaries wrote dissertations on religious topics. Kenneth K. Bailey, whose *Southern White Protestantism in the Twentieth Century*, published in 1964, was a pioneering study of religion in the South, had been one of Professor Swint's students and was something of a mentor to those of us who followed.[1] Two other Vanderbilt dissertations preceded mine and gave some direction to my work. The first, a social history of the Cumberland Presbyterian Church, was completed by Milton Baughn in 1958, and the second, written by my contemporary Rufus B. Spain, was a social history of the Southern Baptist Church and was subsequently published in 1961 under the title *At Ease in Zion: A Social History of the Southern Baptists, 1865–1900*.[2]

My dissertation on the Disciples of Christ was the last of this flurry of religious studies written by Vanderbilt University history graduate students in the

1950s and early '60s. Most of us were also indebted to the encouragement and example of an earlier Vanderbilt graduate who should be regarded as one of the pioneers in the recovery of southern religious history, Walter B. Posey. His early books on the Baptists, Methodists, and Presbyterians in the South, and his later study of religious controversy in the South, were among the earliest efforts to explore the religion of the region.[3] Walter Posey was a mentor to me, as he was to others interested in the history of religion in the South; he presided over many of the early sessions on religion at the meetings of the Southern Historical Association, including my own first presentation at the 1962 meeting, entitled "The Economic Thought of a Southern Frontier Sect."

My dissertation was published in 1966 by the Disciples of Christ Historical Society under the title *Quest for a Christian America: A Social History of the Disciples of Christ to 1866.*[4] With commendable graduate student zeal, I had completed far more research than I could include in one volume, and in 1973 I wrote a second volume entitled *The Social Sources of Division in the Disciples of Christ: A Social History of the Disciples of Christ, 1865–1900.*[5] In those two books I tried to bring a degree of historical detachment and a broader historical perspective to the history of the Disciples movement. In particular, I explored the influence of economic, social, and sectional factors on the major division of the movement at the beginning of the twentieth century that resulted in the separation of the Christian Church (Disciples of Christ) and the Churches of Christ. In a series of articles, the most important being "The Sectional Origins of the Churches of Christ," published in the *Journal of Southern History* in 1964, I outlined the sectional and economic parameters of that division, pointing out that the Churches of Christ were the southern, economically depressed fringe of the movement.[6] My early writings on the Disciples of Christ/ Churches of Christ movement were often judged to be deterministic, though I never dismissed the theological dimensions of the movement's history, and I never imagined that sociological models and theory offered all-sufficient explanations for religious conduct.

I continued to write occasionally about the Disciples of Christ/Churches of Christ movement after the 1960s, though my major research projects have taken me away from the history of my own religious heritage. At the same time, I continued to be an active member of the Churches of Christ, a frequent speaker in churches, and an active participant in some of the more important debates that defined the movement in the second half of the twentieth century. My interest in the history of the movement was rekindled in recent years by the work of a younger generation of historians interested in primitivism in general and the Disciples tradition in particular, especially the writing of Richard Hughes of Pepperdine University.[7]

I had long believed that the sociological patterns that I noted in my social history of the Disciples of Christ movement in the nineteenth century had been replicated in the twentieth century. In 2000, the University of Alabama Press published my book *The Churches of Christ in the Twentieth Century: Homer Hailey's Personal Journey of Faith*.[8] This book combined an institutional history of the Churches of Christ with the biography of one of my father's friends, Homer Hailey. It provided a theological and sociological road map through the schismatic and convoluted history of one of the South's most successful religious groups in the twentieth century. This book is also my most intimately personal piece of historical writing, telling a story in which I am an actor and, at times, a partisan spokesman. For those most interested in understanding the complexities of such an intellectually unstructured movement as the Churches of Christ, I believe that this book tells much about the driving forces behind the incessant feuding and fracturing in the church; I suspect that it also tells much about me.

By 1967, when I became a member of the faculty of the University of Georgia, I had begun to cast about for topics that might have a broader interest than my research on the Disciples of Christ. My next research excursion, which was to lead me from one topic to another over the following three decades, was influenced by the work of my Georgia colleague and longtime friend Willard Gatewood. Willard had helped persuade me to move to Georgia from the University of Oklahoma, and later, in 1981, he urged me to follow him to the University of Arkansas. When I arrived in Athens, Willard was working on a book on fundamentalism that was later published by Vanderbilt University Press;[9] he had also written about racial issues and the black experience in the South. Our daily lunch sessions, generally shared with G. Melvin Herndon, Warren Kimball, Emory Thomas, Will Holmes, and others, often focused on such topics as southern religion and race. In those discussions, those of us who were southerners probed our own southern lives.

Not much was being written about southern religion in the 1960s, but my southern and religious past did not fit well into the scholarly studies that did appear. Understandably, the most prominent studies of southern religion during the sixties explored the dominant white evangelical hegemony—the majority "southern church"—and its almost monolithic commitment to racial segregation. As I thought back on my own forays into the pulpits of black Churches of Christ, and even more, as I remembered the Pentecostal world of my aunts and uncles in South Georgia, it seemed to me that there was another racial and religious cosmos in the South that looked little like the churches described in Bailey's classic *Southern White Protestantism in the Twentieth Century* or in Sam Hill's fervent *Southern Churches in Crisis*.[10] This was an experiential insight, reaching back to memories of my father's intimacy with the black community in Jacksonville, Florida, to my own experiences in Bacon Country, Georgia, when I had lived and labored with sharecroppers and laborers both white and black, and to memories of joyous religious services in which black and white hands reached upward to praise the Lord in unison in the sultry haze of canvas tabernacles.

My quest to expose this underside of southern religion led me first to read the sociological literature that confirmed there was another racial and religious South. The world of southern poor white religion had been explored by Liston Pope in the classic book *Millhands and Preachers*, and a number of other sociological studies had probed the intertwining of class, caste, and religion in the South.[11]

In my 1971 work *White Sects and Black Men in the Recent South*, I told the story of the racial views and behavior of a variety of minority southern religious groups including the Churches of Christ, Free Will Baptists, Primitive Baptists, and an array of holiness and Pentecostal churches.[12] The racial views of these groups rarely mirrored the views expressed by either the middle-class segregationists who dominated Baptist and Methodist congregations in the South or the liberal elites who railed against the prejudices of their middle-class parishioners. I connected the aberrant racial rhetoric and behavior of the southern sects to the complex structure of southern society, arguing that the South was far more culturally, racially, and religiously diverse than the stereotypes imposed on the region by the media and, to some extent, confirmed by most scholarly writing about southern religion. Personally, I felt that I had recovered a piece of my own past; these were the black and white southerners whom I remembered from my days on the farm, people who worked together, social-ized and ate together, and attended one another's church services. Southern poor white society was hardly free of racial prejudice, but it was a place where rigid middle-class taboos were often discarded and egalitarian biblical rhetoric sometimes was taken at face value.

I came away from this research on the racial attitudes of southern sectarians with two compelling insights that I thought deserved further commentary. The first was a reenforced conviction that southern religion was much more di-verse than generally portrayed, as was southern society. I was convinced that the notion that southern religion was a monolithic evangelical Baptist-Methodist-Presbyterian hegemony was misleading. It seemed to me that much of the writing about southern religion was too neat, accepting at face value the claims of educated white ministers (conservatives and liberals) who proclaimed that they spoke for the South. In an effort to highlight the diversity of religion in the South, I coordinated a conference at the University of Alabama in Bir-mingham in 1979, and the proceedings were subsequently published in 1981 as *Varieties of Southern Evangelicalism.*[13]

In my own paper at the conference, entitled "The South: Seedbed of Sec-tarianism," I outlined the explosion of new religious groups in the South in the late nineteenth century, the two most successful being the Churches of Christ and the Pentecostals. In spite of the appearance of huge Pentecostal mega-churches in the middle-class suburbs of the South (and the nation) by the 1970s, most scholars still portrayed southern religion as a solid evangelical hegemony. In subsequent conferences in the 1980s, I pointed out that Baptists and Meth-odists in the South were themselves quite diverse; their churches splintered by class and theological fractures.[14]

A second insight that I gained while writing *White Sects and Black Men in the Recent South* led me out of the South to explore a phenomenon that has changed the religious demography of the world. Among the remote and virtu-ally untapped collections of materials that I visited while doing research on that book was the Holy Spirit Library housed at Oral Roberts University. There I discovered a treasure trove of periodicals and tapes documenting an extraordi-nary post–World War II revival in the Pentecostal subculture. This extraordi-nary and coherent revival was well known to Pentecostals but more or less in-visible to other Americans. Well into the 1970s, public knowledge of the

Pentecostals was pretty well gleaned from condescending journalistic parodies about "holy rollers" and "fake healers."

Once again, my past prepared me to engage the Pentecostal revival at a serious level. My earliest forays into writing about southern sects had often elicited dismay from my colleagues and peers who viewed my writings as irrelevant excursions into religious ephemera. Even if such oddities existed out in the country and in cinder-block slum churches, why study them? My memory constructed a different reality. As a youth, I had attended vibrant Pentecostal services in South Georgia and, just to see the show, had visited an Oral Roberts tent revival in Jacksonville. I could still remember thousands of people flooding the Roberts tent—sitting, standing, and shouting for hours on end awaiting the moving of the Lord. I thought something rather auspicious was happening under the canvas in the 1950s. At the end of the twentieth century, many religious historians judged the booming Pentecostal/charismatic revival that was beginning to erupt under the tents of the healing revivalists to be the most significant Protestant story of the twentieth century.

My 1975 book *All Things Are Possible: The Healing and Charismatic Revivals in Modern America* described the remarkable revival that erupted among the American Pentecostal subculture in the years after World War II.[15] The initial thrust of the revival came from huge healing campaigns conducted by superstar evangelists who, in turn, created lucrative independent ministries. These independent evangelists, including such pioneers as William Branham and Oral Roberts and such later superstars as Jimmy Swaggart, Kenneth Copeland, and Pat Robertson, pioneered religious television programming, exported their message and techniques to thousands of evangelists in the developing world, and built a stunning network of organizations to further the revival. By the 1970s these evangelists, particularly Roberts, had facilitated the spread of the Pentecostal understanding of the gifts of the Holy Spirit into mainstream Protestant churches and the Roman Catholic church, fashioning a booming charismatic movement at the end of the century.

All Things Are Possible rescued the history of millions of people who felt that they had witnessed a move of the Holy Spirit that had changed the world. As it turned out, they were correct. The book became something of a Bible for insiders; after twenty-five years it remains in print, having sold around 50,000 copies. The repute of *All Things Are Possible* among Pentecostals brought me about as close as I will ever expect to come to fulfilling my author's fantasy. For two years in the early 1990s I served as the director of the American Studies Research Centre in India on a Fulbright grant. One evening in 1994, while my wife and I were dining in a Madras hotel, two western couples entered the restaurant. "I'll bet those are Pentecostal missionaries," I told my wife, confident that after thirty years of research I could determine the religious affiliation of most people by their look and manners. After dinner, I walked over to their table and asked: "Are you missionaries?" As I had expected, one of the men confirmed that they were. "With what group are you affiliated?" I continued. "You wouldn't know," he replied. I pressed on, insisting that I might know something about their denomination. He asked, "Have you ever heard of a man named William Branham?" "Actually," I replied, "I think I was the first person who ever wrote about William Branham." After a long pause, he asked, "Are you David Harrell?" They were missionaries from South Africa who had painstakingly studied *All Things Are Possible* at their bible college. They hurried to their rooms to gather cameras and camcorders and returned to record their meeting with the author of their text. Elusive celebrity found me in Madras.

All Things Are Possible was one of those rare and happy literary ventures that enjoyed both wide approval and acceptance among my academic peers and a large popular audience, especially among the people whose history it chronicled. For students of American religion, it gave some insight into the reasons behind the dramatic expansion of Pentecostal religion in the last half of the twentieth century; for insiders, it rescued their past from oblivion. Many of the leaders of the healing revival were pleased with the book because it took them seriously and tried to tell their story fairly, employing a style and tone that was neither dismissive nor judgmental. In the years after the publication of the book, I interviewed many independent pentecostal evangelists who had long been wary of talking with outsiders.

A fortress mentality aimed at protecting themselves from probing outsiders was nowhere more pronounced than on the campus of Oral Roberts University. In the basement of the library of the Tulsa university was a vast archive of materials about the life and ministry of Roberts that had never been cataloged or used—tapes, transcripts, letters, and films. By 1975, I was convinced that Oral Roberts was a seminally important twentieth-century religious leader; he was far more than the caricatured "fake healer" so often portrayed by the media.

Roberts had been the single most important evangelist in the huge Pentecostal healing revival of the 1950s and 1960s, as well as its most respectable and responsible. He had also been the most innovative, ever seeking new techniques of fund-raising, welcoming theological innovation and, particularly, the trailblazing new uses of the media that became the foundation of the massive religious television empire of the last half of the twentieth century. Roberts was also a catalytic figure in moving the Pentecostal message into mainstream Protestant churches and the Roman Catholic church in the 1960s. Beyond his achievements as the founder and builder of a large religious empire, Roberts was a complex and charismatic man whose life explained much about the course of American Pentecostal history.

I had met Oral Roberts casually while writing *All Things Are Possible*, but I had never been able to secure a personal interview. Roberts held me at arm's length, as he did reporters and others interested in writing about him. He had endured a lifetime of ridicule and was understandably publicity shy—unless he controlled the story. I wanted to write a book about him, one that would take him seriously and treat him fairly but at the same time probe the anomalies and inconsistencies in his life and in the Pentecostal subculture; however, that could hardly be done without access to him and to his archives. I made a number of inquiries to Roberts in the last half of the seventies; all of them were rebuffed, and I moved on to other things.

When I moved to Fayetteville, Arkansas, in 1981 to teach at the University of Arkansas, Tulsa and Oral Roberts University lay a tempting three hours to the west. I renewed my efforts to get an interview with Roberts, writing, "Someone outside your own movement should write an objective treatment of your life and impact, because I believe that you are one of the most important Protestant leaders of the twentieth century." The times were right, and the letter got me a luncheon appointment. At some point during a cordial lunch in Oral's office, shared by his wife, Evelyn, and Theology School Dean James Buskirk, Oral made the intuitive decision (as he made all decisions) to give me complete access to himself, his family, all of his close associates, and his massive archival collection. After nearly two years of research, I wrote a large book about Roberts and his ministry, *Oral Roberts: An American Life* (1985).[16] The Indiana University Press sales department and I had visions of Roberts offering the book to his list of two million partners in return for some spiritual reward, but that was a pipe dream. Oral and Evelyn Roberts liked my book and presented me with a moving autographed copy, but the ministry was not interested in a book that portrayed the evangelist, as he put it, "warts and all." On the other hand, although the book received generally good reviews in the national press and from academic readers, many felt that I had been overly generous in my judgment of the world's most famous healing revivalist.

By the time I finished my book on Roberts, Pat Robertson had embarked on a political journey that led him to enter the race for the Republican nomination for the presidency in 1987. After some negotiations, Robertson agreed to grant me an interview and give me access to his staff so that I could write a biography of him. My book *Pat Robertson: A Personal, Religious, and Political Portrait* (1987) was a brief exploration of the religious environment that lay beneath Robertson's political conservatism.[17] The book was intended to clarify for Robertson's friends and enemies the tangled world of evangelical, Southern Baptist, Pentecostal, and charismatic ideas that lay behind his political conservatism and that gave him a political constituency.

In one sense, my excursion into Pentecostalism and the charismatic movement led me away from the South; on the other hand, I always believed that the movements and people I studied in the 1970s and 1980s were an extension of the southern religious experience. Pentecostalism had strong southern roots and flourished in the South in the years after World War II. And I was quite aware that most of the evangelists who graced American television screens in the 1970s and 1980s spoke with a southern accent—Billy Graham from North Carolina, Oral Roberts from the Little Dixie section of southeastern Oklahoma, Jimmy Swaggart from Louisiana, Jerry Falwell and Pat Robertson from Virginia.

In several articles written during these years, I argued that after World War II southern religion had been exported to the entire nation, indeed, to the entire world, by these evangelists through crusades and the use of the media.[18] Jonathan Edwards gave a New England flavor to the Great Awakening; from Charles G. Finney to Billy Sunday, late-nineteenth- and early-twentieth-century evangelism in the United States smacked of an agricultural Midwest in transition; after World War II the South was the breeding ground for world-class preachers. Anthropological theories about the stresses present in cultures in transition offered useful models for understanding the cultural transformation of the South after World War II. The changing South of the late twentieth century exported its writing, its country music, and its rambunctious Holy Ghost religion.

In 1988, I wrote a letter to my old friend Edwin Scott Gaustad, proposing that we write an American history textbook that took religion seriously. That long and laborious work is scheduled to be published in the near future. Other authors became involved through the years, including Randall Miller, John Boles, Randall Woods, and Sally Griffith. Similar to most of my other work as a historian, my proposal to Ed Gaustad undoubtedly was motivated by memories. For many years, I read and taught versions of American history that said little or nothing about the past that I had experienced. Where, I wondered, were the devout, church-going, God-fearing southerners who had populated my childhood—and my adult life? Historians are not particularly to be blamed for this omission. We all write about the past that interests us, that seems important to us, that has some broader consequence. I thought that religion passed those tests. Religion interests me, it is important to know that millions of Americans are still devout Christians, and one simply cannot understand the politics and culture of the United States without taking into account the continued pervasiveness of faith at the beginning of the twenty-first century.

Long before postmodernism and deconstruction raged into the public arena, I think that most historians were quite conscious that we do not pretend to write antiseptic higher truth. On the other hand, neither was I ever comfortable writing with an overt agenda, though I understand that others feel a commitment to do so. I have always believed that all history, and particularly religious history, is best when it is written with a degree of detachment and objectivity, mingled with a sense of respect for beliefs that the author does not share. In the preface to my biography of Pat Robertson, I speculated a bit about how I had tried to approach the writing of religious history. At the risk of appearing naive, I repeat these comments here:

> There are no eternal verities in historical stories, but good historians write as truthfully as possible. A story well told can instruct a wide variety of people. *All Things Are Possible*, a book I wrote over a decade ago, describes the explosive healing revival in post–World War II pentecostalism. To some it is sacred history; to others it is a bizarre tale of ignorance and chicanery. I take some pride in the fact that the book has been used as a text—at Yale University and Oral Roberts University, at the University of North Carolina and at Rhema Bible School.
>
> Telling stories objectively does not imply the absence of interpretation. This book is filled with my interpretations of Pat Robertson's motives, his

meanings, and the forces that influenced him and American society. The validity of those interpretations depends on how logically I have used the evidence. What I have not done is offer overt judgments about the morality or sanity of the story. That, it seems to me, is what a good historian leaves to readers. It is precisely that quality that allows a book to be read by vastly different people, each concluding that here is a true telling of the past.

Not all historians agree with such a definition of historical writing. Much historical writing takes on a tone of polemics, if not propaganda. And, quite properly, most political writing has an instrumental intent. That is all well and good, and I sometimes write polemics myself. But when I am posing as a historian, I try not to plead any case. If I do that job well, the result may be used by a variety of polemicists and moralizers who see the past through different first-principle truths. (vii–viii)

Notes

1. Kenneth K. Bailey, *Southern White Protestantism in the Twentieth Century* (New York: Harper and Row, 1964).

2. Rufus B. Spain, *At Ease in Zion: A Social History of the Southern Baptists, 1865–1900* (Nashville: Vanderbilt University Press, 1961).

3. See Walter B. Posey, *The Development of Methodism in the Old Southwest, 1783–1824* (Tuscaloosa: Weatherford Printing, 1933); *The Presbyterian Church in the Old Southwest, 1778–1838* (Richmond, Va.: John Knox Press, 1952); *The Baptist Church in the Lower Mississippi Valley, 1776–1845* (Lexington: University of Kentucky Press, 1957); *Religious Strife on the Southern Frontier* (Baton Rouge: Louisiana State University Press, 1965); *Frontier Mission: A History of Religion West of the Appalachians to 1861* (Lexington: University of Kentucky Press, 1966).

4. David Edwin Harrell Jr., *Quest for a Christian America: A Social History of the Disciples of Christ to 1866* (Nashville: Disciples of Christ Historical Society, 1966).

5. David Edwin Harrell Jr., *The Social Sources of Division in the Disciples of Christ: A Social History of the Disciples of Christ, 1865–1900* (Athens, Ga.: Publishing Systems, 1973).

6. David Edwin Harrell Jr., "The Sectional Origins of the Churches of Christ," *Journal of Southern History* 30 (Aug. 1964): 261–77.

7. For an overview of Hughes's views, see *Reviving the Ancient Faith: The Story of the*

Churches of Christ in America (Grand Rapids, Mich.: William B. Eerdmans, 1996).

8. David Edwin Harrell Jr., *The Churches of Christ in the Twentieth Century: Homer Hailey's Personal Journey of Faith* (Tuscaloosa: University of Alabama Press, 2000).

9. Willard Gatewood, *Controversy in the Twenties: Fundamentalism, Modernism, and Evolution* (Nashville: Vanderbilt University Press, 1969).

10. Samuel S. Hill Jr., *Southern Churches in Crisis* (New York: Holt, Rinehart and Winston, 1967).

11. Liston Pope, *Millhands and Preachers* (New Haven: Yale University Press, 1942).

12. David Edwin Harrell Jr., *White Sects and Black Men in the Recent South* (Nashville: Vanderbilt University Press, 1971).

13. David Edwin Harrell Jr., ed., *Varieties of Southern Evangelicalism* (Macon: Mercer University Press, 1981).

14. David Edwin Harrell Jr., "Religious Pluralism: Catholics, Jews, and Sectarians," in Charles Reagan Wilson, ed., *Religion in the South* (Jackson: University Press of Mississippi, 1985), 59–82; David Edwin Harrell Jr., "The Evolution of Plain-Folk Religion in the South, 1835–1920," in Samuel S. Hill, ed., *Varieties of Southern Religious Experience* (Baton Rouge: Louisiana State University Press, 1988), 24–51.

15. David Edwin Harrell Jr., *All Things Are Possible: The Healing and Charismatic Revivals in Modern America* (Bloomington: Indiana University Press, 1975).

16. David Edwin Harrell Jr., *Oral Roberts: An American Life* (Bloomington: Indiana University Press, 1985; paperback ed., San Francisco: Harper and Row, 1987).

17. David Edwin Harrell Jr., *Pat Robertson: A Personal, Religious, and Political Portrait* (San Francisco: Harper and Row, 1987).

18. See David Edwin Harrell Jr., "American Revivalism from Graham to Robertson," in Edith Blumhofer and Randall Balmer, eds., *Modern Christian Revivals* (Urbana: University of Illinois Press, 1993), 194–207.

Cusp of Spring

Robert M. Calhoon

I n his preface to *The Royal Governors of Georgia, 1754–1775*, W. W. Abbot drolly recounted a rite of passage: "When the late Professor Charles S. Sydnor informed me [in 1953] that the college at Williamsburg was looking for a colonial historian, I was surprised and delighted to learn that was what I had become. I had not known before that there were different kinds, only American historians and the others who could do foreign languages and became European historians. . . . Now that I am at last publishing a book of colonial history and teaching it as well, I feel a little less a pretender."[1] Even as I accepted John Boles's invitation to write this essay, I felt a lingering sense of being a pretender in a subfield in which I had no formal preparation. By training and appointment I am an early American historian who, a third of the way into his career, began to work with sources on religion in the American South. My professional rite of passage occurred when, as a graduate student in 1960–61, I felt something of the same surprise and delight the young Bill Abbot must have felt, less than a decade earlier, realizing that early American history had its own ethos, its own purpose to link American history to its European origins and to its national future. In 1971 Michael Kammen likened early America to "the barren but sensuous serenity of the natural world in late autumn, before Thanksgiving, containing the promise of rebirth and the potential for resurrection. On bare branches . . . buds bulge visibly in preparation for spring."[2] Like the cusps of autumn and winter, or winter and spring, early American history in the 1950s and '60s invited quiet, deliberate reflection into the processes of historical change. Kammen's overtones of Thanksgiving and resurrection were metaphors for the explanatory force of theology and spirituality in early American consciousness and portents of what I would encounter.

The most important assumptions and experiences I brought to early American history, and later to the study of southern religion, derived from being a child of the late 1940s, '50s, and early '60s, a significant period in American intellectual life. In New York City and Cambridge, Massachusetts, it may have been the era of Reinhold Niebuhr, but in western Pennsylvania, where I grew up, and Ohio, where I got my undergraduate and graduate schooling, it could have been called the era of Howard Lowry. President of the College of Wooster from 1944 until his death in 1967, Lowry was a significant figure in the history of American higher education. A 1923 graduate of Wooster, where he taught on and off while working on his doctorate from Yale, he was, by the early 1940s, a professor at Princeton, an authority on Mathew Arnold, and, in his spare time, director of Oxford University Press in New York. In 1944, his fellow Wooster trustees elected him president. His book *The Mind's Adventure* was an important intellectual defense of liberal arts education anchored to Christian faith.[3] "The turning point of the history in which it is our privilege to share," he wrote, "may well be this growing return of men to their minds and souls. . . . [A]n unmistakable phenomenon of our day, it is much the best thing about us."[4]

Wooster was already a good Presbyterian college, but Lowry transformed the place. He instituted required Independent Study for all students—two seminar papers in the junior year and a senior project equivalent to a good master's thesis in the final year. Wooster already encouraged honors students to write senior theses, but it was Lowry's genius to see that average students, middle-American provincials—potential late bloomers—would be the real beneficiaries of carefully directed independent undergraduate research. In my first two years, I struggled getting Cs and Bs, but as a junior and senior, I found in Independent Study the chance to work on subjects no one had yet fully studied and, at the conclusion of the year, to know as much, and in some respects more, than anyone else about, say, "Kier Hardie and the Origins of the Labour Party," one of my junior year papers written in Edinburgh, or "Lincoln Steffens and the Russian Revolution," my senior thesis. To support Independent Study, Lowry also raised the money to provide regular research leaves for all tenured Wooster faculty—something unheard of in middle western liberal arts colleges in those days. The best departments—chemistry, English, and history, with French, economics, geology, and biology not far behind—flourished and matured into some of the finest undergraduate departments in the country.

When I got to Western Reserve University, in the fall of 1958, the best graduate school available to me considering my slow start in college, I already knew, thanks to Independent Study, how to write a competent research paper. Carl Wittke, the dean of the graduate school and chair of the history department, who taught the American history seminar, was sufficiently impressed with my paper entitled "The Presidential Election of 1836 in the Western Reserve" to earmark an assistantship for me in the fall of 1960. (He knew that I planned to teach in the public schools starting in 1959–60, which suited him fine because all of his assistantships were committed for that year.) Though not a well-known graduate school in history, Western Reserve did have several distinguished senior historians (Wittke and Harvey Wish in American history, Donald Grove Barnes and Arvel B. Erickson in British history, John Hall Stewart and Marion Siney in European history) and two brilliant younger scholars, Jack P. Greene in American colonial history, who arrived in 1959 after I completed my M.A. but before I returned to pursue a doctorate, and Marvin B. Becker in Renaissance history.[5] Wish had directed my master's thesis, and I planned to stay with him for my dissertation. But it seemed a good idea to take at least one course from the energetic and friendly Jack Greene. "What is your dissertation going to be on?" Greene asked during our first conversation. "Something on American historiography since I'm working with Harvey Wish," I replied (Wish was then writing *The American Historian* and had his dissertation students working on particular historians).[6]

"If you write a dissertation on historiography," Greene shot back, "you'll never get your hands dirty in the sources." I sensed instinctively that Greene was right, and suddenly the image of getting my hands dirty in the sources was powerfully inviting. By the end of that semester, I decided to work with Greene on a dissertation about Loyalist motivation, a topic requiring messy involvement in letters, newspapers, pamphlets, legislative records, diaries, and memoirs—one which Greene knew would keep my interest through the dissertation years and well into my academic career and, given the need for a fresh approach to the Loyalists, would make my work publishable. Greene had learned from John Tate Lanning, his colonial Latin America professor at Duke, that the best graduate students were not brilliant but rather average people who dealt with the complexity of history a step at a time and took direction well. History, I realized, suited middle westerners, with their appetite for hard work and provincial hunger for recognition—Lowry's late bloomers.

What prepared me to tackle a topic as complex as Loyalist motivation was the rich fare of post–World War II scholarship that was beginning to influence graduate study in history in the 1950s. Richard Hofstadter, Douglass Adair, Caroline Robbins, Hannah Arendt, Reinhold Niebuhr, Lionel Trilling, David Reisman, Lewis Namier, Gabriel Almond, Jack Hexter, Peter Gay, Perry Miller, and Daniel Boorstin may have received their training in fields like history, law, theology, literature, philosophy, political science, and sociology, but as scholars and public intellectuals they ranged widely across issues of culture, power, and consciousness. Of these, Hofstadter and Miller gave me powerfully influential models of history in which words and ideas were as important as actions and affiliations.

Miller's work on Puritanism, begun in the 1930s but coming to maturity after 1945, Edmund S. Morgan's biographies of John Winthrop and Ezra Stiles in the late 1950s and early 1960s, as well as his essays entitled "The Puritan Ethic and the American Revolution" and "The Revolution Considered as an Intellectual Movement," and Bernard Bailyn's new findings on Revolutionary republican ideology in the early to mid-1960s gradually made religion an integral feature of colonial American history.[7] Religion, we came to realize, may not have been a simple or direct cause of the quest for nationality and political freedom, but it provided some of the language for the debate about that freedom, some of the energy needed to fuel the struggle, and many of the inner connections in the structure of Whig and, for that matter, Tory ideology and British bureaucratic thinking.

Two pieces of writing, a new monograph and an old primary source, collided on my desk in 1969 as I was expanding my dissertation into *The Loyalists in Revolutionary America, 1760–1781.*[8] The monograph was Richard L. Bushman's *Puritan to Yankee: Character and the Social Order in Connecticut, 1690–1765;* the document was a sermon, entitled "The Character and Doom of the Sluggard" by David Caldwell, a Presbyterian clergyman and educator in Guilford County, North Carolina, where I live, who interested me because he tangled with Loyalist neighbors.[9] Bushman used sermons in much the same way as I did, but with more literary power and methodological sophistication, to chart the psychic trajectories of political and social aspiration of radical Whigs, cautious Whigs, and Anglican Tories in Connecticut. Caldwell's seven-thousand-word sermon did something even more ambitious and impressive than the New England sermons Bushman, Alan Heimert, and others had discovered. Caldwell penetrated and diagnosed the dilemma of those Americans who, while uncomfortable in their subordination to British rule, were reluctant to take on the terrifying task of armed rebellion. He then proceeded to demonstrate how the the guidance of the Holy Spirit and insights from Scottish Common Sense faculty psychology could make such flawed creatures into heroic revolutionaries. Read against the backdrop of Bushman's interpretation of early pre-Revolutionary Connecticut, Caldwell's sermon drew me into the psychic maw of Revolutionary contagion in the southern backcountry.

I wondered why and how a sermon so powerful, original, and inventive came to be preached in a society Carl Bridenbaugh assured his readers had only rudimentary cultural and intellectual life.[10] At that very time, in the late 1960s and early '70s, Donald G. Mathews at nearby Chapel Hill was producing a series of articles and conference papers on southern evangelicalism that anticipated themes he would subsequently develop in *Religion in the Old South*.[11] Mathews was looking for points of entry into the *terra incognita* of southern evangelical history: the clergy as a strategic elite, the second Great Awakening as a social process, proslavery Christianity as subversive of slavery, southern Methodism as a form of community protective of the vulnerable.[12] My interests in theology as political language, in churches as nuclei of community, and in conversion and sanctification as stages of religious identity resembled Mathews's concerns. He helped me see that limiting my project to the late eighteenth century was a mistake, that the fierce quarrels over ecclesiology in the South in the 1820s, '30s, and '40s were symptomatic of social tensions and cultural contradictions that dated to the late eighteenth century. I turned my attention to the politics of evangelicalism, that is, the empowerment resulting from conversion and sanctification and the efforts of clerical and lay elites to channel and regulate the energies released by conversion in churches, families, and communities.

My book *Evangelicals and Conservatives in the Early South, 1740–1861*, attempted, with only partial success, to describe and relate the politicizing of religion and spiritualizing of politics.[13] The book may not have been what one anonymous reviewer called "the most badly botched . . . recent work of southern intellectual history," but it surely deserved Mark Noll's gentle complaint about my "tendency to obscure connections between . . . grand themes and . . . detailed sources."[14] To correct those shortcomings, I looked again at the rhythm of religious change during the post-Revolutionary decades—the years of religious upheaval brilliantly re-created by Nathan Hatch in *The Democratization of American Christianity*.[15] Writing about the unlettered and unwashed, Hatch found Christians trying to re-create, in the new nation, the primitive church of the first century A.D. Hatch prompted me to take a closer look at Christian primitivism.

Just as Bushman taught me how to use sermons, another emerging historian of the late 1960s, Bertram Wyatt-Brown, showed me how to place religious primitivism in historical context. I had long admired his article "The Antimission Movement in the Jacksonian South: A Study of Regional Folk Culture" but now returned to it in the late 1980s.[16] Wyatt-Brown depicted the cultural and psychic carnage in rural communities caused by the attempts of newly created Baptist state conventions, especially in North Carolina, to modernize the church through the blessings of bureaucracy and control of print media and a college-trained and professionalized clergy. Rather than pushing religious primitives to the periphery of historical space, Wyatt-Brown made the audacious suggestion that the Primitive Baptists occupied the core of regional folk culture. It was the modernizers who were deviants following the lure of wealth and power away from the core of traditional culture and toward the beckoning new frontier of rationalized, commercialized, bureaucratized religious life.

Primitive Christianity was therefore not primitive in any pejorative sense. It was a theologically rigorous and experientially venturesome Christianity. Indeed, there were two distinct kinds of churches that proudly called themselves primitive and sought to re-create the early church of the Apostles. There were what might be labeled *garden variety* primitives, like the Primitive Baptists or the followers of Methodist schismatic James O'Kelly, who believed they could read the New Testament and collectively submit to the Apostolic example. But another category of nineteenth-century Christians were *confessional* primitives: Lutherans, Episcopalians, and Presbyterians whose churches honored sixteenth-century confessions of faith—respectively, the Augsburg and Westminster Confessions and the Thirty-nine Articles—and who considered those confession statements to be authoritative guides to interpreting biblical texts depicting the early church. With help from Martin Luther Stirewalt Jr., theologian, biblical scholar, and church historian, I came to realize that pastors in the Evangelical Lutheran Tennessee Synod, which broke away from the North Carolina

Lutheran Synod in 1820 in a dispute over adherence to the Augsburg Confession, taught and preached some of the most rigorous and historically authentic theology in all of nineteenth-century America. Gradually in the early 1990s I became aware that the Lutheran churches I had attended since the mid-1960s were heirs of that tradition and that my wife and my numerous Lutheran in-laws had grown up in congregations that, since the nineteenth century, were the heartland of Lutheran confessionalism in America.

Examining the Lutheran theological heritage as part of American religious history and as an ingredient in the history of the Western intellectual tradition, I turned to multivolume historical works that other American historians have used only sparingly—Quentin Skinner, *The Foundations of Modern Political Thought*, and Jaroslav Pelikan, *The Christian Tradition: A History of the Development of Doctrine*.[17] Though Skinner's two volumes are a history of political thought forged on the anvil of religious conflict and Pelikan's five volumes are a history of religious thought hammered out in fierce political and intellectual debates, they concur on the centrality—for both constitutionalism and theology—of the Lutheran paradox of human beings as simultaneously saints and sinners. In contrast with John Calvin's doctrine that the covenant of grace mediated, primarily for individuals, between human frailty and divine justice, Martin Luther emphasized that the divine presence enters human experience collectively, through the church, in sacraments of Baptism and the Eucharist. Though both Calvin and Luther valued the church as a gift of the Creator, Calvinism placed more weight on the individual as the locus of faith, whereas Lutheranism focused on the church, the extended family, and the community as the arena of God's presence on earth.

American historians have been slow to notice that Calvinist and Lutheran strands of the Reformation brought to the New World contrasting political and social theories—an aggressive Calvinist individualism and a more diffuse Lutheran communalism. Calvin classified rebellion and sedition as manifestations of human depravity and public order and security as blessings of Providence, but Calvin's followers soon added tyranny and oppression to their list of sins and threats to the public peace. The Lutheran explanation of God's righteousness—more than Calvin's improvised doctrine of resistance against tyranny—however, became one of Skinner's foundations of modern constitutionalism. The same creative power that caused all matter to exist, Lutheran theology holds, necessarily grieves over imperfections in creation. This divine grief is perfect grief and hence redemptive. Therefore, in Lutheran theology and political theory, power was not an unchecked cosmic force but rather a constituent element in cosmic healing.

By locating the healing presence of the Divine in the Eucharist, Lutheranism instilled in American religious consciousness the sense of religious mystery, which the Calvinist reformation diluted and which the Enlightenment relegated to the periphery of Western consciousness. No less than rationality, mystery is one the great engines of human action. The foundations of Western culture and politics are Aristotelian *and* Augustinian, and this synthesis of Greek humanism and Christian humanism in Western civilization depends for its coherence not only on the radical claims of Greek rationalism but also on the adaptability of Augustine's spirituality. Augustine's view of the world fit with Aristotle's because Augustine himself was steeped in Greek classicism, which detached him from the uncompromising otherworldliness of Near Eastern Christianity. (Eventually, medieval mysticism would channel some of that otherworldliness back into the Western tradition.)

As a radical Augustinian, Luther placed salvation by grace at the center of Christian belief, but as an heir to the Western tradition, he domesticated religious belief by making it part of the warp and woof of everyday life. The social implications of Lutheran doctrine are important for understanding American history because they contrast with the religious psychology of Calvinism. Scottish Common Sense philosophy—a fusion of Calvinism and Scottish faculty psychology—conceived of the pursuit of power as humanizing and ennobling at the onset of political ambition, as creative during the early and middle experience of a statesman, but as ultimately corrupting; there were, therefore, creative intervals—what J. G. A. Pocock calls "Machiavellian moments" to indicate the Renaissance humanist origins of the eighteenth-century concept of civic virtue—during which human beings could, by grace, transcend their own nature and handle power without being corrupted by it. Luther's doctrine of vocation, in contrast, recognized the presence of both responsibility and power in the work God called human beings to perform; taming power, in Lutheran teaching, occurred over and over again because the Eucharist perpetuated the incarnational presence of the Creator in human existence.

Now, as I considered confessional Lutheranism as a belief system and a component of early American culture, my own religious odyssey began to make historical sense. I had grown up in the old United Presbyterian Church—a regional denomination in western Pennsylvania and the Middle West, smaller than the more liberal Presbyterian Church U.S.A. (the Northern Presbyterians) or the similarly conservative Presbyterian Church U.S. (the Southern Presbyterians). The old U.P. Church was the heir to the Scottish Covenanter tradition. Suspicious of revivalism and of conversions not grounded in serious educational ministry, its ministers and laity had refused to participate in the Second Great Awakening. By the twentieth century, the U.P. Church positioned itself between fundamentalism and liberal Protestantism. Deeply commited to its foreign mission fields in Egypt, Sudan, and Pakistan, the church retained the practice of singing, to what seemed to me at the time wretched tunes, a psalm in every service—a throwback to its commitment to the religious and literary education of its largely rural laity.

Living in Mt. Lebanon, a suburb of Pittsburgh, my parents chose the Mt. Lebanon United Presbyterian Church over the northern Presbyterian congregations because it more nearly resembled the southern Presbyterian churches in Missouri and Oklahoma, where they had been raised. The Mt. Lebanon U.P. Church was the largest in the denomination, and its ministers were legendary preachers and formidable intellects. The minister, from 1944 to 1948, was John Coventry Smith, who had been a missionary in Japan from 1929 to 1942 and was then interned in a prison camp by the Japanese for the first six months of 1942. World War II was the most intensive part of my education. On Pearl Harbor Sunday I knew almost nothing about world geography and history; by the end of the war, at age eight, I knew almost as much as I know now. There was little else to do in wartime Pittsburgh than to devour *Time* and *Life* and follow war news in the *Pittsburgh Press*. As liberal and internationalist Republicans, my parents imparted to me their outlook on world affairs. But neither their education nor my own quite prepared me for Smith's series of sermons in September 1945 on the meaning of the war, climaxing on September 16 with his sermon on Hiroshima and Nagasaki. He had gone to Japan in 1929 as a missionary under the auspices of the northern Presbyterian Church because the U.P. Church had, at the moment, no funds to send him and his bride to Egypt. During thirteen years in Japan, Smith became part of a vanguard of Christian missionaries determined to pass leadership of the churches to Japanese clergy and to respect the ways in which Japanese Christians understood and preached theology from their own cultural experience. He knew many members of the Christian community in Hiroshima, including the family of a theology student then studying at Princeton Seminary.

"Two weeks ago, I had to write a letter to my friend in Princeton. What could I say? What would you say to a Japanese Christian minister whose family had been killed in Hiroshima?" It was a painful question to ask his Mt. Lebanon congregation, many of whose members were executives in Pittsburgh industries that had labored prodigiously in the war effort and, like most Americans, greeted Japanese defeat with relief and satisfaction. Mindful of their feelings, Smith conceded that "we have not malaciously and sadistically tortured and killed, but by our scientific weapons we have done that which is terrible and horrible to contemplate." Historian Paul S. Boyer later found a handful of liberal Protestant, Catholic, and Jewish ethical objections, in August–September 1945, to the the atomic bombing of Japan.[18] However, Smith's was the first documented sermon by an *evangelical* Protestant to grapple with the issue.[19]

His text was Romans, chapters 12 and 13, which included Paul's admonition to bless one's persecutors and never seek vengeance, as well as his warning not to resist those in authority. Christians, Smith declared, were not to try to escape persecution and suffering; they were to endure it and recognize, as Smith paraphrased Reinhold Niebuhr's words, that "moral man is in an immoral society."[20] Smith then explained how, with Niebuhr's guidance, he had come to terms with the war: "Now war is one of the parts of an immoral and sinful society. Killing by itself is never a good. . . . But between nations, because we have not yet adopted for ourselves a lawful way, we are condemned to an evil way, the way of war. There is, of course, another possibility—the way of the Cross, accepting shame and pain and death itself. . . . That way is still open to us as individuals, but it is scarcely open to the state, composed as it is by a vast majority not willing to make such sacrifices."[21]

Though few in the congregation could have appreciated it, Smith's quote from Niebuhr was a bold homiletical move. Niebuhr's social activism and his restless goading of American Protestants to examine their ethical conscience were not in favor in most United Presbyterian pulpits in the 1930s and '40s. But partly responding to criticism of his reputation for political liberalism, Niebuhr had written, as World War II erupted, his great work entitled *The Nature and*

Destiny of Man, which rebuked liberals inside and outside of the church for glossing over the reality of sin and human depravity.[22] That was precisely the tenet of Christian theology that Smith wanted to drive home on that September Sabbath morning.

Here Smith alluded to something that only the session of the Mt. Lebanon Church knew, that until the late 1930s he had been a pacifist and that, like Niebuhr, he had wrestled with Scripture and conscience to acknowledge that, in some circumstances, force could be legitimately used against an aggressive, evil tyranny. But that realist conclusion, he insisted, did not get Christians off the hook. War remained "evil, albeit" an evil "we are caught in." He then tried to plumb the depths of that moral captivity: "Those who would modify war by the elimination of its most terrible weapon, mistake the nature of war." The firebombing of Tokyo, like the bombing of Dresden, he contended, was no less evil than Hiroshima and Nagasaki. "The ethical issues of the atomic bomb cannot be separated from the ethical issues of war, but the bomb makes startlingly clear what those issues may be, . . . that war is a terrible business and . . . like sin itself, we go from bad to worse."[23]

During the last years before his internment by the Japanese from December 1941 until his release and return to the United States in July 1942, Smith studied the theological work of Japanese pastors, reversing the normal power relationship of missionary work. He was deeply impressed with a Japanese minister who wrote that "both eschatology and ethics are important to the true Christian life." This insight was crucial to Smith's effort to cleanse his ministry of assumptions of Western intellectual superiority, to acknowledge his debt to a Japanese brother in Christ for confessing that all we know about the future—even a future as uncertain as that in mid-1941—was that God will return in power to vindicate His purposes (the eschaton) and that, in the meanwhile, Christian ethics is the essence of discipleship.[24]

Tracking down the fifty-year-old manuscript of Smith's sermon on the atomic bomb, in his children's possession, during the summer of 1995 suggested other connections between early American and twentieth-century political and religious thought. For my presidential address for the Historical Society of North Carolina, in October of that year, I was drawn to the experience of James S. Ferguson, chancellor at the University of North Carolina at Greensboro (UNCG) from 1965 to 1979, who was also a southern historian with deep roots in North Carolina and Mississippi politics and in southern Methodism. As a courageous racial liberal in Mississippi in the 1940s, '50s, and early '60s, and as chancellor in Greensboro, Ferguson also dealt skillfully with two racial confrontations in Greensboro. Ferguson's mother and grandmother, in early-twentieth-century Mississippi, had been active members of the Methodist Women's Society for Christian Service, "a haven for those who lived in expectation of racial justice," as George Maddox, his colleague at Millsaps College in Jackson, Mississippi, put it.[25] Arthur S. Link recalled that he and Ferguson, as graduate students at Chapel Hill in the early 1940s, "talked a great deal about the racial sitution, and we shared a deep conviction that segregation and all that went with it was morally wrong."[26] A graduate of Millsaps College, Ferguson returned there to teach in 1944. He gravitated to a circle of faculty at Millsaps and, at nearby Tougaloo College, a private school for African Americans, teachers who regularly led their students across the color line to explore firsthand issues of racial justice. The most dynamic member of the group, Tougaloo sociologist Ernst Borinski, a Polish refugee from Nazism, taught Ferguson to think about the aspirations of Mississippi blacks and about white supremacy as "social forces" that had taken on lives of their own and the imminent collision between the two as a reality that social scientists on the scene could diagnose and perhaps channel, with which they could identify, and in which, with sufficient courage, they could even participate.[27]

Ferguson had gone to graduate school at Louisiana State University and North Carolina in the heyday of progressive historiography. Arthur Link recalled their optimistic yearning for modernization to reform the region. Ferguson's dissertation on agrarianism in late-nineteenth-century Mississippi predictably pitted heroic reformers against entrenched, selfish oligarchs. But he also participated in the intellectual cosmopolitanism of the post–World War II era that broke free of progressivism. Borinski, as well as Ralph Linton, an anthropologist at Yale—where Ferguson had a post-doctoral fellowship in 1953—introduced him to social theory and social ethics.[28] Robert Penn Warren's long poem *Brother to Dragons*, about two of Jefferson's drunken nephews, Lilburne and Isham Lewis, who hacked to death their slave George for breaking an heirloom pitcher, deepened Ferguson's Methodist understanding of the imperative of moral action.[29] So did rereading in the winter of 1953–54 William Faulkner's *Intruder in the Dust*. In that novel, lawyer Gavin Stevens, speaking Faulkner's mind, explained that "only a few of us know that only from homogeneity comes anything of a people" and that, as a homogeneous people, southern whites had to acknowledge "that Sambo is a human being living in the free country and hence must be free. That's what we [white Mississippians] are really defending: the privilege of setting him free ourselves which we will have to do for the reason that no one else can."[30] Faulkner compelled Ferguson to acknowledge that teaching the history of race meant confronting for himself—and daring his students to face—the most profound truths about human nature.[31]

When Ferguson returned to teaching in the early 1980s, he turned to Mary Frances Berry and John Blassingame, *Long Memory: The Black Experience in America*, expecting to find a useful synthesis of recent scholarship.[32] *Long Memory* left him deeply disheartened. It presented a racially bifurcated society in which white people existed only as faceless oppressors. Ferguson did not pretend that a small number of whites committed to racial justice somehow balanced the historical record, but he believed deeply that both races shared an enormously complex and tragic common history and that scholars had an obligation to deal concretely with racial encounters like Lilburne and Isham's murderous rampage, the terror of George's last moments alive, and the social changes that placed these people on the Kentucky frontier. As he told a Methodist church gathering in 1973, "we will not be redeemed until matters of the spirit—love of God and respect for the worth of our fellow man—are made the cornerstones of our being. The creature must seek the full dimensions of the life the Creator makes available to him. To live without either is as impossible as applauding with one hand."[33] The Arminianism of Ferguson's Methodist upbringing—that is, the theological position opposed to Calvinist human depravity that recognizes the role of human goodness and a benevolent deity in salvation—remained a constant pole in his historical thinking even as his post–World War II intellectual cosmopolitanism weaned him away from liberal optimism.

To place Ferguson in the context of North Carolina history, I entitled my presidential address "Samuel E. McCorkle and James S. Ferguson: Ideology, Religion, and Higher Education in North Carolina." Like Ferguson, McCorkle was an evangelical Christian; he was a Presbyterian minister and educator in Rowan County. As the founder of Parnassus-Zion Academy in Salisbury and a founding trustee of the University of North Carolina in Chapel Hill, McCorkle

sought to impart to the rising generation of North Carolinians the best learning that Western culture then made available. Just as Ferguson was a southern
liberal at a time when that ideology was in crisis over issues of race, McCorkle
was a classical republican during the post-Revolutionary generation when the
promise of American liberty and virtue required the transformation of the republican discipline of the Revolution into a continuous cleansing social creed
of piety and duty.

McCorkle and Ferguson provided me with lenses through which to examine and compare the religious content of ideology in different centuries. In one
ideologically charged document, McCorkle devised the University of North
Carolina's first rules for student discipline, consisting of twenty-seven regulations that all students were to copy into their notebooks. McCorkle's system
was a comprehensive regime of moral indoctrination governed by a schedule
that ran from morning prayers at sunrise through Sunday evening lectures on
religion and morality.[34] The discipline sought to reinforce McCorkle's proposed
curriculum in which classical languages and texts complemented the study of
moral philosophy and history. Fellow Trustee William R. Davie, like McCorkle
a Princeton graduate, scoffed at the manipulative religiosity of the scheme and
persuaded the rest of the trustees to dilute the Protestant idealism of McCorkle's
rules and curriculum. In what he meant to be a conciliatory gesture, Davie
made William Paley's *Principles of Moral and Political Philosophy* (1785) required reading in the Moral Philosophy course. McCorkle seethed at the proposal, for although Paley was widely admired as an enlightenment apologist
for Christianity, McCorkle feared that his false reliance on rationalism would
wean undergraduate students away from his regime of piety and discipline.[35]
The students did not need Paley to tell them to subvert oppressive regulations.
Openly disrespectful of their professors, they publicly horsewhipped presiding
professor David Ker. Episodes of this kind, and lack of support from faculty
and trustees, finally sent McCorkle back to Rowan County in anger and
humiliation.

Ferguson also encountered rebellious students in Greensboro in the late
1960s, but unlike McCorkle, he exhibited consummate skill in avoiding a violent confrontation between students and police during racial demonstrations
in 1969 and a neoconservative student backlash against UNCG's Neo-Black
Society in 1973. Ferguson's heritage of southern liberalism, exemplified by Frank

Porter Graham, president of the University of North Carolina during Ferguson's graduate student days, provided him with a resource that McCorkle lacked: the concept of public service as something public schooling and higher education could and should institutionalize. McCorkle's classical republicanism assumed that service could only be the product of social virtue, and that social virtue and personal gratification were locked in a dualistic combat for the allegiance of mortal beings. Liberalism, undergirded by Lockean psychology and by nineteenth-century romanticism, taught that service could be enormously gratifying to an individual.

If the liberal devotion to public service was a more useful concept than the republican ideal of social virtue, other features of McCorkle's republicanism compare more favorably with early-twentieth-century southern liberalism. McCorkle's Calvinist theology gave him an understanding of the dynamism of collective behavior that Ferguson acquired only as he outgrew liberal optimism. When Revolutionary warfare in the southern backcountry turned brutish and ugly in 1781, McCorkle courageously condemned Whig partisans for looting and brutalizing their Tory neighbors. He cast his argument in classically republican and evangelical terms, evoking Joshua's condemnation of the Israelite soldier Achan, whose looting "kindled . . . the anger of God against the children of Israel." With fine republican pessimism, McCorkle's condemnation of Whig looting drew a firm line between self-interest and besotted greed. Labelling the backcountry war an "invasive" conflict, McCorkle anticipated late-twentieth-century insights into the character of guerilla warfare.[36] McCorkle's slender hope for the success of the republican experiment rested on attainment of what he called national "happiness"—what evangelicals would soon call "national prosperity"—something more complex and ambiguous than patriotism or economic plenty. For McCorkle, national happiness or prosperity was the spiritual gratification that resulted from sublimation of self in the cause of American piety and virtue.[37] Invasive warfare and national prosperity were dynamic, throbbing historical realities closer to late-twentieth-century notions of cultural change than to the youthful Ferguson's liberal belief in progress.

McCorkle and Ferguson's respective ideologies each cohered by placing opposing values in fruitful tension. At the laying of the first cornerstone of the Chapel Hill campus in 1795, McCorkle declared that the university would have to be both a Mount Zion and a Mount Parnassus—both the mythical mountain where the children of Israel honored the covenant God made with Abraham and the mountain range in ancient Greece where the muses were thought to have first inspired literature. Appealing to historical and mythic events that towered above the rest of human experience, McCorkle announced the potency of metaphor in political discourse. He also understood the potency of paradox and contradiction when he declared that, in the aftermath of winning their independence, Americans read their own history in a mood of "rational rapture."[38] By "rational rapture" he meant a social miracle in which human willfulness in America was in the process of being tamed by the lessons of the past, by the uniqueness of the historical moment, and by the intervention of the Holy Spirit.

"Other than their religious beliefs and involvement in education, what—at a deeper level—bound McCorkle and Ferguson together?" a Roman Catholic layman and student of political philosophy asked me. "Well, for one thing," I heard myself reply, "they were both historic moderates." It was the first time I had ever used the phrase, and I braced myself for the obvious question, "And what do you mean by a 'historic moderate'?" The challenge never came. My questioner nodded in agreement as though—Potter Stewart–like—he recognized historic moderation when he saw it. But if he had pressed me to define the term that night in October 1995, I would have put him off with the excuse "that's a long story."

Mulling over my close escape in my first waking moments the next morning, it suddenly occurred to me, not only that long stories make good books, but also that that political moderation was something I had been studying since I first began looking at moderate Whigs and moderate Loyalists trying to communicate across the divide of independence, or encountered southern evangelicals seeking to tame the passions and excesses of a young, boisterous society or thoughtful conservatives invoking theology as an antedote to reactionary zeal, or came across primitive and confessional Christians disciplining religious zeal with their respect for Scripture and history. Eugene Genovese, Sylvia Frey, Mark Noll, Bertram Wyatt-Brown, and, just before his final illness, the late Arthur S. Link concurred that political moderation in American history deserved a large-scale study of its religious as well as philosophical character.

Where to begin? Here, Quentin Skinner repaid my earlier attention to his

work. Skinner was the first scholar to notice moderate Huguenots and humanist French Catholics reaching out to each other in the early 1570s—the same
time that moderate Anglicans and Puritans did so in England. The politics
forged in the tension and interaction between those contrasting, even conflicting, ideological positions, Skinner suggested, had sufficient weight and vitality
to mediate conflict. Here, in the 1570s, was the historic origin of political moderation as a credo and a system of political ethics. Moreover, the Huguenot,
Puritan, and Anglican diasporas were among the means of transmitting moderation throughout the Anglo-American world. My own work on political ideology pointed to 1713 as the watershed between the embattled moderation of
the seventeenth century and a Lockean consensus about liberty and order that
prevailed for the next two centuries—a moderate age in political thought that
extended to the eve of World War I. Arthur Link confirmed my guess that
Woodrow Wilson was the last American president steeped in the moderate tradition, and that, from his entry into politics through the completion of his first
full year in office, he positioned himself in the middle of an ideological force
field bounded—geographically as well as figuratively—on the South by his
father's conservative republicanism, the North and West by his own and his
family's Calvinism, the Northeast by his appreciation of nineteenth-century liberalism, and across the Atlantic by the British Isles and his fascination with
Burkean conservatism. That middle ground was his moderation and, for my
project, a historical benchmark. Thus, 1913 marked the conclusion of the two
centuries since the Peace of Utrecht as the time when moderation cohered into
a tradition and a palpable element in political culture.

And where to finish? With people I had already encountered by living through
the middle decades of the twentieth century: moderates who, during a turbulent century, remained conscious of their debt to that tradition. The list is not a
long one, but it includes people like the Niebuhrs and their admirers, the Jewish ethicist Abraham Joshua Heschel, jurists such as Lewis Powell, political
advocacy groups such as the Concord Coalition, and, at the dawn of the
postmodern age, religious primitives such as leaders of Restorationist Christian
churches who have long prophesied a coming age of violent extremes requiring mediation by the Spirit—certainly enough material for a twentieth-century
epilogue on the survival of the moderate tradition. Reconstructing this story of
political moderation evokes the same spring-like expectancy I first whiffed al-

most four decades ago getting my hands dirty in the sources of early American history.

Notes

This essay was written with support from a Pew Endowment Evangelical Scholars Fellowship.

1. W. W. Abbot, *The Royal Governors of Georgia, 1754–1775* (Chapel Hill: University of North Carolina Press, 1959), v.

2. Michael Kammen, *People of Paradox: An Inquiry Concerning the Origins of American Civilization* (New York: Alfred A. Knopf, 1972), 298.

3. Howard Foster Lowry, *The Mind's Adventure: Religion and Higher Education* (Philadelphia: Westminster Press, 1950).

4. Quoted in James R. Blackwood, *Howard Lowry: A Life in Education* (Wooster, Ohio: College of Wooster, 1975), 192.

5. Robert M. Calhoon, "Robert M. Weir and the Life of the Mind," *South Carolina Historical Magazine* 99 (April 1998): 180–89.

6. Harvey Wish, *The American Historian: A Social-Intellectual History of the Writing of the American Past* (New York: Oxford University Press, 1960).

7. On Miller, see Robert M. Calhoon, "Perry Miller," in *Dictionary of Literary Biography*, vol. 17, *Twentieth-Century American Historians*, ed. Clyde N. Wilson (Detroit: Gale Research, 1983), 272–85; on Morgan's and Bailyn's early work on religion and the Revolution, see their collected essays: Edmund S. Morgan, *The Challenge of the American Revolution* (New York: W. W. Norton, 1976), chaps. 3 and 4, and Bernard Bailyn, *Faces of Revolution: Personalities and Themes in the Struggle for American Independence* (New York: Alfred A. Knopf, 1990), chaps. 6 and 8.

8. Robert M. Calhoon, *The Loyalists in Revolutionary America, 1760–1781* (New York: Harcourt Brace Jovanovich, 1973).

9. Richard L. Bushman, *Puritan to Yankee: Character and the Social Order in Connecticut, 1690–1765* (Cambridge: Harvard University Press, 1967); David Caldwell, "The Character and Doom of the Sluggard," in Eli W. Caruthers, *A Sketch of the Life and Character of the Reverend David Caldwell* (Greensborough, N.C.: Swaim and Sherwood, 1842), 273–84.

10. Carl Bridenbaugh, *Myths and Realities: Societies of the Colonial South* (Baton Rouge: Louisiana State University Press, 1952), 183–85.

11. Donald G. Mathews, *Religion in the Old South* (Chicago: University of Chicago Press, 1977).

12. On Mathews's early articles on religion in the South, see Robert M. Calhoon, "A

Troubled Culture: North Carolina in the New Nation, 1790–1834," in Jeffrey J. Crow and Larry E. Tise, eds., *Writing North Carolina History* (Chapel Hill: University of North Carolina Press, 1979), 89–90.

13. Robert M. Calhoon, *Evangelicals and Conservatives in the Early South, 1740–1861* (Columbia: University of South Carolina Press, 1988).

14. Review of *Evangelicals and Conservatives*, by Calhoon, *Virginia Quarterly Review* 76 (autumn 1989): 115; Mark Noll, review of *Evangelicals and Conservatives*, by Calhoon, *Journal of the Early Republic* 9 (fall 1989): 394.

15. Nathan Hatch, *The Democratization of American Christianity* (New Haven: Yale University Press, 1989).

16. Bertram Wyatt-Brown, "The Antimission Movement in the Jacksonian South: A Study of Regional Folk Culture," *Journal of Southern History* 36 (November 1970): 501–29.

17. Quentin Skinner, *The Foundations of Modern Political Thought* (Cambridge: Cambridge University Press, 1978); Jaroslav Pelikan, *The Christian Tradition: A History of the Development of Doctrine* (Chicago: University of Chicago Press, 1971–89).

18. Paul S. Boyer, *By the Bomb's Early Light: American Thought and Culture at the Dawn of the Atomic Age* (New York: Pantheon, 1985), 199–201.

19. For Smith's pioneering role in the civil rights movement, see Taylor Branch, *Pillar of Fire: America in the King Years, 1963–65* (New York: Simon and Schuster, 1998), 215–19.

20. Apparently Smith was paraphrasing the title of Reinhold Niebuhr, *Moral Man and Immoral Society* (New York: Scribner's, 1932).

21. John Coventry Smith, sermon preached on 16 Sept. 1945, original manuscript and typescript in the possession of Louise Smith Woodruff, Ypsilanti, Michigan.

22. Reinhold Niebuhr, *The Nature and Destiny of Man: A Christian Interpretation*, 2 vols. (New York: Scribner's, 1941–43).

23. Smith, Sermon, 16 Sept. 1945.

24. John Coventry Smith, *From Colonialism to World Community: The Church's Pilgrimage* (Philadelphia: Geneva Press, 1982), 54–55.

25. George Maddox, telephone interview by author, 21 April 1990.

26. Arthur S. Link, letter to the author, 10 April 1990.

27. James S. Ferguson, "Statement Concerning Ernst Borinski," Southern Sociological Association, Knoxville, Tenn., 28 March 1980, James S. Ferguson Papers, Special Collections Dept., Jackson Library, University of North Carolina at Greensboro.

28. James S. Ferguson, Chancellor's Commencement Address, 4 June 1967, Ferguson Papers.

29. Robert Penn Warren, *Brother to Dragons* (New York: Random House, 1953); see

also Merrill Boynton Jr., *Jefferson's Nephews: A Frontier Tragedy* (Princeton: Princeton University Press, 1976); James S. Ferguson, address to Duke University Divinity School, 21 July 1967, Ferguson Papers.

30. William Faulkner, *Intruder in the Dust* (New York: Random House, 1948), 154.

31. James S. Ferguson, "Lest the Salt Lose Its Savor: Address to the Georgia Institute of Higher Education," n.d. [ca. Sept. 1969], 3, Ferguson Papers.

32. Mary Frances Berry and John Blassingame, *Long Memory: The Black Experience in America* (New York: Oxford University Press, 1982).

33. James S. Ferguson, "The Men Who Go Down to the Sea," Ferguson Papers, Box 85.

34. R. D. W. Connor, *A Documentary History of the University of North Carolina, 1776–1799*, ed. Louis R. Wilson and Hugh T. Lefler (Chapel Hill: University of North Carolina Press, 1953), 2:375–79.

35. Thomas T. Taylor, "Essays on the Career and Thought of Samuel Eusebius McCorkle" (master's thesis, University of North Carolina at Greensboro, 1978), 28–29.

36. Samuel E. McCorkle, "The Curse and Crime of Plundering: A Sermon," McCorkle Papers, Duke University Library, Durham, N.C.

37. Samuel E. McCorkle, "The National and Necessary Connexion between Learning and Religion and the Importance of Religion to the Promotion of National Happiness and National Undertakings," in Connor, *Documentary History of the University of North Carolina*, 1:238–40. See Fred J. Hood, *Reformed America: The Middle and Southern States, 1783–1837* (University: University of Alabama Press, 1980), 7–8.

38. Samuel E. McCorkle, *A Sermon on the Comparative Happiness and Duty of the United States of America, Contrasted with Other Nations, Particularly the Israelites* (Halifax, N.C., 1795), 22.

A Pilgrim's Progress through Southern Christianity

Wayne Flynt

The small town of Anniston, Alabama, where I grew up was not a typical southern community. The town had no roots deep into cotton culture. Residents could not trace their town ancestors back through multiple generations, nor did they live in antebellum mansions. In fact, there was no "antebellum" to Anniston. It was a New South city that sprang to life as a company town in 1872, owned lock, stock, and barrel, or street, school, and church, by the Woodstock Iron Company. Its two founding families, the Tylers and Nobles, were carpetbaggers from the North who came to the foothills of Appalachian Alabama in order to create an iron empire. For a while the excellence of their charcoal-fired iron was so renowned that their community rivaled Birmingham as the South's premier industrial city. Straddling a strategic rail line running from Atlanta to Birmingham, Anniston seemed destined for greatness.

The founders laid out a model town, with each street, school, industry, and church situated where they thought it ought to go. Stonemasons came from England to craft the elegant Church of St. Michael and All Angels. Nearby, the First Baptist Church also emerged from the floor of the valley.

Separating the two parts of Anniston were Noble Street, which contained most of the community's mercantile establishments, and Quintard Avenue, a spacious street whose double lanes were separated by a broad median in which hardwoods and flowering trees were planted. Flanking Quintard were magnificent Victorian houses occupied by the town's wealthiest citizens.

When the city went public in the 1880s, its carefully planned and manicured charm gradually gave way to a century-long modification that finally reduced its Victorian mansions to scrap lumber, to be replaced by fast-food restaurants and service stations. Only the median with its now gigantic oaks and the second-generation sandstone churches survived the city's "progress."

Noble Street and Quintard Avenue, running parallel to each other a block apart, defined Anniston economically, racially, socially, and culturally. On the west side of Noble lay the town's shops, foundries, and textile mills as well as residential neighborhoods for industrial workers, poor whites, and blacks. On the east side of Quintard and running up the side of Tenth Street Mountain, the expansion of the middle and professional classes could be traced through each new architectural generation. East Anniston was not only higher geographically, but it also conceived of itself as towering over West Anniston socially, educationally, and morally. Depending on one's point of view, "over there" in West Anniston "lint heads" in the mill village listened to Hank Williams and the Grand Ole Opry, played baseball in industrial leagues or football for Anniston High School, got "lathered up" at tent revivals or in the backseats of second-hand Fords, and attended emotional churches strong on conviction and weak on reflection. Meanwhile, "over there" in East Anniston, the "country club set" was entertained by touring New York City theater and chamber music ensembles, played golf and tennis, and occasionally attended magnificent churches where they often snoozed through cerebral but uninspiring homilies.

The Homer Flynts carried a west-side culture to the east side of town. In fact, my father had grown up beyond the west side, some twenty or so miles in the country, where his father had been a sharecropper. Growing up on a cotton farm that had become the possession of "old man" Charles Bell, the president of Commercial National Bank and one of the most prominent deacons in Parker Memorial Baptist Church, my father had experienced a hardscrabble childhood typical of tenant children during the Great Depression. While a boy in the 1920s, he had cut his foot and contracted osteomyelitis, causing him to miss a year of school, nearly costing him both legs, and leaving scars that would bequeath a lifetime of pain, both physical and psychological.

Without a high school diploma, Dad seemed destined for a life in the mills. And that was the way he started out, moving to Birmingham with his brother in 1937 and standing in line outside Virginia Bridge Company for four months until finally a personnel man called his name. Once inside the mill, he joined the United Steel Workers of America and proudly helped build the huge gates for dams straddling rivers coursing through the Tennessee Valley.

After his marriage in 1938, Dad aspired to a more stable life than the feast-or-famine, all-day shifts followed by strike-induced layoffs of the steel mill, and he began to sell. His handsome good looks, gift for gab, extroverted personality, and ear for a good story made him a born salesman. Over a lifetime of selling Standard Coffee, Sunshine Biscuit crackers and cookies, Liberty National insurance, Swift meats, and GAF roofing, he never forgot the name of a customer, the punch line of a joke, or what he earned every year of his life.

My early life as the only child of a proud, hot-tempered, but kindly father and a tender, indulgent mother was transitory but happy. Twelve schools in twelve years scattered across towns in two states belied a relatively stable childhood because three of the schools were in Anniston, reflecting the multiple times we lived there. When we first moved to Anniston during the Second World War, we rented rooms in a declining Victorian mansion on Quintard Avenue, the house's exterior elegance refuted by its rapidly declining interior. Next time we moved to the "Model City," Dad cleared enough as a salesman for Swift and Company to move a few streets further east to a bungalow located next to the city golf course in one direction, but in another only a tall wood fence away from a "Negro section" that had migrated east with us.

The third move was the charm. Now installed as manager of Swift's Anniston unit, my father bought a simple frame house as far up Tenth Street Mountain as development extended. True, we resided in the plain houses on the northeast side of the mountain rather than in the mansions on the southeast side, but it made little difference to our status. As soon as any of us spoke or ate a meal or tuned the radio to our favorite stations, it became obvious we were West Anniston people living on the east side of town.

Preference for barbecued pork, SPAM, peanut butter sandwiches, country and gospel music, my mother's constant sewing of clothes, and my father's genius at repairing anything that broke gave us away. So did Dad's prejudices against the "country club set," among whom he lived but lightly regarded. As I approached college age, he allowed me the option of attending Auburn, the state's land grant university, which he had visited and learned to love as an adolescent 4-H Club member; but he solemnly warned me against the University of Alabama, which he regarded as a "play school" dominated by spoiled rich kids whose parents belonged to country clubs and where, to be accepted, one had to join a social fraternity, for which he expressed contempt.

One concession that our family made to social conformity was membership in Parker Memorial Baptist Church. Like us, some Baptists had migrated from West Anniston to the eastern side of town. First Baptist occupied its intended block barely west of Noble Street and not far from the elegant Church of St. Michael. But as poor people moved in and wealthier people moved out, a strange metamorphosis took place. First Baptist was no longer the "first church" of southern tradition. By the twentieth century it might be the oldest white Baptist congregation in town, but it was not the most prestigious. That honor belonged to Parker Memorial.

Parker began as a less august church than it would become when members of First Baptist, who lived east of Noble Street, moved to Twelfth Street and established a new congregation there in 1887 (called simply "Second Baptist Church"). Duncan T. Parker, president of First National Bank, agreed to subsidize the pastor's salary if the church would call Dr. George B. Eager as pastor. The scholarly Dr. Eager, a well-educated Virginian, preached his first sermon in October 1889.

During Eager's pastorate, his benefactor, Duncan Parker, lost both his eldest son and wife. In memory of them, Parker contributed the princely sum of $85,000 to construct a worthy memorial. The magnificent sandstone edifice that rose from the clay lot on Quintard, with splendid wood vaulting and stained-glass windows, did not much resemble a traditional Baptist church, but it did inspire awe among worshipers. Members, properly impressed by their surroundings, dropped the mundane title Second Baptist for the more imposing Parker Memorial (often locals dropped the Baptist denominational designation and referred to the congregation simply as "Parker Church").

From the beginning, Parker's history was marked by curious paradoxes. Its chief benefactor, Duncan Parker, was not even a member, although his deceased wife had been the church's first organist. The congregation prided itself on hiring erudite pastors who were not at all typical of Baptist divines. They were better read theologically, more involved in social reform, and outspoken on matters of public policy. But their outspokenness was not always welcomed by parishioners. Indeed, Social Gospel advocate George Eager resigned as pastor, not because of criticism of his courageous stands on behalf of women's rights or political reform, but because of his criticism of the prestigious Calhoun Club, to which some of his prominent parishioners belonged and which served liquor. Subsequent pastors between 1900 and 1932 served as presidents of the state

Baptist convention, promoted the church to leadership in virtually every ranking (especially gifts to missions), and began a number of social ministries (including a settlement house in the textile community, staffed by a professionally trained female social worker).

Perhaps the greatest paradox came in the early 1930s, when Parker summoned one of its own to pastor the growing congregation. The young bachelor Charles R. Bell Jr. seemed at first glance a perfect fit. Born into the family of my grandfather's landlord, Charlie Bell grew up with all the advantages that a bank president father could bestow upon him. He graduated from Brown University, the cosmopolitan Baptist institution in Rhode Island, not the provincial Baptist college of his home state. He continued his education at Southern Baptist Theological Seminary, in Louisville, where he chose as teacher-mentors two of that institution's most liberal faculty (W. O. Carver and H. W. Tribble). Widely read and even more widely traveled, Bell returned home as full of dreams and visions as a fall muscadine is full of juice.

Strongly influenced by the Oxford Group or Buchmanite Movement during his formative years as a ministerial student, Bell led the formation of a local group of young people who were committed to mutual confession and restitution. However much their confessions may have unburdened them, other persons involved in their publicly confessed sins were not so liberated. Such naïveté had another downside as well. Older members accused young Charlie of building a clique of self-righteous people laying special claim to holiness. They were not impressed.

Worse revelations were in store for Parker. During a six-month sabbatical in 1936 to travel and study, Bell observed firsthand the rise of fascism in Europe, poverty in India (where he conferred with Mohandas Gandhi), and militarism in Japan (where he met with Christian pacifist and Socialist Toyohiko Kagawa). Deeply moved by what he saw and heard, Bell returned to Parker and formed a cooperative farm, developed a warm friendship with Clarence Jordan, the founder of Koinonia Farm near Americus, Georgia, conducted camps for black children, participated in the organization of the Southern Conference for Human Welfare, and entertained blacks in his home as social equals. He considered the New Deal too timid in tackling urgent social and economic problems, urged repeal of the poll tax, and abandoned Franklin D. Roosevelt for Socialist party presidential candidate Norman Thomas.

Parker members tolerated all this iconoclasm with varying degrees of patience. His crossing of venerable racial boundaries led not only to grumbling among his members but to hate mail and calls for his resignation.

But Charlie was not the church's first controversial pastor, and the congregation took perverse pride in its differentness from other congregations, Baptist and otherwise. In contravention of Foreign Mission Board guidelines, Parker sponsored its own missionary, J. Christopher Poole, in Africa. While Charlie studied abroad, the church welcomed in his place Dr. John W. Phillips, a native of England and graduate of Andover Newton Seminary, who held a Ph.D. in Egyptology from the University of London. In fact, Phillips, who was pastor emeritus of First Baptist Mobile, had scandalized the 1931 Southern Baptist Convention in a keynote sermon that challenged many basic tenets of biblical orthodoxy. Despite Phillips's reputation as a heretic, Parker Memorial's historian pronounced Phillips's sermons "among the most compelling ever heard from the Parker Memorial pulpit."[1]

Then again, the church historian was not a typical member of the congregation. Harry M. Ayers published the *Anniston Star,* one of a handful of consistently progressive Alabama newspapers. The son of T. W. and Minnie Ayers, who had been pioneer members of the church, Harry was deeply involved in both state and national Democratic party politics. His physician father had founded both the local paper and the *Alabama Medical Journal,* led the Good Roads Association in Alabama, worked in the Democratic party, and served as the first physician missionary for the Southern Baptist Foreign Mission Board. He, his wife, daughter, and son all served lengthy missionary terms in China and bequeathed Parker an international vision rare for the time in any region of America. Families such as the Ayers and Bells might not always agree with Charlie's advanced social and political attitudes, but they did defend him from detractors.

Even his enemies conceded that Charlie Bell could preach. His thoughtful analysis and international application of Christian principles were wedded to a spell-binding oratorical skill that left listeners riveted to his sermons. And crowds came as much to hear what he had to say about Christ as about controversial public issues.

Bell, who had married a wealthy wife and had survived a series of church crises occasioned by his unorthodox theology and social views, seemed to have matured sufficiently by the 1940s to take his place as lifetime pastor at Parker.

Then the onset of the Second World War propelled him in a totally new direction. Renewed interracial meetings in his home stirred rumors throughout the town in 1944. But it was his pacifism that finally did him in. His brother Tartt Bell had attended Tulane University and the University of Chicago and had become active in the Fellowship of Reconciliation, a national pacifist organization with roots in Quakerism. Charlie had always favored pacifism but had not made it a central issue in his church. But when church members determined to hang a plaque honoring Parker's members who served in the military and display an American flag in honor of the righteousness of the nation's cause, Bell objected to what he considered national idolatry. He managed to postpone the confrontation until D-Day in June 1944. As news of the European invasion blared from radios, Parker members resolved to celebrate the invasion in nationalistic terms. Overwhelmed by patriotic parishioners, many of whom were soldiers training at nearby Fort McClellan, Bell resigned.

He had no trouble finding pastorates in the American Baptist Convention, first in Madison, Wisconsin, and later in Pasadena, California. He returned to Parker to preach on anniversaries and other special occasions, and when he did, throngs of curious citizens turned out to hear their controversial local son.[2]

To replace Bell, the church chose a former navy chaplain. B. Locke Davis was a native Texan, a history graduate of Baptist-affiliated Hardin-Simmons University in Abilene, and had pastored a large Missouri Baptist church that was dually aligned with the Southern Baptist Convention (SBC) and the American Baptist Convention. He was pondering a move to a congregation in Detroit, Michigan, when Parker called him. Davis's long tenure in Anniston was as tranquil as Bell's had been stormy. Aside from a brief imbroglio when he publicly opposed John Kennedy for president in 1960, Davis enjoyed a secure and successful tenure. He was cut from the same cloth as Parker's early pastors. He fiercely advocated separation of church and state, played a prominent role in the state Baptist convention (serving two terms as president), and presided over the steady growth of his middle-class congregation. Ecumenical in the sense of maintaining close relations with pastors of other denominations even though he was opposed to church union, he played a major role in the interdenominational ministerial association. Still blessed with more than its fair share of Anniston's business and political leaders, the church flourished. Davis's sermons were thoughtful and carefully reasoned, although not memorable.

It was during the later Bell and early Davis ministries that I grew up in Parker

Memorial. Although I recall the annual revivals, I better remember the excellent and highly disciplined choir and the scintillating Sunday school class for college students, taught by one of Charlie Bell's disciples from his infamous Oxford Group. Although I took little notice of it at the time, I should have recognized the merging of personal piety and social justice that Alex Sawyer instilled in me in that class. And no one who ever knew Locke Davis could forget his passionate sermons advocating separation of church and state, particularly during the 1960 presidential race.

Thinking back, I am amazed at how few troublesome religious issues impressed me while I was growing up. After I felt "called" to the ministry, I had ample opportunity to preach at youth day services at my home church as well as to countywide youth rallies. I do not remember arguments over biblical authority, although I do recall admonitions against the handful of "independent" Baptist churches in Calhoun County that had withdrawn from the SBC because of the denomination's alleged liberalism. And when I was ordained, I remember the relief with which Locke Davis greeted my historical analysis of Baptists as an offshoot of the Protestant Reformation, rather than the "one true church" created by Jesus Christ in A.D. 33. Davis had no intention of encouraging what he considered historically inaccurate Baptist Landmark heresies that had flourished in the South during the century between 1850 and 1950.

My matriculation at Baptist-affiliated Howard College (now Samford University) in Birmingham, one of the more conservative denominational schools of the eastern seaboard, provided scholarly reinforcement for a path down which I had already started. Though some ministerial students were single-mindedly and dogmatically fundamentalist, my circle of acquaintances and friends adhered to the moderate course expostulated by all the religion faculty, most of whom were graduates of the progressive (by Baptist standards) Southern Seminary in Louisville. In Bible classes, my professors tried hard to reconcile what, to many of my friends, were seeming contradictions between science and religion (evolution with the first chapter of Genesis). They had been imbued with neo-orthodox theology at Southern and dispensed it freely at Howard. It all made sense to me, and I thrived on the works of Reinhold and Richard Niebuhr. Preaching regularly on Sundays in rural and small-town churches reinforced my perception of the kindness of ordinary Alabama Baptists for a "Howard boy" trying to make himself into a preacher. But even then, I think my style was a bit too academic for their tastes.

Certainly my attitudes on race did not sit well. I cannot remember when I departed from southern racial orthodoxy. I do not remember any time after I began reading the Bible that segregation made sense to me. At first my fierce pride in southern history and southernness kept me from completely rejecting the South's racial culture. But by my senior year in college, 1960–61, when the Freedom Riders came through my hometown and their bus was firebombed by local thugs, I was furious. My first letter to the editor of the *Anniston Star* was an unkind rebuttal to a fellow citizen who claimed the Bible as a mantra for segregation.

Whether it was because my racial views were diverging dangerously from my 1960s culture, or because my crowd of debaters were notably less fervent Baptists than my ministerial friends, I began to consider an alternative career. The most logical course seemed to be teaching, and the most obvious subject was history.

Scholarships were required because neither my family nor I had adequate financial resources. And my marriage in 1961, to a Baptist preacher's daughter whose family was even poorer than we were, compounded that problem. Fortunately, the National Defense Education Act had been passed recently, thanks primarily to the efforts of two liberal Alabama Democrats, Senator Lister Hill and Congressman Carl Elliott. So, after careful consideration of Vanderbilt, Duke (where I would have studied Latin American history), and Florida State Universities, I decided on Florida State (where the option was U.S. history). My Howard College mentor, Hugh Bailey, advocated FSU as an up-and-coming graduate program with a mix of well-regarded senior scholars such as Weymouth Jordan and promising young professors such as William W. Rogers, James Jones, and William I. Hair.

Bailey was correct, and I was not disappointed. FSU between 1961 and 1965 was neither the best graduate school in the South nor the most highly regarded, but it had just what a first-generation college and graduate student needed: wonderful mentoring, superb teaching, a bevy of excellent graduate students, a youthful faculty hungry for success. In fact, I learned more history at the Mecca, a campus hangout, while nursing a cup of coffee and arguing politics, religion, and especially race relations and southern history than I did in seminars. Almost never did Rogers, Jones, or Hair turn down my invitation to spend part of an afternoon in such informal tutoring.

The Mecca did not long remain our rendezvous for such conversations. The decision by its management to deny access to FSU's small contingent of African American students led to a boycott, which we all fervently observed. Our bull sessions moved down the hill to more racially accommodating eateries.

As hungry for success as my father before me and aware that I was not the best prepared graduate student ever (my transitory career in chronically underfunded and poorly staffed Alabama public schools had not prepared me well academically), I learned to compensate by discipline, organization, and hard work. The course work and reading reminded me of the Br'er Rabbit story of the briar patch: I had been thrown into a paradise of new ideas, challenging professors, and like-minded graduate students.

Unfortunately, those new ideas did not include southern religion. None of my history professors seemed interested in the subject, though Bill Rogers was a preacher's son. Like many southern intellectuals of that generation, they correctly viewed organized white Christianity as a bastion of racism, and even the religious among them had largely disengaged from institutional Christianity.

But Dorothy and Wayne Flynt had not disengaged. We found a congenial home at Tallahassee's First Baptist Church and a circle of graduate school friends who, with the important exception of James T. Baker (who later became a distinguished scholar of southern religion at Western Kentucky University), came from disciplines other than history. Or rather, we found a congenial home until 1964, when the church by a vote of some 540 to 527 rejected access to African Americans. I literally wept for my denomination, and I never again set foot in Tallahassee's First Baptist Church. My wife and I attended a Missouri Synod Lutheran Church for our remaining time in Tallahassee, and amidst church bombings and escalating violence in Alabama, I vowed never to return to Alabama or join another Baptist church.

Life often plays tricks with our more fervent resolutions, and so it did with mine. About this time in my life, I bought a copy of Harper Lee's novel *To Kill a Mockingbird* (1960).[3] Both author and novel were a revelation. Here was a person who thought like me, who actually applied biblical Christianity to a social context. Both author and setting involved Monroeville, Alabama, a world I understood and had once loved for its sense of community, history, and place. How many Harper Lees were there left in that world befuddled by Wallacism? Could the others be converted? Was it possible to be a "minister" if one's platform was a classroom podium rather than a church pulpit? Perhaps, in fact, academe would tolerate prophetic utterance, something most Southern Baptist churches had proven conclusively they would *not* tolerate.

In 1965, whether out of accident or design (my resilient Calvinism still views the act as providential), Dr. George V. Irons, head of the history department at my alma mater, newly renamed Samford University, asked me to return to teach history. But with Hugh C. Bailey as a rising star in southern history and with the war in Vietnam escalating, what the department really needed was someone to teach East Asian history. Fortunately, many small liberal arts colleges had the same need, schools that could not attract the small number of specialists graduating from Yale or Berkeley or the University of Washington. So the Ford Foundation had begun funding intensive summer-long institutes in East Asian Studies, one of which happened to be scheduled at FSU in the summer of 1965. With my new Ph.D. in hand, I turned down a one-year position at FSU and a tenure-track job at an impressive, newly established Baptist school—Kentucky Southern College—in order to return to Alabama and, even more amazing, to the folds of Alabama Baptists.

My brief immersion in Asian studies that summer was a revelation. I had already been enthralled by a course at FSU taught by political scientist Robert C. Bone, who had been a diplomat in Indonesia. Now the Ford grant brought to FSU scholars like Charles O. Hucker from Michigan, Minoru Shinoda from the University of Hawaii, Albert M. Craig from Harvard, and Oliver Edmund Clubb, one of the State Department's last "China hands." The postdoctoral grant also purchased for us an impressive personal library of books on East Asian history and culture, which I devoured, especially volumes on Taoism, Buddhism, Confucianism, and Shintoism. At Samford University and later at Auburn (which at the time had no East Asian specialist), I taught modern East Asian history. In time that interest was to lead to a merging of two fields.

In my new job at Samford University in Birmingham, I taught hordes of students from backgrounds similar to my own. As part of a generation determined to make history relevant, I shamelessly used my classroom to make them consider the ethical, moral, and religious dilemmas of a Bible Belt evangelicalism that coexisted with the most racist, poorest, demagogue-driven subculture in the United States.

Always fascinated with politics, I encouraged students to express their discontent with Alabama politics in concrete ways. I became faculty sponsor of the Young Democrats (quite a change for me; I had become an Eisenhower Republican as an adolescent, had served as southern coordinator of College Youth for Nixon-Lodge in 1960, and had led a Republicans for LBJ movement at FSU in 1964). We initiated a voter registration canvas in the black neighborhood of Homewood, the Birmingham suburb where Samford University was located. I also organized a joint venture of the Young Democrats and the Baptist Student Union to tutor high school students at Homewood's wretchedly underfunded black high school. And from that tutoring program at Rosedale High School came Samford's first African American student. I also spent hours with United Mine Workers volunteers in 1976 working to elect Jimmy Carter, whose Baptist affiliation, neo-orthodox theology, and social reform agenda so closely paralleled my own.

Just as important as my new political party was my new scholarly interest. FSU had not been a compatible environment for studying religious history, but Samford could hardly have been better. The Alabama Baptist Historical Archives, though seldom utilized by scholars, contained a huge treasure trove of resources. Across town, the Methodist state archives at Birmingham Southern College were equally rich and similarly ignored. At FSU I had taken the advice of Weymouth Jordan, initially my major professor (although I finished under the direction of W. W. Rogers with help from W. I. Hair), and had written a political dissertation on U.S. Senator Duncan U. Fletcher that in 1971 would become my first book.[4] My second book (1977) was a collateral study of Sidney Catts, the Alabama Baptist preacher turned Florida governor, a racist/nativist reformer who perfectly captured the ambiguities of southern evangelicalism.[5]

Meanwhile, I staked out my newfound interest in southern religious history in a series of journal articles and chapters in anthologies.[6] All the anthologies resulted from symposia on southern religion, where I came to know and respect the impressive scholarship of John Boles, David Harrell, Samuel Hill, Charles Wilson, and other pioneers in the study of Bible Belt Christianity. Indeed it was Harrell, with whom I would later be united at Auburn, who first asked me to write about southern poor whites for a series he was co-editing.[7] Although most scholars during the 1960s were drawn to poor whites by Marxist economic theory or interest in folk culture, I was attracted by questions of religion, ethics, and social justice. And I saw poor whites through the lens of my own father, mother, and grandparents, not as hapless victims but as proud, resilient survivors.

Initially my interest in the application of Christianity to social ethics and public policy drove my scholarship. If southern evangelicalism had produced Harper Lee, my religion professors at Howard College, Charlie Bell and B. Locke Davis at Parker Memorial, all those idealistic, deeply committed Christian students whom I taught at Samford and in my college Sunday school class at Vestavia Hills Baptist Church, and myself, might there be a dimension to such religion that scholars had either ignored or underemphasized? The more original sources I read, the more "deviants" from the stereotypical norm I encountered. My conclusions certainly did not contradict the dominant interpretations of Hill, Boles, Wilson, and company, but my research did refine and modify their conclusions. As the work of John P. McDowell and others increasingly made clear, southern evangelicals had not existed in a time warp impenetrable to new currents of religious thinking. If most southerners rejected liberal theology and Social Gospel ethics, some received it gladly, though with whatever "southernizing" it took to make it palatable to their cohorts. At least in Alabama (which became the most industrially diverse of the southern states), urban and industrial problems not unlike those of Pennsylvania or Michigan demanded similar social applications of Christianity. Emerging from the dark and largely untouched recesses of dusty manuscript collections and uncounted reels of microfilm were influential Baptist, Methodist, and Presbyterian ministers, theologians, and laypeople who had not only heard of Walter Rauschenbusch, Shailer Matthews, and Richard Ely but had even read them, met them, and invited them south to lecture at a hundred obscure meetings of social service commissions and Baptist, Methodist, or Presbyterian churches and college classrooms. And these denominations were producing enough of their own iconoclasts to convince conservative and fundamentalist brothers that the entire orthodox southern empire was threatened by traitors from within. Although few scholars had entertained the idea, it occurred to me that perhaps fundamentalists within the Southern Baptist Convention, Methodist Episcopal Church, and the Presbyterian Church in the United States (the southern branch of Presbyterians) might be correct: moderate and neo-orthodox ideas were indeed infiltrating these last bastions of the faith once delivered to the saints.

There was no doubt in my mind as to which side won this theological battle for the religious soul of the South during the twentieth century. Conservatives and fundamentalists captured the SBC after a long and bloody struggle and proceeded to drive out as many moderates as would go. And that was a fortuitous development for Southern Methodists, Presbyterians, and Episcopalians, where secession by conservatives and falling membership would have been even greater except for alienated moderate Baptists who, fed up with the growing intolerance of the SBC, joined alternative denominations, probably making both them and the SBC more conservative by their migration.

As for this old, gray, grizzled crusader, I decided to stay and fight; I remained in Alabama and stayed a Baptist. Perhaps in every Baptist psyche there is the making of a martyr to some cause or other. Plunging into politics and public policy, I made hundreds of speeches, some even in Alabama Baptist churches and at unappreciative governor's prayer luncheons, about child and adult poverty, racial and economic injustice, shabby and demeaning treatment of women, and other issues of social justice. I signed on with the American Cancer Society to help draft policy on cancer among America's socioeconomically disadvantaged. I served as expert witness in the state's equity funding lawsuit, testifying that the state discriminated against black, poor white, rural, and mentally or physically impaired public school students. I used my historical research and my training in theories of persuasion to keynote a statewide series of town meetings promoting tax and education reform. When Governor James Folsom Jr. and Circuit Judge Eugene Reese asked me to facilitate a compromise between plaintiffs and defendants in the state's equity funding lawsuit, I spent four months in meetings with lawyers trying to resolve this elemental question of social justice. I helped organize Voices for Alabama's Children, the Alabama Poverty Project, and A+ (Alabama's educational reform coalition) and spoke as often off campus as on campus after leaving the chairmanship of Auburn's history department. I served as senior policy adviser for the platform committee of the Alabama Democratic party. Once a week I still proclaimed the biblical message of grace and social justice to members of the Pilgrim's Sunday school class at Auburn's First Baptist Church, whose social ministry provided Blue Cross and Blue Shield health insurance to twenty children of employed but poor parents whose companies did not provide health insurance.

Finally able to focus my scholarly interest on religion, I agreed to help a colleague in East Asian history complete a collective biography of Alabama missionaries to China. I also accepted an invitation from Marlene Rikard, a former graduate student of mine and chair of the Alabama Baptist Historical Commission, to write a new kind of denominational history. The resulting books, *Taking Christianity to China* (1997) and *Alabama Baptists* (1998), gave me the most complete opportunity to explore the issues that first perplexed me in the 1960s.[8] Although a gestation of three decades is much too long a pregnancy, my relief at the final delivery of these books matched the lengthy conception. Being asked by the University of Alabama Press to co-edit a new series, Religion and American Culture, was simply frosting on the cake.

Whether or not all my research ever sees the light of day is problematic, given the aging of both body and energy. If I do not complete the task, then someone else will rummage through the fat files I have collected on all those southern Baptists, Methodists, and Presbyterians who across the decades have, like the author of this essay, believed that a warm, evangelical, missionary-centered Christianity of grace can be reconciled to a gospel of social justice and compassion for the poor.

The ancient Hebrew prophets proclaimed such a message. Christ defined that message as the function of his life. It is therefore not surprising that a substantial minority of southern evangelicals have occasionally believed the message and have even tried to change their society to conform to it.

Notes

1. Harry M. Ayers, *Parker Memorial Baptist Church, 1937–1968* (Anniston, Ala.: The Church, 1968).

2. Wayne Flynt, "Growing Up Baptist in Anniston, Alabama: The Legacy of the Reverend Charles R. Bell, Jr.," in Jerry Elijah Brown, ed., *Clearings in the Thicket: An Alabama Humanities Reader* (Macon, Ga.: Mercer University Press, 1985), 147–82.

3. Harper Lee, *To Kill a Mockingbird* (Philadelphia: Lippincott, 1960).

4. Wayne Flynt, *Duncan Upshaw Fletcher: Dixie's Reluctant Progressive* (Tallahassee: Florida State University Press, 1971).

5. Wayne Flynt, *Cracker Messiah: Governor Sidney J. Catts of Florida* (Baton Rouge: Louisiana State University Press, 1977).

6. Wayne Flynt and William Warren Rogers, "Reform Oratory in Alabama, 1890–1896," *Southern Speech Journal* 29 (winter 1963): 94–106; Wayne Flynt, "The Ethics of

Democratic Persuasion and the Birmingham Crisis," *Southern Speech Journal* 35 (fall 1969): 40–53 (my outside field at FSU had been rhetoric and theories of persuasion, which have remained a lifelong interest); Wayne Flynt, "The Negro and Alabama Baptists during the Progressive Era," *Journal of the Alabama Academy of Science* 39 (April 1968): 163–67; Wayne Flynt, "Dissent in Zion: Alabama Baptists and Social Issues, 1900–1914," *Journal of Southern History* 35 (Nov. 1969): 523–42; Wayne Flynt, "Sidney Catts: The Road to Power," *Florida Historical Quarterly* 49 (Oct. 1970): 107–28; Wayne Flynt, "Organized Labor, Reform, and Alabama Politics, 1920," *Alabama Review* 23 (July 1970): 103–80; Wayne Flynt, "Alabama White Protestantism and Labor, 1900–1914," *Alabama Review* 25 (July 1972): 192–217; Wayne Flynt, "Religion in the Urban South: The Divided Religious Mind of Birmingham, 1900–1930," *Alabama Review* 30 (April 1977): 108–34; Wayne Flynt, "Southern Baptists: Rural to Urban Transition," *Baptist History and Heritage* 16 (Jan. 1981): 24–34; Wayne Flynt, "Southern Baptists and Reform, 1890–1920," *Baptist History and Heritage* 7 (Oct. 1972), 211–23; Wayne Flynt and Wallace M. Alston Jr., "Religion in the Land of Cotton," in Brandt Ayers, ed., *You Can't Eat Magnolias* (New York: McGraw-Hill, 1972), 99–123; Wayne Flynt, "One in the Spirit, Many in the Flesh: Southern Evangelicalism," in David E. Harrell Jr., ed., *Varieties of Southern Evangelicalism* (Macon, Ga.: Mercer University Press, 1981), 23–44; Wayne Flynt, "Alabama," in Samuel S. Hill, ed., *Religion in the Southern States: A Historical Study* (Macon, Ga.: Mercer University Press, 1983), 5–26; Wayne Flynt, "Feeding the Hungry and Ministering to the Broken Hearted: The Presbyterian Church in the United States and the Social Gospel, 1900–1940," in Charles R. Wilson, ed., *Religion in the South* (Oxford: University of Mississippi Press, 1985), 83–137.

7. This initiative resulted in J. Wayne Flynt, *Dixie's Forgotten People: The South's Poor Whites* (Bloomington: Indiana University Press, 1979).

8. Wayne Flynt and Gerald W. Berkley, *Taking Christianity to China: Alabama Missionaries in the Middle Kingdom, 1850–1950* (Tuscaloosa: University of Alabama Press, 1997); Wayne Flynt, *Alabama Baptists: Southern Baptists in the Heart of Dixie* (Tuscaloosa: University of Alabama Press, 1998).

Growing Up a Historian

Frederick A. Bode

M y background did not point in an obvious way to an academic career, much less to one more or less devoted to the religious history of the South. I spent most of the first two decades or so of my life in southern California, and although that placed me technically below the Mason-Dixon line, I would never set foot in the "real" South (if suburban Washington, D.C., even counts) until almost the end of my eighteenth year. My parents and I, their only child, had joined the early post–World War II migration to the western land of opportunity, in our case from the Middle West. One might suppose that Wheaton, Illinois, where I spent the first five years of my life, would prove more promising in shedding light on my future interest in evangelical religion. But in 1939, the year before my birth, the eponymous site of Wheaton College (and now the home of the Institute for the Study of American Evangelicals) was beginning to assume its predominant character as a pleasant outer suburb of Chicago whose new and inexpensive housing had lured my parents from the confines of a flat on the near North Side. The college, I suspect, entered their consciousness mainly as an impediment to the purveyance of alcoholic beverages in the town.

Even more remote from my chosen field or the likelihood of pursuing an academic career were my parents' backgrounds. My father, born in 1899, had immigrated from Germany in 1912, along with his parents, four brothers, and one sister (another brother and sister, twins, were born shortly thereafter). My grandfather had been a cabinetmaker in Germany, and after a brief spell in Iowa eventually set himself up in business in Milwaukee, where he achieved only modest success. My mother was also of German ancestry but was born in Lafayette, Indiana, in 1904 of middle western–born parents, growing up in a large family of six children, all but one of whom were girls. Unlike my father, who was nominally Lutheran, she was raised in a Roman Catholic household, and a rather strict one at that. My grandfather had tried his hand at various small businesses, but it was his good-natured camaraderie and involvement in local Democratic politics that eventually secured his appointment as superintendent of city parks. (It was many years later that my budding historical consciousness led me to seek out the bronze plaque that linked his name with New Dealer Harry Hopkins at the city swimming pool built by the Works Progress Administration.) Moreover, no one in my parents' families was educated beyond high school, and most of them did not even get that far. My father eventually secured a high school diploma at night school, but my mother left school around the sixth or seventh grade (it was never quite clear).

Yet my parents did aspire to upward mobility. My father, who decided early in life that he would never make a living working in overalls, trained himself as a young man to be a draftsman. By a combination of hard work and Germanic perfectionism he established a reputation for himself first in Chicago and then in Los Angeles as someone who could be counted upon to take on complex and difficult projects. He eventually moved from woodworking firms to architectural offices in the 1960s and continued to work almost full-time as a consultant until he was over eighty, achieving real prosperity late in life. My mother toiled during most of her married life in jobs ranging from "salesgirl" at Marshall Fields Department Store to telephone operator during the war to clerking in a drug store. I thus grew up in a household in which everyone was expected to contribute (I at a paper route, as drug store box boy, and as Edison Company meter reader) to the maintenance of a modest middle-class way of life. But there was something more than a mere expectation of upward mobility that characterized my family and that pushed me to excel in school and, finally, toward an academic career. My father, alone among his numerous siblings, had a craving for books, with all the lacunae and distortions unsystematic reading can bring. He had always wanted, he told me, to be a professor. My mother's taste ran to romantic novels, but she was a shrewd judge of human nature and had real political instincts. Despite the fact that she held down a job, she threw herself into community work, especially the PTA. Although she had difficulty composing a grammatical sentence, she managed to serve several terms as an elected member of the local board of education. My parents took it for granted that I would go to college. Fewer than a third of my numerous cousins did so.

I spent my school years in Inglewood, a suburb of Los Angeles, whose rapid growth during and after the war depended largely on employment in the nearby aircraft industry. Although now featured in Quentin Tarentino movies as the home of assorted African American desperados pursing their own version of the American dream, it was earlier a white working-class and middle-class community, where most people traced their origins to mainly Protestant "old immigrant" stock, and most were first- or second-generation migrants, like my family, from the Middle West or the South. There was a respectable minority of Catholics and "new immigrant" Italians, Eastern Europeans, and even Jews. The small number of Latinos found in Inglewood then were referred to as "Mexican" if they lived near the railroad tracks and "Spanish" if they looked white and owned a home, as a few did, in a decent neighborhood. There were even a few East Asians, but no blacks. My parents, like many others, moved to Inglewood in part because it was both affordable and white. It had even been the scene of Ku Klux Klan activity during the 1920s, and the city's ordinances were still said to contain a provision forbidding blacks to be on the streets after 8 P.M. This was a variety of racism that would not have been out of place in many working-class neighborhoods throughout the North. However, by the time I was in high school, between 1954 and 1958, the conventional wisdom I absorbed there regarded discrimination as un-American and disapproved of those southerners, Governor Orval Faubus being the prime example, who sought to flout the law. Like other northerners, we saw racism as a southern problem that had little to do with us. After I left Inglewood, the issue of busing emerged and racial conflict flared, only to be "solved" by massive white flight that changed the character of this city of 70,000 in less than a decade.

Unlike African Americans, white southerners were not an abstraction for me. The occasional southern accent could be heard in the classroom or on the playground, but such accents were more common among my peers' parents, who had been part of the migration westward going back to the Great Depression. Some still endured epithets like "Okie" and "Arkie," which applied without much discrimination to "poor white" southerners generally and carried connotations of laziness, malnutrition, and old jalopies parked in the yard. But on the whole, southerners, though a minority among the middle westerners, were absorbed into the respectable part of the community. The parents of one of my best friends and the mother of another were southern born, all of them Georgians and Baptists to boot. They regularly attended the First Baptist Church, which, though it adhered to the northern American Baptist Convention, had a distinctly southern cast to it. (There was, in fact, a Southern Baptist Church in Inglewood, but since its membership was decidedly poorer, the upwardly mobile Baptists regardless of origin tended to favor the First Baptist Church.)

Some of the friendships I made in high school (and in one case in the fourth grade) have persisted over the years. We were a very close group that provided me with something of a refuge for my own social insecurity and that was remarkably fecund in ways that have influenced me to this day. We debated all manner of things and prided ourselves on our knowledge of politics and current affairs. We were academic achievers and in subtle ways even competed against each other. All of my small group of friends finished in the top ten of our graduating class of close to four hundred. At the time, I considered myself a partisan Republican, and that meant I could support what I regarded as the party's historic commitment to freedom. I opposed segregation almost as vehemently as I denounced the New Deal and all its works. To one who craved acceptance and upward mobility, the Democratic Party meant scruffy labor bosses, the taint of communism (yes, there was a time I thought the junior senator from Wisconsin, Joe McCarthy, was fighting the good fight), perdition-bound Roman Catholics, and—southerners. In my senior year United States history class I argued regularly about segregation with a new girl from Arkansas. By the end of the year she was visibly pregnant, thus confirming the worst about southern "hillbillies." Even more fun were the debates I pursued with my friend Peter's Savannah-born mother almost every morning before walking to school. She was an ardent Democrat, loyal Baptist, patriotic Georgian, and firm defender of the folkways of the South. (Her husband was an English-born doctor, one-time Seventh Day Adventist, admirer of Nietzsche and Aldous Huxley, and indulger in all manner of esoterica.) The Georgian parents of my friend Kaye (Homer Kaye III, to give his full Christian name) could hardly have been more different—though each seemed recognizably southern. His mother was a kind, self-effacing, churchgoing lady who made excellent fried chicken. His father, also a churchgoer, was usually loudly denouncing some conspiracy directed against decent folk or defending some bizarre scheme destined to save humankind. Never, as I recall, did he engage in a racial diatribe. Kaye planned to study art and become a painter. (After returning from the University of Illinois, he gained occasional entry into the arcane world of Hollywood. I owe to him an abiding interest in art and film.) So, by accident of friendship, things southern entered my consciousness and remained there—partly a bundle of prejudices and partly a miscellany of trivial knowledge, like the ability to name almost every southern senator.

Most young people I knew in Inglewood acknowledged a denominational affiliation. To be a Methodist or a Presbyterian was still part of one's persona even if church attendance was sporadic. To satisfy my maternal grandfather, to whom he was devoted, my father consented to have me baptized in a Catholic church, but that was the limit. Since he would never let his son be subjected to the blandishments of popery, I was raised and confirmed a Lutheran, in a church whose members bore names like Jensen, Gabrielson, and Hallberg and where the accents of Minnesota were thick on the ground. My father was a Mason and something of a freethinker for whom God was manifest in the deserts and mountains of southern California. My mother always harbored some resentment that she allowed herself to cease being a practicing Catholic, but she did so to please my father. Both attended church occasionally since it seemed in my interest that they do so. Although our church did not adhere to one of the conservative synods, our pastor was fairly traditional and taught us straight from Luther's *Short Catechism* during two years (yes, *two*) of confirmation classes. Since I took religion, like everything else, with seriousness, I accepted the teachings of the catechism with utter literalness. I must have missed the point, however, of the doctrine of *sola fides*, since the absence of any inward acceptance of faith never seemed to trouble me. My best and oldest friend, Bill, was a Disciple of Christ. We frequently attended each other's church (and sometimes the Baptist church of our other friends) and regularly debated such questions as the proper mode of baptism and the propriety of wine as opposed to grape juice for communion. I was convinced that Bill's parents were model Christians who never drank, never swore, never fought, and never missed church. As a result I was embarrassed on account of my own parents, who did all of those things. Bill's family was, moreover, more affluent. Never mind that Bill frequently ended up at my house for dinner and overnights and that friends were always eager to accompany my father and me on our hiking and camping trips. Because Bill planned to become a minister, I too had to become a minister, as I announced to my startled parents at about the age of about fourteen. My religion, then, grew out of insecurity, and dogma replaced faith.

In my senior year of high school my career plans changed. I had already begun to shed my quasi-fundamentalist beliefs, and since I had never experienced anything like a "call" to the ministry, the change entailed no soul-searching. Under the influence of my government teacher, and a similar decision by my friend Peter, top student and leading high school intellectual, I decided on a career in the foreign service. Since our teacher had gone there, both of us planned to enter George Washington University (GW) in the fall of 1958. By midsummer Peter had backed off and decided to stay home and enter the government program at the University of Southern California (USC). Still insecure and following the lead of an envied friend, I submitted a last-minute application to USC and was accepted. But then something happened that I cannot entirely fathom or explain. Toward the end of August I informed my parents that I intended to go to GW after all and would leave home in less than two weeks. The decision was liberating and, as I look back, one of the most important ones I ever made. My freshman roommate turned out to be a Jew from Miami, a couple of years older than I. There were a few Jews at Inglewood High School, none of whom seemed very different from the rest of us. But Al was something else. He sounded different, sort of New York, or at least what I had imagined from movies that a New York accent would be like. He was a liberal Democrat whose hero was Adlai Stevenson, he read the *New York Times*—and he was the first person I had ever met who proclaimed a disbelief in God. I began my Sundays in Washington as a regular communicant of Reformation Lutheran Church on Capitol Hill, but I also sought out Al and his Jewish friends, and after a while my church attendance became more sporadic. Like so many college freshmen before me, I was beginning to question my certainties. My politics were becoming less conservative and my religious beliefs less secure. During my second year at GW I learned that my uncorrected vision would disqualify me for a foreign service appointment. While I expressed some regret, inwardly I was pleased. Since I had always loved history, I decided, with the rather vague aim of becoming a teacher, to switch my major and return to California to complete my two final undergraduate years at the University of California, Los Angeles (UCLA). (Bill became and remains a Disciple's minister. Peter left the Baptist fold, became an Episcopal priest, and has since moved to England, where he took Roman Catholic orders.)

By the time I graduated from UCLA in 1962 I was a full-fledged liberal and agnostic. Much of the student body there was Westside Jewish and liberal, especially so, it seemed, in history. My professors at GW now struck me as older and stodgier; many of those at UCLA were young, brilliant, and intellectually provocative. Robert Winter's courses on twentieth-century America provided us with a delectable menu that included generous portions of Lewis Mumford, Alfred Kazin, Lionel Trilling, and C. Wright Mills, along with slide lectures that ranged from Chicago School architects to the abstract expressionists. Instead of straight political history, we learned about Populist folklore and Progressive status anxieties from Richard Hofstadter's *Age of Reform*. Donald Meyer's course on intellectual history was something of a *tour de force*. Our textbook was V. L. Parrington's *Main Currents in American Thought*, but Meyer had studied at Harvard and had learned from Perry Miller that the intellectual historian need not despise an American "mind" heavily freighted with Calvinist theology. Moreover, Meyer had just published his Harvard doctoral dissertation, entitled *The Protestant Search for Political Realism*, which included a penetrating analysis of the political evolution of Reinhold Niebuhr.[1] Parrington's unidimensional celebration of "democratic" writers and thinkers and his denigration of anything that smacked of Puritanism did not stand a chance against Meyer's slyly understated but witty and, for a Niebuhr scholar, appropriately ironic lectures.

My interest in the South took a back seat at UCLA, but "Negro history" and the problem of civil rights (the sit-ins had begun, but the "movement" was only in its infancy) occasioned more than a passing glance. The election of John Kennedy, which caused palpable excitement among my liberal professors, brought renewed hope that despite "massive resistance" in the South the achievement of equality and justice was possible. Moreover, I was convinced by C. Vann Woodward's argument in *The Strange Career of Jim Crow* that segregation was not an eternal and ineradicable southern folkway but of relatively recent origin.[2] My teacher in the senior methods seminar was a historian of the old school, Brainerd Dyer, who had written biographies of William Evarts and Zachary Taylor, and for whom my regular references to Woodward elicited the testy comment, "Well, C. Vann Woodward may be a good historian, but that doesn't mean he's right about everything" (or words to that effect).[3] While I wanted to choose a topic on "the Negro" for my senior essay, Dyer suggested that I do something on my (and his) home state of Illinois. By way of compromise we agreed that I would produce a research paper on "The Negro in Antebellum Illinois." Among other things I learned that prejudice and discrimination had never been just southern problems. My first footnote citation was to an essay Woodward had just published entitled "The Antislavery Myth," from which I quoted the following: "[an] elaborate aspect of the antislavery myth is the legend that the Mason and Dixon Line not only divided slavery from freedom in antebellum America, but that it also set apart racial inhumanity in the South from benevolence, liberality and tolerance in the North."[4] Although many students thought Dyer old-fashioned, I came to appreciate his nuts-and-bolts approach to historical research. I learned how to compile a bibliography, read my sources critically, be aware of differing interpretations, take notes, get my footnote format right, and finally put everything together more or less coherently.

Meanwhile, new career plans began to take shape. I had never thought seriously about the prospect of graduate work in history. Yet both Meyer and Winter pushed me in that direction, nominated me for a Woodrow Wilson fellowship, and urged me to apply to the best graduate schools. To my surprise I received not only the Wilson but favorable responses to all of my grad school applications except one—Harvard. Yale was my first choice, partly because Woodward was there, although I had by no means committed myself to southern history. Nor did the possibility of religious history occur to me, even though my attention to religion remained strong. Reading Meyer's *Protestant Search* over the summer led me to the work of Reinhold Niebuhr at a time when the influence of that theologian over historians and intellectuals generally was at its height. Moreover, the examples of Meyer and Niebuhr seemed to show that it was possible to pursue an interest in religion without being in any conventional sense "religious." After I opted for Yale, I learned that my friend Bill had decided to continue his theological training at Yale Divinity School. The fact that he had chosen a leading "liberal" graduate school led me for a time to underestimate the depth of his Christian faith. His religious trajectory was in fact quite different from my own. Peter's turn to Episcopalianism (he was also nearby at Episcopal Divinity School in Cambridge) introduced me to a church where, it seemed, one could adhere to traditional forms but at the same time avoid precise theological commitments and lay aside worries about anything that might interfere with a good time. This was a superficial view, but it was not—these were the days of Bishop Pike's notoriety—altogether mistaken. Since

I still *enjoyed* attending services, if ever I felt the need for a quick liturgical fix, I would head toward an Episcopal church, the higher the better.

My first year of graduate school was a baptism of fire. Every student I met gave the impression of being more sophisticated than I, more enlightened about the arcane mysteries of doing history, and more articulate in seminar discussions. In short, I was terrified, convinced I would never make it to the end of the year. In a very practical way, however, I discovered my métier in John Blum's seminar on the United States in the twentieth century. On the first day he simply presented a list of research topics on the American homefront during the Second World War from which we had to choose with scarcely a moment's reflection. To my good fortune one of them dealt with religious opinion on postwar plans for Germany. I ended up comparing the views of Niebuhr and Charles Clayton Morrison of the *Christian Century*, a topic that allowed me to pick up where Meyer had left off in 1941. In all, Blum was a model seminar director, who returned draft after draft of our papers until we got it just right— and had eliminated all those passive verb constructions that he could not abide.

Religious topics became something of a mainstay for me and helped ease the problem of choosing essay topics. In Hajo Holborn's seminar on modern German history, for example, I did a paper on the role of the Protestant churches in Germany under the Nazi regime. But it was in Woodward's seminar that I made the commitment to southern history. During the first term I produced a paper on the Episcopal Church and the Negro during Reconstruction, using the *Southern Churchman* of Richmond as my principal source. This was my first exposure to a nineteenth-century denominational newspaper, which at this stage of my training I found disappointing since inevitably it said far less about my topic than I imagined it would and indeed little about anything that seemed historically important. Only slowly did I realize that, if properly read, the denominational press could provide a whole range of insights into the cultural and intellectual world of southern Protestants. The results of my effort were also less than I expected. Woodward praised the research but was unconvinced that whatever southern Episcopalians said about the problems of Reconstruction really mattered very much. During the second semester, when we switched our attention to the post-Reconstruction South, I resolved to try again with a religious topic, this time looking for evidence of the Social Gospel in the annual proceedings of the Southern Sociological Congress (1912–20). From

Woodward's point of view, however, such organizations did little more than consider the symptoms, rather than probe the fundamental causes, of injustice in southern society. My paper, although a good, workmanlike job, did little to change Woodward's mind about the marginality of a southern Social Gospel.

Between 1962 and 1964 I completed my coursework, which included an American religious history seminar with Sydney Ahlstrom. Like Donald Meyer, he proved that religious history could be an intellectually challenging field. I chose to do my major paper on Methodism and society in Georgia between 1880 and 1900, looking particularly at the role of Atticus Haygood. Having read Timothy Smith's *Revivalism and Social Reform*, I applied too uncritically to the Georgia scene his argument that Wesleyan perfection had paved the way for the Social Gospel.[5] Still, I tried to take the Methodist tradition seriously (something with which I had no personal connection whatever), as Ahlstrom insisted I must. I was pleased with what I had written, and so was Ahlstrom, who urged me to pursue my interest in postbellum southern religion. I decided to continue my search for a southern Social Gospel, and Woodward, despite his skepticism, generously agreed to supervise my doctoral research, with Ahlstrom as a member of my committee.

Starting out in southern "church history" (as it was still usually denominated) in the 1960s meant that there was very little serious historical work on which one could build. About the only respectable monograph in my area was Hunter D. Farish's *The Circuit Rider Dismounts*, a study of southern Methodism in the New South published in 1938. I did not know at the time that matters were about to change. The publication of Kenneth Bailey's study of twentieth-century southern Protestants and Donald Mathews's book on slavery and Methodism was imminent, and Samuel Hill's enormously influential *Southern Churches in Crisis* would appear in 1966. John Boles and John Eighmy were also beginning or about to begin their own pioneer work on southern religion.[6] So I continued to plow through denominational histories, biographies, and other published sources to search for whatever evidence of social concern and engagement among southern ministers I could find. I made regular trips into New York where the public library, remarkably, held a sizeable—and rapidly disintegrating— collection of southern denominational newspapers running roughly from about 1880 to the 1910s.

While at Yale I had watched the civil rights struggle from a distance and was not involved in any political activity although I knew some students who identified in one way or another with "the movement" and were already dissenting from American policy in Vietnam. My knowledge of the South and understanding of the racial conflict had always been theoretical. In the spring of 1965 I went to the South on my first research trip, and it was the first time I had journeyed beyond northern Virginia into the Old Confederacy. Although I happened to be in Montgomery shortly after the Selma march, I can hardly say that the trip was a revelation. It did not particularly raise my political consciousness or change the way I conceived of doing history. To the outsider the most egregious manifestations of segregation were no longer obvious. Apart from the accents, universities such as Emory, North Carolina, and Duke, where I spent my time plowing through manuscript collections, did not seem much different from what I knew in the North. The few black faces I observed on these campuses (for that matter, not many fewer than at Yale or UCLA) suggested that progress was being made. Driving through the South I saw a lot of rural poverty, but to me Lyndon Johnson's Great Society seemed on the right track to solving outstanding problems.

Something else was starting to gnaw at me as my note cards accumulated: my research lacked a focus. I found considerable material that suggested some clerical engagement in social issues, but most of it seemed to be detached from the fundamental problems of race and class that Woodward emphasized. Yes, there were the Haygoods, the McKelways, and the Murphys, but they seemed stuck in what we might today call a New South discourse. Their criticism, so I was beginning to think, lacked bite. I could gather more information on what the ministers or the denominational press had to say about social problems, but as Woodward rightly warned, I risked writing a dissertation that was little more than a catalogue of pronouncements on this or that issue. Ahlstrom insisted that I try harder to get at the "ethos" of southern Protestantism—I, who had never attended a service in a *southern* Baptist church! I did have the good fortune of being a teaching assistant during 1965–66 in a course on southern history, taught by Staughton Lynd, who was beginning a short and stormy career at Yale. Lynd, who came from a radical Quaker background, had been active in the civil rights movement and was now an outspoken opponent of American support for South Vietnam. Always tolerant of diverse points of view, he made no bones about his own position, as a historian searching for evidence of radical dissent in the American past or as an activist seeking to redeem the American present. Although I am more cautious now about the desirability of pursuing such agendas as a historian, working for him at the time set me on the road to reexamining some of my own ideological commitments and ultimately the direction my research would take.

It took a while before the spell of uncertainty broke. While reading issues of the *North Carolina Christian Advocate* I discovered among Methodists deep divisions that somehow related to the political controversies agitating that state during the 1890s. After poking around a bit, I decided to give up the idea of searching for an elusive Social Gospel. It would be more worthwhile, I now thought, to focus on this one state during a decade of political turmoil that included the Populist revolt and the white supremacy campaigns. Woodward queried whether I would have enough to go on. Would I really discover anything new? Woodward himself had given only cursory attention to southern religion. From his perspective the churches were mainly an impediment to addressing more fundamental issues of class and race. I was now inclined to take Woodward's opinion more seriously; but if he was right, I wanted to find out exactly how the churches stood in relation to concrete issues and in what ways, if any, they influenced the course of political and social change. On another research trip in the spring of 1967 I met several historians at the University of North Carolina (UNC), and then, shortly after I returned to Yale, Woodward asked me if I would be interested in a three-year appointment as an instructor in the history department at UNC. (How differently things were done in those days!) As a result of floundering for a year and half with an unmanageable topic (I still have boxes of unutilized note cards), I was not yet close to finishing my dissertation. I had written very little, and there was still more research to do. What better place could there be than Chapel Hill? And so I eagerly accepted the offer.

I quickly discovered that a heavy teaching load, especially during the first year, limited progress on my dissertation. And there were other distractions, namely the war and a growing mood of black militancy that manifested itself during my third year at UNC in a full-scale strike by the black cafeteria workers. Caught up in the spirit of the times, I committed a good deal of energy to both issues and became a founding member of the local chapter of the explicitly radical New University Conference (which regarded itself as the "faculty arm" of the Students for a Democratic Society), much to the chagrin of many of my senior colleagues. I became friends with several younger colleagues and graduate students who were politically active and had at least a passing interest in Marxism. Since the time I had worked for Lynd I had become aware of a number of younger scholars who were developing a more radical perspective on American society and applying Marxian categories to the study of American history. I was especially excited by Eugene Genovese's recently published *Political Economy of Slavery*, which developed a sophisticated analysis of southern slave society, distinct from and antagonistic to northern bourgeois capitalism.[7] It nicely complemented Woodward's account of the postbellum period that traced the rise of a new bourgeoisie that largely displaced the antebellum planters as the South's dominant class.

My engagement with Marxism generally and Genovese's work in particular was an intellectual turning point for me. Their impact remained powerful even after I began to question Genovese's argument that planters as a class stood opposed to decisive aspects of bourgeois ideology and practice. More to the point, Genovese led me to the concept I needed to make sense of the role of North Carolina's religious leaders and institutions during the 1890s. This was the notion of hegemony, first articulated in the writings of the Italian Marxist Antonio Gramsci. It provided a way to understand how every stable class society, for example, requires a historically distinctive framework of institutions, practices, and ideological assumptions widely held to be legitimate. Specifically, I tried to show how denominational leaders in North Carolina used their control of such institutions as colleges and newspapers to provide ideological support for those political forces that favored moderate reform under the auspices of a pro-business leadership. Religion, I concluded, helped secure the hegemony of what V. O. Key called North Carolina's "progressive plutocracy" or, in the phrase of George Tindall, "business progressivism."[8] Despite my political activism, I managed by early 1969 to send off a draft of the thesis to Woodward, whose suggestions for revision were relatively few.

In looking back on my three years in North Carolina, I in no way regret the stands that I took. At the same time, my political ideas were often naive. Those of us who saw ourselves as part of the New Left seriously overestimated the possibility of radical change in America, while we had too little confidence in the effectiveness of the democratic process for achieving more proximate goals.

Yet fear of dissent and even repression were also realities. As UNC tried to head off the unionization of its black employees, and especially after the Kent State massacre in the spring of 1970, it was easy to believe that the university was complicit in racism and was part of a system that made the war in Vietnam possible—an object lesson in hegemony. I had, however, neglected the lessons I had earlier learned from reading Niebuhr, that political aims, however desirable in themselves, may be deflected or thwarted by the realities of power and by our own very human limitations. I eventually concluded that ideologies like Marxism, in seeking to construct societies free of inequality and conflict, often end up having to impose those conditions of perfected virtue that we as human beings stubbornly resist and thus risk creating deadly caricatures of their idealistic aims. I also remained too isolated from colleagues who would have enriched my time at UNC. I was skeptical of the effectiveness and even good will of many of those I regarded as "so-called" liberals. These attitudes were not always fair, and I should have been willing to show more openness to and respect for a world I had never known firsthand.

Since there was no question of my contract being renewed at UNC, in 1970 I had to look for another job. Despite everything, I actually had two offers. The one I accepted was an appointment at Sir George Williams University (now Concordia University) in Montreal, whose history department had a reputation for a Marxist bent. Eugene Genovese had taught there for two very controversial years.[9] I knew that George Rudé, the distinguished British Marxist, had also been recruited. Moreover, a young colleague at Duke, who had been politically active in Durham, had gone to Sir George the year before. Also arriving from Duke in 1970 was Don Ginter, with whom I would undertake several years hence a very fruitful scholarly collaboration. Together with a recent Duke Ph.D. (and son of a Southern Baptist minister), we made up quite the North Carolina contingent. A period of rapid expansion at Canadian universities during the 1960s and '70s led to the hiring of many foreign academics, especially Americans. Later, especially as budgets became tighter, a reaction set in, but among my generation of academics in Canada the proportion of Americans was high. Probably many of us thought that we would eventually return to "the States," but, in fact, most of us stayed in Canada, especially since job opportunities were shrinking everywhere in North America. I eventually became a Canadian citizen.

My move to another country greatly reduced my activism. Although for a time I regretted this state of affairs, I gradually realized that a life devoted more, so to speak, to the theoretical side of things was more suitable to my temperament. I kept busy preparing for classes, reading widely, seeing lots of movies, and preparing my dissertation for publication. Meanwhile, during my second month in Montreal at a departmental party, I met Janice Simpkins, an undergraduate in her final year. Discovering we had much in common, including a love of European travel, reading, and good food, we saw more of each other and got married the following July. After several years of simply enjoying life together, we had two children, Paul and Sarah, born in 1980 and 1983. My marriage also helped me reach a degree of maturity that gave me a more objective perspective on my life, including my years at Chapel Hill. My political views became more moderate as well.

My revised dissertation was published in 1975 under the title *Protestantism and the New South*.[10] Like any author, I looked forward to the reviews with great trepidation. I was greatly relieved that all but one of the reviews were favorable. The most penetrating criticism came later, notably in work by Wayne Flynt and David Harrell. Their principal objection was that the book focused on denominational leaders, who might have been expected to identify with other elites in political and business life, while it neglected the life blood of the churches, ordinary men and women whose religion was less compromised by the requirements of power. Their faith not only sustained them in trying times but could even provide a sense of urgency to such protest movements as Populism. (I do take some comfort that Flynt judged my book to be the "best example of this kind of elitist analysis.")[11] I must, of course, plead guilty to emphasizing the role of elites. I did so in part because some denominational leaders possessed a relatively coherent vision about the directions in which they wanted to take their churches *as institutions*. I would still argue that their efforts had important political implications that the Marxian concept of hegemony helped me illuminate. I also showed that the most powerful criticisms of the churches' conservatism came from within, by men (I certainly did ignore women) whose social vision was strongly informed by their religious faith. What I did not appreciate was the importance of church records as a grass-roots source; nor did I take into account the growth of holiness and Pentecostal movements as possible indications of popular disaffection from denominational establishments.

Although I continued to keep up (more or less) with the literature on southern religion, my interests for a time turned elsewhere—first to the antebellum South and then to the hoary question, raised anew by Genovese's work, of southern distinctiveness. Since so much of the recent quantitative work, especially by the "new" economic and political historians, bore on issues in which I was interested—the particular features of southern social structure and political behavior—I followed the debates in those fields quite closely. Although I remained duly skeptical of behavioralist explanations, I was prepared to accept that behavioral models and quantitative methods could shed light on discrete historical questions. Why, for example, did some plantation regions appear to favor secession while others did not? Did plain-folk support for the slave regime depend upon some expectation of upward mobility? Were there measurable social and economic correlates to party choice? I also decided to limit my research to one state, and Georgia, because of its regional diversity (not to mention old youthful associations), seemed a good bet.

My colleague Don Ginter, though a historian of eighteenth-century England, was doing work on rural social structure in Yorkshire that in some ways paralleled my own interests. As a joint project we decided to develop a computerized census database for Bibb County, Georgia, and in the process we learned a great deal about the problems and pitfalls of using the enumerator returns. In the course of our reading we were struck by the contradiction between the contention of Roger Ransom and Richard Sutch in *One Kind of Freedom* that postbellum tenancy was virtually unprecedented and our own contrary impressions drawn from the 1860 census.[12] Because the problem of farm tenancy in the antebellum South had been largely ignored since the early work of Frank Owsley and his students, we turned aside from Bibb County and undertook the research that resulted in the book that Don and I coauthored, *Farm Tenancy and the Census in Antebellum Georgia*.[13] Our findings on the extent and variety of antebellum tenancy suggested an important element of continuity between a South that relied heavily on slave labor and one that after the Civil War depended on a modified form of free labor. I already suspected that antebellum southern society and the ideological assumptions of its dominant class of planters were less inimical to capitalism and bourgeois values than Genovese's model of a slave society based on admittedly distinctive class relations allowed.

As Genovese himself recognizes, the antebellum South was strongly tied to an international capitalist market and deeply embedded in a larger national structure that valued (at least for whites) democratic political institutions. The problem was to try to sort out and weigh the relative influence of these various and contradictory tendencies. I now thought Genovese emphasized one side of things too strongly.

Again I had to take stock of what I wanted to achieve as a historian. I knew I did not want to become a full-time quantifier. In the tenancy book, quantification clearly relegated more traditional forms of historical analysis to the sidelines. It was good training and continues to serve me well, but not to the exclusion of other methods and approaches. Marxism also represented an important stage in my development as a historian. I could now regard it, too, as a source of useful insights about class and society, but not as a total theory of history, much less as offering a blueprint for social change. I had long been interested in what gave southerners—whether slaveholders, slaves, yeomen, poor whites, men, or women—some notion of identity or community, partly among themselves as discrete groups but also across seemingly impervious divides, as between slavery and freedom. Or to put it another way, I wanted to understand more about what sustained—or weakened—formidable structures of power, tradition, and legitimacy. This was to raise again the old problem of hegemony, perhaps in a new form. My more immediate task was to find some way to define a viable topic or series of topics around which I could organize my research and especially how I could make use of the considerable material I had accumulated for the area around Macon and Bibb County. During the course of my work I discovered local church records. As I immersed myself in them, a conception of the moral basis of community began to take shape in my mind. The urge to do religious history returned with full force.

Other concerns influenced the way my personal recovery of southern religious history took shape. While work on the tenancy project was underway, Janice and I made the decision to have children. As the birth of our second child approached in 1983, we began to consider the desirability of raising our children in a religious tradition. Janice had not attended church since she was a child, when her parents sent her to Sunday school at the local United Church of Canada. Although I had not regained certainty about my own religious faith,

I had rejected materialism as equally dogmatic. I suppose I could best have been described as an open-minded agnostic ready to give religion another try. After searching around a bit, we settled on a small—but high—Anglican church in our neighborhood that over the years has been struggling to stay alive. (Church attendance generally in Quebec, this onetime bastion of ultramontane Catholicism, has dramatically declined since the so-called Quiet Revolution of the 1960s. The traditional "English" churches have additionally suffered from the ongoing exodus of the anglophone population since the 1976 electoral victory of the sovereignist *Parti Québecois*.) Our children were baptized in the church, and Janice and I have remained active in the parish. We participate in a community of people from diverse backgrounds ranging from francophone *Québecois* to refugees from Africa and the Seychelles Islands, and we have made some good friends among them over the years.

What does church membership say about my religious faith? Not a lot. Yet despite the lengthy gap, being in a church has provided my life with some continuity. At the same time it appeals to my historian's yearning for continuity with a particular tradition—in my case Christian and Western along with both the contradictions and sometimes pleasant surprises that Christian and Western imperialism have made so apparent in my own parish. While I cannot pretend that the transcendent aspects of Christianity have much meaning for me, I can find no better set of metaphors for the human condition or better understanding of our restless striving than those contained in the Christian drama of consciousness of sin and the quest for redemption. In short, while faith remains problematic, I find personal value and satisfaction in situating myself somewhere, however tenuously, within the Christian tradition. Participating in the life of a church has also brought me greater maturity as a historian. In a setting where complacency and hypocrisy regularly contend with heartfelt faith and a desire to do God's will, the complex and contradictory qualities of human nature are nowhere more evident. Historians should try to explain these complexities and contradictions as best they can, but they must begin by taking them seriously. In looking back on my first book, I do not think that it entirely lacked this dimension of understanding (religion had always been too much a part of my consciousness), but it was certainly overshadowed by other, albeit legitimate, concerns. One of the incidental contributions of the "new" religious history has been to remove religion from the "superstructure," as something that needed to be explained (often in practice, explained away), and to restore it to the "base" of fundamental human concerns.

By 1989 or so my work in church records had led me to the minutes of Stone Creek Church, located in Twiggs County about twelve miles or so southeast of Macon. This was the largest Baptist church in the county, and its records were complete, full of information, and easily legible on microfilm. I decided that Stone Creek would make a good case study of how church records could be used and how much information used in conjunction with other sources such as the census could be teased out of them. Eventually I distilled a mass of material into an article that appeared in the *Journal of Southern History* in 1994.[14] I found that church adherence not only crossed lines of class and race but was far higher than I had expected. Notably, by 1860 the great majority of Twiggs's richest men were members of Baptist and Methodist churches and dominated positions of lay authority. Where Genovese discerned a growing self-consciousness of sectional difference and Bertram Wyatt-Brown discovered an older tradition of honor, the values that these slaveholding communities tried to impart through exhortation and discipline were those of hard work, temperate living, respect for legitimate authority, a sense of community, and benevolence.[15] These were, of course, traditional values, but not very different from those espoused by evangelicals everywhere. Antebellum churches became strongly committed to the maintenance, and indeed strengthening, of a slaveholding society and were dutifully suspicious of a northern reformist agenda tainted by abolitionism. Yet this widely espoused conservatism could not altogether obliterate the contradiction between an ethic of benevolence and individual self-discipline and one that insisted on the legitimacy of holding men and women in bondage.

I have kept my distance from the various feminisms, particularly those that tend toward essentialism or a postmodern form of discourse that regards forms of knowledge as little more than linguistic constructs. I still believe that class (and perhaps religion!) is a more powerful analytical tool than gender. In the course of my research, however, I had accumulated a good deal of material relating to gender and religion throughout Georgia, and so I decided to try my hand at gender analysis. I discovered that I could do it rather well and make it work for my own purposes. In an article that appeared in the *Georgia Historical Quarterly* I argued that important elements of southern evangelical belief and practice were at odds with the admittedly powerful constraints that slave society placed upon white women.[16] Even a feminized language, as well as feminized standards of behavior, pervaded southern evangelical discourse and stood in sharp contrast to the masculine ideal of honor. I was pleased that the article received the E. Merton Coulter Prize of the Georgia Historical Society, although I hardly think the man who carried the standard for the Dunning School of Reconstruction history far into the era of revisionism would have been amused.

Years of learning about the South have also taught me much about myself, and like Quentin Compson's Canadian roommate in *Absalom, Absalom!*, Shreve McCannon, caught somewhere in midconversation, I still yearn to be told more. Although I have never participated in southern churches, I do believe that the standpoint of an outsider can provide valuable critical distance. I hope I have learned over the years to exercise some humility in the face of people who lived long ago and were part of a tradition I never knew firsthand. I try to have no particular emotional investment in particular outcomes, whether these illustrate the strength of human sympathy and understanding or selfishness and cruelty. My lesson from Marxism is never to underestimate the potential for conflict that is rooted in the structure of society. But the origins of conflict lie also in ourselves. Marxists who tended to reduce human nature to social determinants underestimated both the reality of what Christians call sin and our potential for love. Outcomes, then, are likely to partake of irony. That, I believe, is the lesson of the Christian tradition. Since the myriad voices of Georgian evangelicals have not yet exhausted their patience with me, I will impose on their hospitality a while longer. The contradiction between religion as a moral basis for community and the powerful constraints of class, race, slavery, and gender continues to fascinate. Central and Middle Georgia remain an almost inexhaustible repository of material for a lifetime of projects: for analyzing rural-urban differences, changes in the patterns and languages of conversion and discipline, and the politics of race and status within individual churches; for tracing religious influence on political behavior (an almost untouched subject in the South); for interpreting perceptions of the family and social order; and for understanding the way authority was exercised and resisted. Thanks to a younger generation of historians of religion, as well as a growing number of "secular" historians in whose work religion now figures centrally, we know incomparably more about how to approach these issues than when I entered the field three decades ago.

Notes

I wish to thank John Faithful Hamer for his careful reading of the manuscript and for his penetrating comments and suggestions.

1. Richard Hofstadter, *The Age of Reform: From Bryan to F.D.R.* (New York: Alfred A. Knopf, 1955); Vernon Louis Parrington, *Main Currents in American Thought,* 3 vols. (New York: Harcourt, Brace, 1927–30); Donald B. Meyer, *The Protestant Search for Political Realism, 1919–1941* (Berkeley: University of California Press, 1960).

2. C. Vann Woodward, *The Strange Career of Jim Crow* (New York: Oxford University Press, 1955).

3. Brainerd Dyer, *The Public Career of William M. Evarts* (Berkeley: University of California Press, 1933); and Brainerd Dyer, *Zachary Taylor* (Baton Rouge: Louisiana State University Press, 1946).

4. C. Vann Woodward, "The Antislavery Myth," *American Scholar* 31 (spring 1962): 316.

5. Timothy L. Smith, *Revivalism and Social Reform in Mid-Nineteenth-Century America* (New York: Abingdon Press, 1957).

6. Hunter Dickinson Farish, *The Circuit Rider Dismounts: A Social History of Southern Methodism, 1865–1900* (Richmond, Va.: Dietz Press, 1938); Kenneth K. Bailey, *Southern White Protestantism in the Twentieth Century* (New York: Harper and Row, 1964); Donald G. Mathews, *Slavery and Methodism: A Chapter in American Morality, 1780–1840* (Princeton: Princeton University Press, 1965); Samuel S. Hill Jr., *Southern Churches in Crisis* (New York: Holt, Rinehart and Winston, 1966); John B. Boles, *The Great Revival, 1787–1805: The Origins of the Southern Evangelical Mind* (Lexington: University Press of Kentucky, 1972); and John Lee Eighmy, *Churches in Cultural Captivity: A History of the Social Attitudes of Southern Baptists* (Knoxville: University of Tennessee Press, 1972).

7. Eugene D. Genovese, *The Political Economy of Slavery: Studies in the Economy and Society of the Slave South* (New York: Pantheon Books, 1965).

8. V. O. Key Jr., *Southern Politics in State and Nation* (New York: Alfred A. Knopf, 1949), esp. chap. 10, "North Carolina: Progressive Plutocracy," 205–28; and George Brown Tindall, *The Emergence of the New South, 1913–1945* (Baton Rouge: Louisiana State University Press, 1967), 224.

9. Genovese dedicated a collection of essays to seven Sir George colleagues (including Aileen Kraditor, who also spent two years in Montreal) who "fought the nihilist perversions [of the New Left] and made possible the restoration of a genuine political movement." Eugene D. Genovese, *In Red and Black: Marxian Explorations in Southern and Afro-American History* (New York: Pantheon Books, 1971), v.

10. Frederick A. Bode, *Protestantism and the New South: North Carolina Baptists and*

Methodists in Political Crisis, 1894–1903 (Charlottesville: University Press of Virginia, 1975). An earlier version of chap. 3 appeared as "Religion and Class Hegemony: A Populist Critique in North Carolina," *Journal of Southern History* 37 (Aug. 1971): 417–38.

11. Wayne Flynt, "One in the Spirit, Many in the Flesh: Southern Evangelicals," in David Edwin Harrell Jr., ed., *Varieties of Southern Evangelicalism* (Macon, Ga.: Mercer University Press, 1981), 36 n. 20. See also David Edwin Harrell Jr., "The Evolution of Plain-Folk Religion in the South, 1835–1920," in Samuel S. Hill, ed., *Varieties of Southern Religious Experience* (Baton Rouge: Louisiana State University Press, 1988), 42.

12. Roger L. Ransom and Richard Sutch, *One Kind of Freedom: The Economic Consequences of Emancipation* (Cambridge: Cambridge University Press, 1977), 88.

13. Frederick A. Bode and Donald E. Ginter, *Farm Tenancy and the Census in Antebellum Georgia* (Athens: University of Georgia Press, 1986). Another publication to come out of our joint labors was Bode and Ginter, "Regional Patterns of Intercounty Farm Investment in Antebellum Georgia," *Research in Economic History* 10 (1986): 241–69.

14. Frederick A. Bode, "The Formation of Evangelical Communities in Middle Georgia: Twiggs County, 1820–1861," *Journal of Southern History* 60 (Nov. 1994): 711–48.

15. Bertram Wyatt-Brown, *Southern Honor: Ethics and Behavior in the Old South* (New York: Oxford University Press, 1982). For Genovese's more recent understanding of the contradictory nature of southern thought, see Eugene D. Genovese, *The Slaveholders' Dilemma: Freedom and Progress in Southern Conservative Thought, 1820–1860* (Columbia: University of South Carolina Press, 1992).

16. Frederick A. Bode, "A Common Sphere: White Evangelicals and Gender in Antebellum Georgia," *Georgia Historical Quarterly* 79 (winter 1995): 775–809.

Coming of Age
in the Bible Belt

John B. Boles

hirty-three years ago, writing my dissertation in my early twenties, I had a fleeting sense that there was something vaguely autobiographical about both my choice of topic and my fascination with it. In the midst of reading southern evangelical sermons from the 1790s and the first decade of the nineteenth century, I was at first struck with how familiar they seemed. Then I realized that I had heard very similar sermons—the basic theology, the structure, the actual Bible-drenched vocabulary—my whole life in the Southern Baptist churches I had attended. But in the late 1960s, with the Vietnam War, two tragic assassinations, and political and racial turmoil abounding, I was more caught up in the tumultuous present than in my own rural past, and I thought little about how my life experiences might be shaping not simply my choice of dissertation topic but how I approached it and the interpretations I advanced. In more recent years my appreciation of the often unconscious relationship between one's personal history and one's historical writing has grown. Looking at the southern religious past from my own perspective as a white child of the Bible Belt alerted me to certain aspects of that past and perhaps blinded me to others. The history I wrote—what I chose to emphasize—reflected to a degree my own experiences.

It seems ironic that I was born in a Catholic hospital in Houston, because my parents were emphatically small-town Protestant southerners. But as wartime labor needs expanded in the early 1940s, my parents, Billie and Mary Boles, left the small East Texas town of Center to move into an apartment house in Houston occupied by several other Center families, including my aunt and uncle. Other relatives lived nearby. My father had come to a job at the huge

Todd Shipyards that built Liberty ships, and when my mother became pregnant (with twins, it turned out), their newly chosen Houston obstetrician delivered babies only at St. Joseph's Hospital, where at the time approximately 40 percent of all babies born in Houston were born. But as soon as the war was over, my parents (and my aunt and uncle) returned to their small hometown and resumed life in a cultural and social backwater where time—certainly as compared to booming Houston—seemed to stand still. It was there, in the part of Texas where the penumbra of the Old South was most apparent, that I grew up. Although we lived in the small town of Center until my brother and I (a little sister had come along by this time, and two years later another brother) reached the fourth grade, most of our relatives lived in rural areas, and we felt like country folk. Then in 1952 my parents bought a small farm five miles out what was named Cotton Ford Road—a reminder of the days when wagons loaded with cotton eased across Flat Fork Creek on their way to Shreveport. There we first raised cotton along with corn and a garden, and later we turned to the commercial production of chickens. My father continued to work in Center as the town's only taxi driver, and when too many people had their own cars, leaving him with insufficient business, he found work in a local plywood mill. But our identity was with the farm, which for several years we cultivated with mules and absolutely minimal technology.

Childhood memories, of course, bring back many images of family, of school, of work and play. Religion was intertwined in nearly every activity. I can remember attending Sunday school and church from at least age four, and I have fond memories of most of us high school–age students sitting together (and apart from our parents) in a far back corner of the nave. Socializing was for us as much a part of the service as worship. And there was church on Wednesday nights and on Sunday nights, too, with week-long summer revival meetings featuring a visiting preacher. Sermons were always the center of the church service, and every sermon was aimed at winning converts even if it was hard to imagine there was anyone in the pews who was not already a member. Sunday after Sunday the service always ended with an invitation to confess one's sins, "accept" Christ, and join the church. With the congregation singing a song like "Just As I Am" or "Softly and Tenderly," the minister would leave the pulpit, come and stand directly in front of the first pews, and press the invitation with a skill that utilized psychological and social pressure and obvious heartfelt earnestness.

Summers were also the time for vacation Bible school, and Sunday school classes had parties, picnics, and various sorts of outings. Often our Sunday school teachers were our public school teachers on weekdays, so we never doubted that what was said on Sunday had applicability on the other days, too. Teachers, doctors, and lawyers were nearly all active churchgoers. Hence higher education and advanced learning—such as I encountered—were clearly associated with religion and church participation. Practically everyone I knew attended either a Baptist or Methodist church, although several individuals were Pentecostals of various sorts. My home town then had no Episcopal, Catholic, Presbyterian, or Lutheran churches, and obviously there was no synagogue, although I understood that an elderly man who worked in the men's clothing department of one of the stores was Jewish.

In retrospect it seems my whole society was shrink-wrapped in evangelical Protestantism, but it felt perfectly natural and unexceptional to me at the time. School opened every day with a prayer over the intercom, and it would have been astonishing had the prayer one day not concluded with "in Jesus' name, amen." Football games opened with a prayer, the rodeo opened with a prayer, the Rotary Club opened with a prayer. In fact, I do not remember and cannot imagine any public event not opening with a prayer, and if any minister was seen in the audience, the moderator would always ask "Brother Jones [or whoever] to lead us in prayer." And, of course, most businesses except certain gas stations and some so-called convenience stores were closed on Sundays, with perhaps a drug store open for several hours mainly to fill prescriptions. Many people felt mildly embarrassed about going to a movie on Sunday afternoons or evenings, and few would even do work around the house on Sundays (or if they did so, they were careful not to be seen). Evangelical religion was as all-encompassing as the air we breathed, and I never heard anyone utter a comment that could be interpreted as agnostic or atheistic—if anyone entertained such thoughts, they were sensible enough to keep the thoughts to themselves.

Most of the time we drove the five miles on the paved farm-to-market road to attend services at the First Baptist Church, Center's largest and, at least in our minds, most prestigious church; its steeple was the highest point in town except for the water tank. Sunday school attendance was often over six hundred, and in a town with a population of just less than five thousand people, that represented a very large church. Every person I looked up to in town and at school was an active churchgoer, and many of these were people, men and women, who demonstrated kindness and love and support to me as a child from a relatively impecunious background who did well in school and whose parents were recognized as good, honest people. Later it would puzzle me to understand how prominent citizens who were apparently devout Christians and who certainly acted toward me in a Christ-like manner could simultaneously be blatant, even hateful, racists with regard to the blacks in our town—a moral complexity that still bothers me. I never heard our segregated world criticized—on any grounds—by any relative, minister, teacher, or person in authority. People were apparently able to compartmentalize their lives, with the unseemly parts sealed off from the proper parts. For example, the bootleggers' wives attended church, too, and no one mentioned the illegal sources of their income—or demanded that the sheriff close down their husbands' operations. One could have identified the home of the bootlegger who lived near us from an airplane because the tire marks from a constant stream of customers darkened the road to his driveway. I later learned that an uncle who was almost like a second father to me was a bootlegger: I had wondered why, when talking about religion, he had supported so vigorously the doctrine of "once saved, always saved."

For one period in our life we attended a tiny rural Baptist church, called North Jericho, near our farm, I think because its minister at that time was a man who worked with my father at the plywood mill. This small, one-room church, with outdoor privies, was on the site of one of the first Baptist churches in the county, and its picturesque graveyard contained weathered tombstones of almost a century in age. For me they seemed like relics from ancient times. And on occasion we visited my mother's childhood church, called Lone Cedar Baptist Church, with a huge cedar tree out front surrounded by a low wall upon which we children loved to sit. At both North Jericho and Lone Cedar Baptist Churches the sermons were less sophisticated and the music simpler (only an upright piano for accompaniment, for example; there was no organ) than at First Baptist. I can remember that during prayers at Lone Cedar especially, elderly men would get down on their knees, and their "amens" would sprinkle the sermon in acknowledgments of assent and emphasis.

Two special events occurred annually at many such rural churches. The one we children liked best was called homecoming, a sort of churchwide reunion that helped keep kinship ties and congregational friendships intact despite geographical separation. Most of the present members and many former members, often coming from long distances with children in tow, attended the home-comings, and though there were special sermons and programs, what we looked forward to were the "dinners on the grounds." Wide plank tables were put up under the trees in the churchyard, and every family seemed to try to outdo the others with the food they provided. The children especially did not feel obliged to confine their choices to what their families brought, and I still recall with pleasure roaming up and down the tables, picking out choice pieces of fried chicken, potato salad, corn on the cob, and several deserts, and competing to see how much we could pile on our paper plates. At least in my memory, I never ate so well as on those hot summer days among the cousins, neighbors, and folding chairs in the shade of churchyard trees. After the festive and filling din-ner, we children would rummage in the trash piles behind the cemetery's back fence, searching for rectangular pieces of Styrofoam that had once held flower arrangements. We fashioned unsinkable toy boats and battleships from these and played with them for days back home.

Another special church occasion was what we called the "afternoon sing-ing." The Shelby County Gospel Singing Association sponsored or authorized or at least sanctioned these events that featured not only the best singers, solo, duo, and quartet, from the local church but groups from churches throughout the county. The county sheriff (with the unlikely name of Charlie B. Chris-tian) and his family were popular performers at such musical events. Accom-panied by piano, the various singers performed a repertoire of standard hymns, and the local radio station, KDET (DET stood for Deep East Texas), sent a mobile van that set up several microphones inside and erected a small broad-cast antenna out beside the truck. The station was low wattage and signed off every day at sundown, but on Sunday afternoons it filled the county's airwaves with the sounds of old-time gospel singing, a form of music, especially the quartet singing with the intricate interweaving of parts, that to this day pleases me. As a boy I was as intrigued with the spectacle of a remote broadcast unit outside as with the harmonizing inside the church.

This evangelical culture was totally and completely segregated by race, with odd exceptions always defined by whites. We hunted and fished together with blacks and could work side by side in the fields all day, but we could not eat together at the kitchen table. Of course, churches and schools were totally seg-regated; even the janitors and cooks were white. Blacks could not try on clothes in the department stores on the town square, they could not eat in the cafés, and even at hamburger stands, where there was usually a small opening at the rear at which blacks could inconspicuously order food, they were expected to walk or drive away to eat. Blacks could not come into the lobby of the movie theater even to buy tickets (much less popcorn and soft drinks); instead, at the back of the ticket booth there was a small window opening into an outside alley. Blacks purchased their tickets there, walked up an outside staircase, and sat in the balcony where an eight-foot-tall wooden wall, with chicken wire stretching to the ceiling, separated the black section of the balcony from the white section. In retrospect it is interesting that my father's cab served both whites and blacks, and no white passenger seemed to mind that perhaps the previous rider had been black.

The Trailways buses that stopped in town had separate waiting rooms for blacks, and blacks sat at the back of the buses. My father's taxi stand was at the bus station, and my twin brother and I occasionally stayed around the station with him as he awaited customers. One afternoon I was surprised to see an apparently white teenaged girl sitting in the black section of the waiting room, and then I noticed she was getting in the black section of the bus. When I overheard her speak, I was even more shocked by her black accent (at the time I did not realize that my own accent would later shock northern acquaintances). In disbelief I asked my father why that white girl was getting on the bus with the blacks (though I am sure I used the crude vernacular at that time), only to be told that she was black. Thus I became aware that "race" was not just a matter of biology but was what later I found out scholars called a social construct. This phenotypically white girl was "black" as much because of her behavior and speech patterns as because of her genes.

The residential patterns in Center were segregated, and the section where all the blacks lived, which everyone called "the nigger quarters" or, more politely, "the quarters," still had mostly unpaved streets, no running water, and no sewage system. Ironically, this section of town was adjacent to the several streets where the most affluent whites lived. The countryside was more integrated, even though the distance between homes was far greater. A mile behind our farm home, through the woods, was a dirt road along which there still were a number of wooden shacks that had once been sharecroppers' cabins, and immediately adjacent to our farm property was a small black elementary school and a black church. There were two sets of school buses, one that picked up older black children and brought them to C. H. Daniels Colored School in Center, and another that picked up white children and took them to either the white elementary school (grades one through eight) or the high school. The black church, which was located about one thousand feet from our home, had far more impact on my life than did the black school. A black neighbor, with whom I discussed religion, informed me that the church was of the denomination called "The Triumph of the Lord Jesus Christ over His Enemies on Earth Church."

The black church was an unpainted, squat building about forty feet square; it had no steeple, no sign, no Sunday school rooms. There were plain plank pews, with an open section in the front containing some chairs to the left and several short pews to the right placed perpendicular to the rest of the pews. Two or more black guitarists sat at the front on the chairs, their big amplifiers behind them. To the right were a half-dozen or more women, often wearing loose-fitting robes, who seemed to be the spiritual energizers of the congregation. On my many visits to look in and watch, I never saw anyone preaching or anyone who was an apparent leader. Instead, the guitarists kept up a steady, loud rhythm, congregants hummed and shouted, and usually several of the robed women were standing, dancing, their arms waving, beating a tambourine against their open hand or against their thigh, with their faces transfigured in evident spiritual ecstasy. Often some of the women especially became so caught up in the music, singing, and spirituality that they would collapse on the floor in a swoon, which was called "getting sanctified." These services went on practically every night and lasted almost until midnight.

For us, sitting in our backyard swing (these were the days before air conditioning and television in the rural South) or lying in bed with the windows open to catch any possible breeze, the deep bass sounds of the guitars and shouts of glory were the only sound we could hear. My response to witnessing these services, and hearing that beat of the guitars pound on hour after hour, was mixed: the dancing, which often became frenzied, and the falling unconscious on the floor both repulsed me and filled me with awe. I could recognize an extraordinary degree of faith, yet its expression seemed so exotic and extreme, certainly as compared to the eleven o'clock services at First Baptist, that I wondered if it were something only emotional blacks were capable of—hence revealing an attitude toward blacks that was common among southern whites at the time.

When in September 1961 I left Center, Texas, for Houston and Rice University, I left as a rural white southerner, a Protestant evangelical who had never seen an immigrant, never eaten in a restaurant other than a Dairy Queen, never had any ethnic food other than spaghetti and meatballs, never flown in an airplane, never heard segregation criticized or challenged. I was about as country as one could be in the post–World War II South, yet several wonderful school teachers had awakened in me a thirst for learning. These men and women loaned me books, let me skip classes in high school so I could read and learn at my own pace, and arranged for me on some evenings to ride with them the thirty-two miles to Nacogdoches, where they were taking night courses at Stephen F. Austin State Teachers College. I would wander through the library there, reading books and periodicals while they were in class, and then would ride back to Center with them; they would then take me to my farmhouse out in the country. A handful of teachers opened up a world to me that I otherwise would not have known existed: a world of books, of learning, of ideas. And because Rice University was then tuition free, I could afford to go once I completed high school. Dedicated teachers and a richly endowed university changed my life, but I still do not know why my parents consented to let me go to the supposedly dangerous big city of Houston (I even remember warnings about bop music) and a culture-threatening university (the family dentist warned my parents that there were atheists and Communists at Rice). Perhaps they agreed for me to go because we had close relatives in Houston, and like most Texans, then and now, they had an awed respect for what had previously been called the Rice Institute. Still, I remember my father telling me years later that the saddest day of his life had been the day when he deposited me as a freshman at my Rice dorm room.

If I could have passed Math 100 at Rice, I might have become a scientist. My freshman year in high school the Russians orbited Sputnik, and suddenly all schoolchildren who made good grades were urged by their teachers to go into science so we could defeat the Communists in the space race and hence guarantee the victory of freedom and Christianity. I accepted this patriotic assignment and was, in fact, interested in the books I read about space stations orbiting the earth, but despite myself I found I was more interested in history—perhaps because Joe Ellis was such a good teacher. My small high school had no advanced classes, had no operable science labs, and did not offer calculus. But when I got to Rice, as a math and physics major, so I thought, I quickly discovered that practically every other student had been in advanced classes and had taken calculus. I was drowning from the start; actually, at the first calculus tutorial, when another freshman began asking about alternative proofs of Rolle's theorem, I had a sinking feeling. Along with a goodly number of my classmates, I failed that year-long math class. It has always given me great pleasure to realize that although I eventually got tenure at Rice, that math professor did not. Early in my first semester, while taking chemistry, calculus, and physics taught macho-like, as though hard equaled good, I also was taking an English course and an excellent but demanding course in United States history taught by William H. Masterson and Louis P. Galambos. These two courses confirmed my interest in the humanities and convinced me to switch majors, and I subsequently took a number of courses in American history and literature. But I quickly learned that American history as taught in universities, and the textbooks they used, privileged one section of the country and did not often help me understand my own life experiences.

It was not just that most of the nation's history was compressed into the history of the Northeast, but that when I sought to understand southern religion, for example, it seemed, according to the lectures and reading, ephemeral to the region's history when not malignant. We spent much time studying the Puritans, and Transcendentalism, and the Social Gospel, but very little on religious developments outside New England. The textbook assigned for my freshman course, which I still consider a magnificent survey of the nation's history, especially as compared with modern-day versions with their diminished vocabulary and lowered expectations of students, had only a paragraph or two on religion in the antebellum South, where it was depicted as a force for intolerance. In volume two, the discussion of religion in the South centered on the Scopes trial, where religion represented "militant and organized ignorance."[1] I objected, not because I did not accept these interpretations, but because I thought the topic deserved more substantial treatment in the more than 1,300 pages of text. After all, I was aware that the South of the 1960s was called the Bible Belt, but I could not—based on my coursework—determine when or why it became so. All my reading suggested that New England should be the Bible Belt. The South that I knew, where religion was still extremely important, seemed inexplicably absent from the university curriculum.[2] Absent, that is, until second semester of my senior year, when I took an anthropology course entitled Primitive Religion.

The eminent professor for the class, Edward Norbeck, was an elegant, prim man (I could never imagine him doing fieldwork, which he obviously had done) with careful diction who talked about religious practices in faraway lands, practices so bizarre that they seemed somehow a different category of experience from the religions that I knew about in mainstream white America. One evening, casually reading our textbook (written by Norbeck), *Religion in Primitive Society*, I came upon a brief discussion of a revival in Kentucky at the beginning of the nineteenth century that was said to be "remarkable from the standpoints of the violence of the bodily seizures of members of the congregations and the numbers of individuals affected." Several pages later the text described revival participants in Kentucky "'treeing the devil,' running about on all fours and emitting sounds called 'holy barks.' More remarkable were the 'jerks,' violent whip-snaps of the body which sometimes resulted in injury or, if accounts of the time are to be credited, occasionally death from a broken neck."[3] Professor Norbeck elaborated slightly on the text in class lectures, but when I went by his office later to ask about the events in frontier Kentucky, he told me little had been written on the subject, and I followed the footnote suggestions in the book to fill out the story. Still I was disappointed by how little I found and was doubly intrigued because the physical manifestations of religious fervor described in early Kentucky reminded me so forcefully of what I had witnessed at the nearby black "Triumph" church as a boy—I had assumed such behavior was peculiar to blacks, and here it was described among white southerners at the opening of the nineteenth century. I had previously been admitted to do graduate work in history at the University of Virginia at the very beginning of my final semester at Rice, and I had intended to study some aspect of Thomas Jefferson's life or career when I applied. A course entitled Jeffersonian and Jacksonian Democracy taught by Sanford W. Higginbotham had introduced me to the scholarship of Merrill D. Peterson, Bernard Mayo, and Dumas Malone, and all three were at Mr. Jefferson's university in Charlottesville.

During the graduate student orientation meeting, the graduate dean, historian Edward Younger, told us to choose a dissertation topic early, the earlier the better, he said. I suppose because the Norbeck course on primitive religion was still on my mind, I decided on a topic within a few days. But it represented a slight shift away from concentration on Jefferson himself to an aspect of the Jeffersonian-era South. I would study the Kentucky revival and try to pinpoint when and why evangelical Protestantism became dominant in the South despite Jefferson's prediction that Unitarianism would gain preeminence in the region. That fall semester I took Mayo's class and wrote my first graduate paper; my topic was James McGready, a Presbyterian minister closely identified with the famous, or infamous, Cane Ridge camp meeting in Bourbon County, Kentucky, in August 1801, at which supposedly twenty thousand backwoods people had congregated and participated in the wildest kinds of revival excesses. At the time the prevalent interpretation went no further than saying that frontier southerners liked their whiskey raw and their religion red hot, so the revival "exercises," as they were called, were assumed to be normal for such conditions. That initial paper, and several others in the seminars of both Mayo and Peterson, became the basis of my 1969 dissertation and 1972 book, *The Great Revival*.[4]

It quickly became obvious that the ministerial leaders, along with most of the parishioners, in frontier Kentucky had migrated there from the seaboard states, so it seemed logical to begin my study of the Kentucky revival by examining the religious background in the older states. The Alderman Library at the University of Virginia had an outstanding collection of Americana in its Tracy McGregor Library, and this rare book collection featured one card catalogue that listed items in chronological order of publication. I set about to read, in chronological fashion, every account I could that mentioned the South and religion, and a dissertation fellowship from the Woodrow Wilson Foundation provided travel funds that allowed me to go to every significant southern archival collection. My goal was to read every sermon, ministerial diary, associational document, travel account, and any other primary source I could find that shed light on religious attitudes and practices. I simply assumed—perhaps I was shaped by my own experience in which religious people had ideas, a general comprehension of theological precepts, and did not just feel but rather, on occasion at least, thought—that there was more to southern religion than red-hot emotion, and perhaps somewhat defensively I wanted, as a kind of poor man's Perry Miller of the South, to find a world of ideas, abstract concepts, yes, even theology, behind practices that had been depicted so disparagingly in most histories.

Soon I constructed what seemed to me a persuasive set of religious ideas, beliefs about how God controlled the world, how people interpreted their world in the light of those ideas. In short, I laid out a theological system involving a belief in divine providence and what I called the expectation of a providential deliverance from a self-diagnosed religious declension that lay behind the revival that erupted on the Kentucky frontier. I actually had read a good bit about the anthropology of religion and was familiar with Anthony F. C. Wallace's theory of revitalization movements, but laboring in the misguided belief that one should hide the theoretical underpinning of one's narrative, I quite consciously abjured all but the faintest hint of such matters. Implicit in my 1972 account, and made explicit in later versions, was a three-stage explanatory scheme. I argued that before such a regionwide revival could occur, there had to be in place a network of churches and ministers, a widely accepted set of beliefs about how God worked in history, and a perception of a social crisis so intense that presumably only Providence could effect a resolution.[5] Much of the narrative of my Great Revival book was involved with documenting the meeting of these prerequisites; then there followed a detailed description of the spread of the camp meeting revival across the South. The concluding chapter, an attempt to step back from the immediate topic and survey the larger implications of the early-nineteenth-century revivals, suggested that the revivalists quickly learned to downplay theology and to emphasize the importance of the conversion experience itself. This, I proposed, became the essence of southern evangelicalism.

I suppose it would be easy to contend that I was arguing backward from what I had experienced in the First Baptist Church of Center in the 1950s and early 1960s and finding its origins in the southern past. I also asserted in that concluding chapter that southern evangelicalism was strikingly individualistic with very minimal concerns for anything like a Social Gospel, and that southern evangelicalism had become a bulwark against social change. I still believe that the historical evidence supports these broad conclusions, but I am willing to concede that the southern evangelical world I knew personally made such an interpretation seem doubly valid. Both research and experience, I believed, confirmed my analysis.

Another issue with which I had to come to terms was the tragic matter of race. Like most white southerners of my generation, I had grown up in a completely segregated world. My home church each Christmas season had placed a large wash tub on the table at the front of the nave that was used for communion preparation (carved on the edge of the table were the words "This do in remembrance of me"), and people came forward and placed in the tub contributions to the Lottie Moon Christmas Offering to support missionaries around the world; later, doing research at the Southern Baptist Seminary in Louisville, I had visited the Lottie Moon Memorial Room, and in Charlottesville I had visited the Baptist church that had been Lottie Moon's home church. By the time I was in graduate school, my eyes having been opened to southern racism by such books as John Hope Franklin's *Reconstruction: After the Civil War* and C. Vann Woodward's *Strange Career of Jim Crow*, I grasped the irony of the fact that while my home church members gave generously to spread the gospel to the so-called heathen of Africa, if one of those converted Africans had come to our church to thank us, the church deacons would not have let him enter the building.[6] I simply assumed that biracial worship had never occurred in the South. I read books on the history of slavery in my graduate course taught by Paul Gaston, and the then definitive study by Kenneth M. Stampp mentioned that whites and blacks often attended the same churches in the South, but he so exclusively argued that such religion was a means of social control that the presence of blacks in the pews seemed forced attendance rather than worship and shared belief.[7] Stampp also made clear that slave marriages were not recognized as legal contracts but existed at the whim of the masters. Moreover, Stampp emphasized that "In law there was no such thing as fornication or adultery between slaves; nor was there bastardy, for, as a Kentucky judge noted, the father of a slave was 'unknown' to the law."[8]

This personal and academic background helps to explain my reaction when I began reading church minutes from early Baptist churches especially. I was simply astonished to read of slave members, of slaves taking communion with whites, of slaves being admitted either by letter or by confession of faith, of blacks and whites being addressed as brother and sister, of blacks participating in church disciplinary hearings and even giving testimony in cases regarding whites—I knew from my history courses that in the civil courts of the day blacks could not testify against whites. Then I discovered blacks being convicted of adultery in the church disciplinary hearings and subsequently being removed from the church rolls. But how could this be, I wondered, since I had learned in class that slave marriages were not recognized in law and all slave children hence entered the world as bastards. I remember excitement welling up within me as I slowly realized that the relationship of blacks and whites in the antebellum churches was more complex than I had been led to expect or would have ever imagined.

But I was doing this research, and finding this information that was new to me, in 1968 and 1969, years of chaos and confusion inside the academy as well as without. Henry F. May of the University of California at Berkeley was at the University of Virginia in 1968 doing research for his book on the enlightenment in America; as part of this project he was studying religion in the South, and someone on the history faculty sent him to me.[9] We began a long series of conversations, the joint aftermath of which was that I gave him access to my huge bibliography on southern religion, and he graciously agreed to read and comment on my eventual dissertation manuscript. In the course of our conversations about the topic, I mentioned the material I was uncovering on what I termed *integrated* (Katharine L. Dvorak later helped me to see that *biracial* was the more accurate term) churches in the Old South. He agreed with my interpretation and with the significance of the findings, but he cautioned that perhaps the times were not ripe for a southern white, educated at a southern university, to publish such findings. Almost simultaneously Willie Lee Rose, also a mentor at Virginia, warned me similarly. She had been dragged into the controversy over William Styron's novel *The Confessions of Nat Turner* and the insistence by some young black scholars that whites could not understand black history and had no business meddling in it.[10] After I witnessed the animosity directed toward Styron by several black scholars at the 1968 annual meeting of the Southern Historical Association, I decided to limit my dissertation (and first book) to whites only.[11] I think my decision was a combination of cowardice, a genuine dislike of conflict, and due deference to the sensitivities of black scholars.

By the early 1970s it seemed to me that the intellectual climate had changed. Clearly, the topic of black history was rich enough to support every interested scholar. And in academic year 1973–74, Willie Lee Rose, who by then had moved from the University of Virginia to Johns Hopkins University, presented a talk at Towson State University in Baltimore, where I was then teaching, in which she described the lessening of tensions in the field of black history. I was pleased to have my own sense of the situation confirmed by someone like Professor Rose, in part because I had been asked by the University Press of Kentucky to write a small volume on religion in Kentucky for their Kentucky Bicentennial Series and was already hard at work on it. That little book, published in 1976, had a chapter entitled "Black Christianity" and another entitled "White Churches and Black Slavery."[12] Here I talked about blacks worshiping in so-called white churches, and I argued that in them, blacks found a greater degree of equality than they did anywhere else in antebellum southern life. I did not argue that slaves actually found full equality here or elsewhere, although several later readers seemed to believe I implied as much. I later amplified these views both in a brief synthetic history of slavery and in a book of collected essays by several other scholars on the general topic of biracial churches.[13] I realized that slaves usually sat together either in the back of the church or in a balcony or perhaps listened through the windows on those rare occasions when whites occupied all the indoor seats, but I believed there was no evidence that blacks wanted to sit with their masters rather than with fellow blacks drawn from all the farms and plantations nearby. In fact, I think that these safe times together with blacks from the larger neighborhood were an important moment in the creation of a sense of black community.

To what extent have I emphasized these biracial worship experiences and possibly even exaggerated their significance because I wanted to find a tradition of biracial worship with which to implicitly chastise and correct the segregated worship I experienced in the 1950s when, as the cliché had it, 11:00 Sunday morning was the most segregated hour in America? I believe the juxtaposition of the evidence from the antebellum period with my own past highlighted the existence of biracial worship in my mind, but I do not think scholars have yet fully come to terms with its importance either for whites or blacks in the antebellum period. Despite the racism and the white condescension toward blacks of that era, many slaves found genuine faith and had meaningful, authentic worship in the biracial churches. I would like to believe that someday in the future, southern whites and blacks can recover and improve upon their earlier biracial practices and jointly create a community of faith.

Of course, my career has not been influenced solely by events from my rural youth. On the first day of graduate school I met another beginning graduate student, Nancy Gaebler. She had come from Baltimore and college in Pennsylvania to study southern and colonial history, and she, too, was interested in religion. Her M.A. thesis became a biography of Devereux Jarratt, an Anglican minister who cooperated with the early Methodists and almost became a Methodist himself. Nancy and I immediately discovered we shared many interests, and we soon decided to share our lives. She received her M.A. in June 1967; we were married in September of that year; and as I continued research on my dissertation, she worked as assistant curator of the Rare Book Division at the University of Virginia. Later she would serve as a careful reader and critic of my writing, and in those days when dissertations were still typed and carbon paper was the primary means of copying, she helped type several versions of my manuscript on a small portable typewriter. We were both surprised when my first job was at Towson State University, located about a mile from her parents' home in the Baltimore suburb of Towson. But as we prepared to move to Towson, they were preparing to retire to Florida. Soon Nancy parlayed her history degree and her library experience into a position as manuscript curator at the Maryland Historical Society in downtown Baltimore. This was an ideal job for her, and in fact it brought us both great pleasure. I managed to get a small office off the manuscript reading room, and we often spent Saturdays there together, she doing her work and I using the fine collection of historical materials at the society's library.

We both met Richard Duncan of Georgetown University, who served as editor of the *Maryland Historical Magazine*, which was published by the society. Dick soon began sharing the pleasures of editing with me, asking me to become the book review editor of the *MHM* beginning with the spring 1972 issue. Nancy, too, was involved in a series of book publications sponsored by the society, and we often spent long evenings together editing and proofreading each other's projects. In 1973 Nancy retired from the society and soon gave birth to our first son, David. At the very end of that year Dick Duncan decided he needed to devote more time to his own work. Consequently, beginning with the spring 1974 issue, I became editor of the *MHM*. With a new baby and a new magazine, our lives had never been busier or more fulfilling. Until this time I had taught the United States survey course at Towson State, a survey course in U.S. religious history, and a course in historiography and methodology required of history majors. The chair of the department, Mary Catherine Kahl, had long taught the Civil War course and, before becoming chair, had offered a course in the history of the South. She was understandably reluctant to give up her southern history course, and I was understandably eager to find some way to teach the same material. Then I realized that there was on the books a course entitled Interpretative Problems in History, and the problems could vary according to the instructor. Hence I began teaching a version of that catch-all course that I labeled Southern History as an Interpretative Problem in American History, a course heavily historiographical in approach that long influenced my teaching even after I left Towson State.

Through an extraordinary coincidence in the fall of 1976 I had confirmed an intriguing part of what I had always considered essentially a tall tale related by my paternal grandfather, Vessie Boles, who lived with our family in the mid to late 1950s. We were poor, but my grandfather was poorer, and he often spoke about his father being murdered in the woods of East Texas at the turn of the century. My paternal grandmother's father was shot dead out of a locomotive engine in a great labor strike in the early 1900s, but my grandfather also talked about his grandfather, who he called "old man Joe Boles." According to the tales, this Boles had been so affluent that not only did he give all his children a farm, but he also gave all his former slaves land, too. I wondered about this for several reasons, not the least of which was what could have happened to all that supposed wealth because no one in our extended family then had much of anything. About that time, my father decided he needed some help on the farm, so he arranged with an elderly black man named Mark Cartwright and his wife to come and become sharecroppers. My father bought an old sharecropper's house that was located on the dirt road a mile behind our farm, had it moved to a corner of our farm, and added a room to the back; then the Cartwrights moved in. When Mark Cartwright met my grandfather and the two began talking, they both realized that sixty years before they had played together on my great-grandfather's farm: Mark had been the child of Ossie Cartwright, who had been a sharecropper on "Cap" Boles's farm.

Then in 1976, while I was studying anthropology at Johns Hopkins University with Sydney Mintz, courtesy of a National Endowment for the Humanities Fellowship for College Teachers, I discovered there was a university book sale at the campus book store in which books were being sold by the pound. Scrambling among the sales tables and filling my arms with bargains too good to miss, I stumbled upon a book entitled No Quittin' Sense, the oral autobiography of an elderly black Pentecostal minister in East Texas. Thumbing through the book hurriedly to see if I should buy it, my eyes caught a fascinating passage: "Uncle Ossie Cartwright was Mama's oldest brother. He lived over east of Shelbyville, in a community called Possum Trot. I'd never been to his place, but I'd heard Mama say he had a big house and lots of land. The house *was* big. It had four rooms. And he had forty acres, some of it still in woods. When he was young, right after he wasn't a slave no more, he had worked for a white man named Joe Boles, and when Uncle Ossie was ready to get married Mr. Boles had give him forty acres of timberland."[14] I bought the book. This fragment of the story of the Cartwright and the Boles families strengthened my interest in post–Civil War southern history, especially the institution of sharecropping that continued in attenuated form into my own lifetime.

Then in 1977 I was fortunate enough to be appointed visiting editor of the *Journal of Southern History* at Rice University, the result of my *Maryland Historical Magazine* editing experience and my southern history teaching at Towson State. I loved my year in Houston, as did Nancy and David, and although we then moved to what we assumed would be our permanent home at Tulane University in New Orleans, the attractions of Rice and the journal lingered in our minds. Three years and another son, Matthew, later, following Frank Vandiver's resignation from Rice and Sanford W. Higginbotham's eminent retirement, I was brought back to Rice both to teach southern history (Vandiver's course) and edit the journal (Higginbotham's primary assignment). On the occasion of Hig's retirement, assistant editor Evelyn Thomas Nolen and I arranged a major symposium of former members of the journal's editorial board, and they gave historiographical papers on the major topics in southern history. Evelyn and I later edited those papers into the book entitled *Interpreting Southern History*.[15]

As much as I enjoyed editing the *Journal of Southern History* and working with its excellent staff, I found the position to be essentially full-time all year long. I had only one course per semester to teach, but graduate students and the journal left little or no time for extensive research in distant archives. Moreover, reading the hundred or more annual submissions to the journal on every conceivable topic of southern history—including topics that I would otherwise never have read—forced me to become more broadly familiar with the field than would have been my normal inclination. And, of course, all the books we reviewed and all the periodicals whose table of contents we searched for possible entries in our annual bibliography published in the May issue came across my desk. I must confess to finding this mass of mail exhilarating. Even as a boy

I looked forward every morning to the identifiable whine of the postman's car tires on the pavement announcing the arrival of the mail and the daily *Shreveport Times*. For a mail freak and a student of southern history, I had the ideal job. Now I had to parlay this into a means of continuing to publish. I had no time for extended visits to other libraries and no long blocks of time for writing, but were there projects that could benefit from the range of material that I necessarily had to read as part of my editing responsibilities? I decided that I had a unique opportunity to comprehend the whole of southern history and therefore should attempt to write a general, interpretative history of the South, incorporating the newest scholarship and, I hoped, introducing students and possibly even a larger public to the riches of that scholarship. *The South through Time* was the result, published in 1995 and now available in a revised, updated edition.[16] I do not know if I want to be tied forever to revising this long book every four or five years, but along with editing the *Journal of Southern History* and directing the work of graduate students, I do know that I expect to be immersed in southern history for the remainder of my career.

Notes

I wish to thank Patricia B. Bixel, Nancy G. Boles, and James Shields for reading this essay and offering helpful suggestions.

1. Richard Hofstadter, William Miller, and Daniel Aaron, *The American Republic*, 2 vols. (Englewood Cliffs, N.J.: Prentice-Hall, 1959), 2:438.

2. I missed taking Frank E. Vandiver's course on the history of the South because the year it was scheduled to be offered, he was serving as Harmsworth Professor at Oxford University.

3. Edward Norbeck, *Religion in Primitive Society* (New York: Harper and Brothers, 1961), 85, 90.

4. John B. Boles, *The Great Revival, 1787–1805: The Origins of the Southern Evangelical Mind* (Lexington: University Press of Kentucky, 1972).

5. These prerequisites were spelled out in John B. Boles, "Evangelical Protestantism in the Old South: From Religious Dissent to Cultural Dominance," in Charles Reagan Wilson, ed., *Religion in the South* (Jackson: University Press of Mississippi, 1985), 13–34, esp. 15.

6. John Hope Franklin, *Reconstruction: After the Civil War* (Chicago: University of Chicago Press, 1961); C. Vann Woodward, *The Strange Career of Jim Crow* (New York: Oxford University Press, 1955).

7. Kenneth M. Stampp, *The Peculiar Institution: Slavery in the Ante-Bellum South* (New York: Knopf, 1956), 156–62, but see 373–74 for a glimpse of something more authentically religious.

8. Ibid., 198, see also 340–41.

9. The resulting publication was Henry F. May, *The Enlightenment in America* (New York: Oxford University Press, 1976).

10. William Styron, *The Confessions of Nat Turner* (New York: Random House, 1967); and John Henrik Clarke, ed., *William Styron's Nat Turner: Ten Black Writers Respond* (Boston: Beacon Press, 1968).

11. The session, entitled "The Uses of History in Fiction," was a panel discussion moderated by C. Vann Woodward and included Styron, Robert Penn Warren, and Ralph Ellison. All the criticism came from the floor of the packed ballroom; Ellison defended the character and writing of Styron.

12. John B. Boles, *Religion in Antebellum Kentucky* (Lexington: University Press of Kentucky, 1976). One reader for the press said I devoted too much attention to blacks, but the press agreed with my coverage.

13. John B. Boles, *Black Southerners, 1619–1869* (Lexington: University Press of Kentucky, 1983); and John B. Boles, ed., *Masters and Slaves in the House of the Lord: Race and Religion in the American South, 1740–1870* (Lexington: University Press of Kentucky, 1988). See also John B. Boles, *The Irony of Southern Religion* (New York: Peter Lang, 1994).

14. Reverend C. C. White and Ada Morehead Holland, *No Quittin' Sense* (Austin: University of Texas Press, 1969), 40.

15. John B. Boles and Evelyn Thomas Nolen, eds., *Interpreting Southern History: Historiographical Essays in Honor of Sanford W. Higginbotham* (Baton Rouge: Louisiana State University Press, 1987).

16. John B. Boles, *The South through Time: A History of an American Region*, 2d ed. (Englewood Cliffs, N.J.: Prentice Hall, 1999).

The Gentlemen
Theologians Revisited

E. Brooks Holifield

I feel quite honored to find myself among such distin-guished company in these pages, especially since my contribution to the discussion of religion in the South has been limited, for the most part, to one modest book that occupies a space somewhere near the margins of current historical interests. *The Gentlemen Theologians* (1978) attempted to combine intellectual history with other methods that might clarify the social setting of the ideas, but it dealt with an elite body of urban clergy, and its center of gravity—at least as I saw it—was the discussion of their "rational orthodoxy."[1] Neither clerical elites nor theological abstractions of that sort elicit widespread enthusiasm at the moment. Yet perhaps for this very reason, the book might serve as a helpful occasion for an essay on the relationship between scholarship and life experi-ence. Why would I have chosen such a topic? Looking back now, I find an odd mixture of motives and interests in the background of the book. It reflected something about my own history as a southerner who grew up in the family of a Methodist minister and who chose to remain closely linked to my religious tradition despite some ambivalence about it. The book itself was, beneath the surface, partly an expression of that ambivalence.

Surely there were inner impulses connected with the writing that were hid-den to me then and remain hidden to me now. It is equally certain that at least some of the motivation for the project grew out of contingencies of the most everyday sort. I had begun teaching in 1970 in Emory University's Candler School of Theology, a place where theological ideas—even if not the theologi-cal ideas of antebellum southerners—were taken seriously. The school had a library, moreover, that made some of the sources immediately accessible. And the topic also gave me a chance to work on some historiographical puzzles that interested me then and continue to interest me now, such as the relationships between what people think—the ideas they hold—and the other dimensions of their lives: their region, class, education, gender, race, institutional commitments, and "role" (with "role" being the self-definition and behavior that result from perceptions of the expectations of admired reference groups). And yet I also cannot deny the subterranean links between the writing of the book and my own history.

One is often surprised by reviewers, but none surprised me more than a mildly supercilious reviewer for a British journal who came away from the reading of *The Gentlemen Theologians* convinced that he had found a benighted soul devoted to the defense of southern antebellum rational orthodox theology.[2] According to his interpretation, my intent was to tout the originality of the southerners and defend them as first-rate theologians. The truth was closer to the reverse: I found the theology interesting partly because it was so alien to what I had come to think theology should be. I actually shared my reviewer's judgment that the gentlemen theologians were—with one or two exceptions— imitative and second-rate thinkers. But I did not conclude that therefore they told us nothing about religion in the antebellum South.

I had been raised in Arkansas as a liberal pietistic Methodist with a warm heart but little knowledge of the Christian tradition, minimal awareness of biblical scholarship, and only the vaguest sense that serious theology mattered much at all. I had faithfully attended Methodist churches, involved myself in youth groups, felt the emotional tingle (along with more earthly joys) at church camps, and attended the annual revival services, though by then the revivals in larger urban Arkansas Methodist churches had become more a matter of enjoying the rhetorically gifted, witty, and anecdotal visiting preachers than of struggling for a breakthrough into the circle of the converted.

By the time I graduated from high school, I had decided to follow my father's footsteps into the Methodist ministry. I liked to speak in public and organize young people's activities, and it seemed more or less a natural step to take. I expressed my sense of call to the ministry in an aphorism characteristic of the Methodism of the 1950s: one was called when one's talents and interests intersected with a clear need in the world. I cannot say much about the talents, but I was interested in the things ministers did and the kinds of relationships they

formed with people, and the church had been an important source of my sense
of identity. By the time I graduated from college, I thought about this vocation
in slightly different ways. I understood it as a response to what I perceived as a
need for skillfully led face-to-face communities in which people take some responsibility for each other, continue a tradition that has, at its best, enriched
human life, and share with each other in the asking of questions about how to
live and how to understand the world around them. The less accessible reasons I entered the ministry could probably never be disentangled from my family dynamics, but these notions of vocation gave me a way of thinking about it
that fit my self-understanding for a long time.

   As a student at a small Methodist-related Arkansas school, Hendrix College,
I took a couple of religion classes, found them less than fully engaging, and
turned my attention to literature and philosophy. In my philosophy classes I
discovered the Boston personalism that had become a fixture in some strands
of Methodist liberalism, and the personalist idea of a finite God struggling against
evil made sense to me for years. I was also intrigued, though, by the critics of
religion, and I wrote my college honors project on existentialist themes in the
fiction of Jean-Paul Sartre, Albert Camus, and Fyodor Dostoyevsky, a project
that now seems outrageously broad and unmanageable but one that was fully
consonant with the academic ethos of the early 1960s. At the same time, I began to read, though only partially to understand, the theology of Paul Tillich,
who offered a religious vocabulary that seemed consistent with these existentialist ideas. His *Courage to Be*, which I read as a college senior, provided a way
of thinking about the "God beyond God" that carried me a step beyond the
pietism in which I had been nurtured.[3]

   During this period, I was also serving as the lay pastor, licensed but not ordained, of small Methodist congregations in the rural areas surrounding the
college. I was nineteen when I started, still minimally knowledgeable about
the Christian tradition, only slightly more aware of biblical scholarship, and
utterly unschooled in the subtleties of human relationships that seminary students learn to recognize in their first year of study, but I spent a couple of Sundays a month for two and a half years in isolated rural Arkansas communities,
preaching, visiting with people, organizing youth groups, driving to hospitals,
leading church meetings, sitting with the dying, conducting funerals and weddings, and learning something about what religion meant to people with expe-

riences far different from mine. I met some fine people, learned how to relate
to some contentious personalities, and garnered some insights about small communities. I once administered the Lord's Supper using Nehi grape soda (the
communion steward owned a small grocery store that was out of grape juice,
and Methodists never used real wine), went bird hunting with the men (and
experienced a little of the ethos of southern "honor" about which Bertram Wyatt-
Brown would later write), and stumbled my way through some of the intricacies of living in two worlds at the same time, reading Jean-Paul Sartre's plays
and novels at school while appropriating the language of rural southern Protestantism in my tiny churches. I was far too naive to be thrust upon people in the
midst of their family conflicts, their suffering, their disappointed ambitions, and
their struggles to make a living, but it helped me understand things that I never
would have understood otherwise.

The summer of 1963, before I entered Yale Divinity School, I read and outlined the first two volumes of Tillich's *Systematic Theology* (the third volume
did not appear until later that year), but I was to find that most of my teachers
at Yale had little sympathy for Tillich.[4] At Yale, I read the theology of Karl Barth,
audited a course with visiting professor Daniel Day Williams on process theology, found myself especially drawn to the courses on the history of the church
and American religious history, and discovered that I responded happily to Yale's
inclination to teach students theology by having them read the classic historical sources. In the systematic theology course, we read John Calvin's *Institutes
of the Christian Religion* in the first semester and Friedrich Daniel Ernst
Schleiermacher's *Christian Faith* in the next.[5] Calvin was the seminal source
for much of the Reformed piety that I had seen around me (without quite knowing what it was) while growing up in Arkansas; Schleiermacher was the seminal source for the ways of thinking that had attracted me after I began my college studies. Each in his own way depicted life in the world as a fragile endeavor
in which we try to secure our existence by absolutizing our values—Calvin
called it idolatry; Schleiermacher, captivity to the sensuous consciousness—
only to find that we gain a wider vision when we are somehow enabled to accept our finitude and discover ourselves opened to a sense of interconnectedness
with a larger unity that transcends our narrow individuality.

The theologian who left the strongest imprint on me at Yale was H. Richard
Niebuhr, who had died the year before I entered the divinity school but whose
lingering influence permeated the place. Especially through my courses in

Christian ethics with James M. Gustafson, whose lively knowledge of historical theology also encouraged me to read the classical sources, I began to attend
to Niebuhr's ethical and theological writings and to learn a way of thinking about
theology that had little to do with the rational proofs and evidences of the sort
that had preoccupied the antebellum southerners, or with the philosophical
idealism that stood behind the personalist tradition, or with the more sentimental
forms of liberal pietism that had shaped my religious life as a youth. Niebuhr
represented for me a modern and compelling voice who stood, albeit critically,
in the tradition of both Calvin and Schleiermacher.

Niebuhr's "radical monotheism" conveyed to me an idea of Christian theology as a response to the mystery of the reality that had drawn us into existence,
that manifested itself in every worldly event, and that remained when all else
passed away. Implicit in Niebuhr's images was a somber, chastened understanding of human life and its possibilities, and what struck me as the intellectual
humility of it seemed consonant with my own growing awareness that I would
never have any answers to the big questions. I was attracted by Niebuhr's contention that everyone lived by one or another practical faith, one or another
center of value; that most of us implicitly placed our trust in an ever-changing
polytheistic or henotheistic array of gods, ranging from our isolated selves to
such gods as wealth, class, race, nation, or religion; and that while all these
gods were destined to pass away, it remained possible to be drawn in trust to the
reality that transcended and relativized them. With such a vision, theology
became a pointer to a way of living in the world before God with a sense of
humility, care for one's neighbor, and responsibility.

Niebuhr's *Meaning of Revelation* informed the way I would think about the
meaning of Jesus as the elusive figure in the gospel narratives whose story—
always an interpreted story, subject to continuing reinterpretation throughout
the centuries—became for the Christian community the story that illumined
other stories and so revealed a way of living responsibly in the world.[6] Niebuhr
taught me that all communities look to revelatory events—moments in their
inner history that provide an image by means of which other significant occasions of their common and personal life receive a meaning—and that the Christian community was one that had been drawn by the biblical images of Jesus
into a distinctive understanding of God as the one beyond the many who acted
upon us in every action that befell us.

For Niebuhr—and this also impressed me—theology was resolutely confes-

sional. He meant by this that it was not the task of theology to offer justifica-
tions for Christianity, to try to prove that it was the best religion, or to defend
claims on the part of the church to superior knowledge or some other excellence. Christian theology was, rather, the effort of Christians to speak of what
had happened to them in their community, how they came to trust, and what
they saw from their point of view. To substitute the sovereignty of Christianity
for the sovereignty of the God recognized in Christian faith was to fall into a
type of idolatry.

One can therefore imagine my surprise at learning from the review in that
British journal that I seemed to be defending antebellum southern rational
orthodoxy. As I understood them, the rational orthodox theologians about whom
I wrote had been preoccupied with responding to the Enlightenment critique
of Christianity by showing that reason could marshal evidences to authenti-
cate the Christian revelation as the exclusive source of religious truth. I had
come to believe that such an enterprise was misplaced and futile.

And yet I would probably have to concede that I was engaged in some sort of
"defending" when I wrote the book, even if I failed fully to recognize it at the
time. Let me try to explain what sort of defending might have been going on.

My wife Vicky and I lived in New Haven for seven years. One of our two
children was born there. We loved the region. We liked the proximity to New
York City, and I made many trips to work in the McAlpin Collection of British
History and Theology at Union Theological Seminary, managing always to
spend some of the time that should have been spent in the library just walking
the streets of Manhattan. The seven years taught me some things about both
myself and my identity as a southerner. I recall the fun of reading Willie Morris's
North toward Home, the account of a Mississippian who moved to New York
and became a distinguished editor and writer, whose stories about growing up
in the small-town South gave me images and anecdotes that interpreted my
own experience.[7] I was so grateful for the book that I wrote Morris a thank-you
note. I still laugh aloud at some of the stories. But it was a symbol of the broader
experience of living elsewhere. From New Haven, I could see the South as a
different place, different from what I had known when it was the only place I
knew, different from the New Haven that I was now beginning to explore. I
had other experiences, too, that taught me about the South and perceptions of
it, including one conversation with a middle-class couple in Milford, Connecti-

cut, who asked me (it was a serious question) if I had worn shoes while growing up. I was already aware that the South was not the intellectual center of American life—in fact, I was convinced for my first few months at Yale that I, as a graduate of a small Arkansas college, had no right to study at such a place and that I would surely reveal my cognitive deficit every time I opened my mouth—and a couple of my friends assumed a special responsibility for reminding me periodically that there was something slightly comical simply about having had the misfortune to be born in a place like Arkansas.

During my graduate training in the Department of Religious Studies, however, I thought little about the South. My chief mentor, Sydney E. Ahlstrom, was completing his magisterial *Religious History of the American People* (1972), which reflected his conviction that the Puritan impulse flowed through virtually all American religious history.[8] Ahlstrom talked about the South, especially its Baptist traditions, as the last great repository of Puritanism in America. But he saw Puritanism almost everywhere else in American religious history. It seemed to follow that the priority for a fledgling historian of American religion should be immersion in that Puritan tradition. At the same time, another of my important mentors at Yale, Edmund S. Morgan in the history department, was producing bright and lively studies of early colonial history that confirmed my conviction that the seventeenth century was the place for me. Morgan had written some short pieces on the South, but he had not at that time published his *American Slavery, American Freedom* (1975), which did so much to clarify the paradoxes of southern colonial life.[9] To my later regret, I skipped the seminar with C. Vann Woodward because the gossip among graduate students was that he discouraged papers on religious topics, and those were the topics that interested me.

So I remained ignorant about most of southern religious history. I knew that seventeenth-century Virginia Anglicans had a tough time, that camp meetings were entertaining to read about, that revivalism spread across the region in the later eighteenth century, that the churches waffled on slavery before finally deciding to support it, and that Confederate chaplains won a lot of converts in battlefield altar calls. I also knew about the Scopes trial. But I recall one conversation with a fellow graduate student in which I had to admit that I had never heard of the influential and learned Presbyterian theologian James Henley Thornwell. All of this is a little embarrassing to relate. I should have been reading more widely than I was. I wrote my Yale dissertation on seventeenth-century Puritan thought, more specifically on sacramental thought and piety, and I spent the next two years after leaving Yale revising the dissertation while trying to begin a teaching career.

It is ironic that an offhand comment in one of Sydney Ahlstrom's lectures comes to mind still as a clue to what drew me later into the research on southern religious thought. Ahlstrom was the historian who had first elicited my interest in theology in America—an interest that has stayed with me—and it would be no exaggeration to say that he had little special interest in southern thinkers. In talking briefly in one lecture about religion in the South, however, he once made a few funny references to the nineteenth-century Baptist James R. Graves, whose polemical satire against Methodists, *The Great Iron Wheel; or, Republicanism Backwards and Christianity Reversed* (1856), along with the reply by "Parson" William G. Brownlow, *The Great Iron Wheel Examined; or, Its False Spokes Extracted* (1856), illustrated what Ahlstrom took to be the folksy and simplistic quality of nineteenth-century antebellum southern religious polemics.[10] Ahlstrom had a wonderfully engaging sense of humor, and in this instance it served his pedagogy: the comment stuck in my mind.

Since this was the idea that stuck, I found it something of a surprise when I later began to run across the writings of the people I would call the "gentlemen theologians." Here was a collection of writings that did not seem to fit my own stereotype. The more I poked around in the library, the more I thought that maybe I had a book topic that could make an interesting point—the South had been home to a group of influential and sometimes relatively learned clerical theologians, and very few historians had bothered to give them a second look.

One has to remember that in 1973, when I began the research, serious studies of southern religion were not overflowing on the library shelves. The 1950s saw the appearance of several good denominational histories; scholars during the '60s produced a number of serious books on religion and slavery. During the '70s some remarkable studies of religion and race, ranging from H. Shelton Smith's *In His Image, But* (1972) to Eugene D. Genovese's *Roll, Jordan, Roll* (1974), were marking a new era in the study both of white religious attitudes and of black religion. One could also find some serious studies of the camp meetings and of revivalism and its effect on southern religious culture, ranging from Charles Johnson's *Frontier Camp Meeting* (1955) to John B. Boles's *The*

Great Revival (1972). But someone seeking insight into the history of theology in the South had few places to turn. Arthur S. Link and Rembert W. Patrick had published in 1965 a 444-page book on southern historiography—*Writing Southern History*—in which they devoted slightly more than a page to general works on religious history and not quite a paragraph to historians who had looked at any of the figures who had attracted my attention.[11]

At Emory I was teaching the history of American Christianity, though with broader teaching responsibilities for the history of Christianity from the sixteenth century to the twentieth in Europe as well. Since I taught mainly theology students, I was working each day with people for whom religious ideas mattered. Something in the setting of a theological school keeps alive at least a degree of continuing interest in the history of what people have thought about some pretty abstruse matters. On the other hand, I was also working in a tradition—southern Methodism—in which theological ideas, especially complex, difficult, challenging, threatening ideas, had often seemed a bother, an intrusion, or worse. A significant, visible group of Methodist seminarians always entered—and graduated from—the school with a disposition thoroughly formed by the anti-intellectual currents of the tradition and the region. These students sought a type of technical training in which they could learn as quickly as possible how to accomplish certain administrative, liturgical, and pastoral tasks. They found courses in theology, ethics, and history little more than hurdles to be jumped or ordeals to be endured.

When I wrote *The Gentlemen Theologians*, therefore, I was, to some modest degree, subjecting to criticism some of the anti-intellectualism in my own tradition. I was saying that theology—which required an attempt to think seriously about some ideas that were not always immediately practical—was part of the southern heritage, too. This was one of the reasons I tried to take seriously styles of thinking with which I felt otherwise little affinity. While I was writing the book, and after it appeared, more than one colleague in the historical guild expressed astonishment that I would waste my time on these antebellum southerners. One shamed me a little for paying that much attention to people who held slaves or legitimized the pretensions of other slaveholders. Another greeted the publication of the book with the sarcastic observation that I had obviously found my niche within the provincial. But I thought that it was not entirely a vacuous enterprise to speak from within the context of the southern church (where my seminary position located me) with a reminder that part of the southern religious heritage included a tradition in which people had valued the effort to think about important matters, a tradition in which ideas counted for something. Whether they had been right or wrong, successful or unsuccessful, was not the point.

One of my friends in the profession once remarked to me, upon ferreting out some of my more liberal sympathies, that at least I had tried to be fair to people who thought differently from me—people who in his judgment, by the way, also thought far more rigorously than some of the nineteenth-century religious liberals for whom I had expressed more liking than he thought justified. I took the comment as a compliment. I did try to be fair, to avoid cheap shots and a too facile moralizing. In several ways I did respect the antebellum southern theologians. They were surely, from my perspective, flawed thinkers: I found their ideas wrong, their defense of slavery troubling and tragic, their polemical vehemence overdone, and their disdain for most nineteenth-century biblical criticism shortsighted. But they took ideas seriously. They accepted the discipline of thinking as part of the religious life. And for those virtues, if for nothing else, I was, at least implicitly, offering some kind of defense.

From another perspective, though, I really did not think about the book as a defense of anything. Considerations of that sort never much entered my mind as I was traveling to libraries throughout the South, reading long tomes that were often less than scintillating and plowing through manuscript census returns. I was simply trying to learn better the craft of a historian. I was having fun trying to put the data together into a single story. And the topic itself offered a historiographical challenge. It gave me a chance to think about the relationship between the history of ideas and at least a modest form of social history. When I found that most of the clergy whose writings I was reading had been urban ministers and that they had sometimes linked their intellectual aspirations to their sense of their urban setting, I decided that part of the engagement of the research and writing would be in the effort to link the social location and the thought.

In this endeavor, the social theories of Robert King Merton at Columbia University offered help, especially his descriptions of social role and reference group theory. He had outlined a theory of role as a pattern of behavior formed by a group's perceptions of what others expected them to be and do.[12] An article in the 1960 volume of *Public Opinion Quarterly* by Herbert H. Hyman on "reference groups"—the people whose expectations shape those perceptions—led me further along in this direction.[13] I also read in 1975 Thomas C. Cochran's *Railroad Leaders, 1845–1890* (1953), a book that had used role and reference theories to understand the decisions made by railroad managers who looked to the top officers and presidents of their companies and to powerful entrepreneurs for clues as to how they were to behave.[14] Methods of this sort seemed tailor-made for what I was beginning to find in the letters and biographies of the urban clergy. The gentlemen theologians clearly looked upon the educated classes of the towns—and especially the other professional groups in the towns—as people whose opinions mattered. They worried that the clergy had failed to keep up with the other professions; they also encountered in their urban churches an expectation, often articulated openly, that they should always exhibit both a gentility of manner and a certain rationality of mind that would distinguish them and their congregations from the unlearned exhorters of the countryside. The theoretical ideas helped me discover a consistent way to interpret their journal entries and their admonitions to one another.

At the same time, the theories also made sense to me because they illumined aspects of my own past as a child growing up in a clerical household in the South. For my father, just as for many of the clerical gentlemen, the ministry had been a route of upward social mobility, and he, like them, had been sensitive to the force of a community's expectations. No minister can successfully lead a congregation without learning to work—however uneasily and sometimes subversively—within the definitions of the minister's "role" that implicitly shape congregational relationships. And I had seen the ways in which the expectations of certain highly educated and wealthy professionals can be especially powerful in such situations. In his *History Primer* (1971), J. H. Hexter talked about the way in which the "second record" of historians—their own experience of the world around them—could sometimes lead them to see things in the past that might otherwise be overlooked.[15] I think he was right and that this part of my own second record helped me see things in the data that I might not otherwise have seen. Some of the tensions I was able to discern in my father's life had more than a passing resemblance to the tensions I could see in the comments of the antebellum genteel clergy.

I had experienced, in a different way, some of those same kinds of tensions.

I had my own awareness of how subtle assumptions present within a community can establish perceptions that affect how one lives and works. In the first
place, no community has a more demanding set of role expectations than research universities. One is continually told, in both subtle and blunt ways, that
the university expects certain specifiable forms of behavior, including the publication of research. In the second place, stereotypes flourish in universities as
much as anywhere else, and nothing is easier to stereotype in a university—at
least among a segment of the faculty—than religion, religious leaders, and
schools of theology. When my wife, Vicky, enrolled in several biology courses
available on the Emory campus, one of her teachers—a talented scholar—asked
me one day in the lunch line if her interest in biology worried me. His assumption was that if I taught in a school of theology I must certainly harbor negative
attitudes toward the biological sciences and also hold to metaphysical assumptions that he, as a scientist, would be bound in integrity to reject. I assured him
that I did not deeply lament my wife's interest in biology. We did not discuss
the further matter of whether my metaphysical assumptions were all that different from his—if indeed either of us thought much about our metaphysical
assumptions when we did our work, in any case—but such experiences helped
me to understand, I think, at least some of the psychological dimensions of the
effort of the antebellum clergy to suggest that Christian theology need not be
construed merely as an obscurantist refusal to recognize the insights derived
from other sources of knowledge. I did not think that these clergy had found a
solution that resolved the issues. In fact, I thought that they had proposed solu-
tions that exacerbated the problems. But I could understand why they felt the
need to address the questions.

It was harder, though, for me to understand their deep investment in a slave
society. One of my later regrets was that I did not spend more time in the book
trying to understand this. I included a chapter on their moral thought in which
I tried to unearth some of the presuppositions that surfaced in their thoughts
on slavery, and I used one theologian, Thomas Smyth of South Carolina, as a
case study of the biblical defense of slavery, but this strikes me now as inadequate. In the writing of this essay I glanced back over some of the reviews of
the book. One reviewer began with a clever epigram that I had to admire: "*The
Gentlemen Theologians*," he wrote, "is itself a little too genteel."[16] That was probably right. And one way in which it was accurate, although the reviewer was

making another point, is that the book failed to plunge deeply enough into the tragedy of this intermingling of Christian theology and a slave order. It failed to explore the point that the theologians were proposing a rational and serene theodicy—a justification of the world's ultimate orderliness and justice—just at the time when the surrounding society was constructing a palpably unjust and authoritarian order in which human beings were mistreated because their culture and color were different. Christian theologians had supported slavery for centuries, but it was nonetheless striking that so few of the southern thinkers were able to see that the injustice of it was just about to lead to a cataclysm in which the society itself would be destroyed.

The southern racial tragedy had been for me a source of shame and distress. I had attended segregated schools all the way through high school. My college had been racially segregated until my senior year. I never had a serious conversation with a black person of my own age until a youth conference sponsored by the Methodist Church in 1960 on Mount Sequoyah in Fayetteville, Arkansas, brought black and white young people together in one of the unpublicized retreats that the denomination sponsored to help prepare the South for the changes that were underway.

On racial matters, my family had been southern liberals, with all of the virtues and vices that white liberalism on racial matters involved in the mid-1950s and early 1960s. My father had so vigorously opposed Arkansas's demagogic, race-baiting governor Orval E. Faubus that someone called once and told us they were going to bomb our house. When my father offered the invocation at the opening rally for the gubernatorial campaign of Lee Ward, a moderate from northeast Arkansas who tried to unseat Faubus, he lost friends and received admonitions from leaders of Arkansas Methodism whom he had greatly admired. The closing of the schools in Little Rock in 1957 was an event of great shame for us, and it reconfigured our lines of friendship and association, since whites who felt differently about the issue now were often uncomfortable with each other.

My college years came during a period of revolutionary change in racial relations, and I was deeply moved by the civil rights movement, though largely as a bystander. I was impressed by the courage of the freedom riders who began in 1960 to integrate the bus stations and appalled by the mob insurrection at Ole Miss in 1962, the brutality that greeted voting rights organizers in the South from 1962 through 1964, the blunders of Public Safety Commissioner Bull Connor in Birmingham in 1963, the killing that same year of Medgar Evers, and the white southern resistance to the Selma March in 1965. I was also dismayed by the religious arguments for racial segregation that one could find in a few Arkansas bookstores. The civil rights movement convinced me, if I needed convincing, that religion could operate powerfully in a culture both to defend injustice and to resist it.

When I undertook the research for the book, the racial ethos had changed. The calls for Black Power that Stokely Carmichael and Willie Ricks started to issue in 1966 signaled the emergence of a black nationalism that had little use for white liberals. The violence that began in the Watts area of Los Angeles in 1965 and then spread to other cities over the next three years seemed to symbolize the hopelessness of it all—a hopelessness intensified by the assassination of Martin Luther King Jr. in 1968. In writing *The Gentlemen Theologians*, I was always aware that the religious presuppositions of southern whites had helped to create this dilemma, and I should have been both more venturesome and more explicit in looking at the links between religion and race.

The heavier emphasis in the book was on social class, which was the topic, implicitly and explicitly, of the first two chapters. Those chapters focused on the ideals and pretensions of urban southerners who were, for the most part, of relatively high social standing in their communities. It looked at expectations of people who were conscious of their status as townspeople and of their own aspirations for rationality, elegance, and refinement. Part of the argument of the book was that such expectations helped form the setting in which a "rational orthodox" theology would find a congenial setting. In making this argument, I was also aware of another form of ambivalence in my own history.

Like most Americans, I had always simply thought of myself—as soon as I became aware of the classifications—as *middle class*. But I was also aware that the term told only part of the story. My father had been the son of a rural minister who, after the early death of my grandmother, had transferred from the old Protestant Methodist Church to the Methodist Episcopal Church, South. The story that passed down the generations suggested, though not in terms quite as crass as this, that he made the move because he wanted to move up socially, the Protestant Methodists having occupied a niche ever so slightly lower on the scale than the Southern Methodists. In any event, he was not a man of wealth, and my father, who had grown to maturity during the Great Depression, had struggled to escape poverty. My maternal grandfather, in turn, had been a small farmer who lost his house and land after a disastrous fire and had to become a sharecropper. His seven children knew what poverty meant as well, and they had few of the opportunities that even modest affluence can bring, especially after his early death left his wife alone to raise them by herself. During the years of the Great Depression, my parents had been among the economically dispossessed. They had seen a way out through education, and by the time I was born my father had managed, at considerable personal cost, not only a college education but also a seminary degree from the Perkins School of Theology at Southern Methodist University—an educational journey that was rare for clergy in Arkansas, or anywhere else in the South, during the 1930s.

They had escaped the poverty, but they had also been scarred by it, and they could never escape a feeling of discomfort in the presence of the privileged, a nagging sensation of inferiority, accompanied always by a sympathy for people who, like themselves, had been compelled to work their way up without many advantages. Much of this I absorbed, and when I wrote the chapters on the pretensions of town dwellers in the antebellum South, I wrote with an ironic distance that was born of my own heritage as a child of parents whose childhood had been unprivileged. And yet my parents had also yearned for self-improvement, had struggled for some of the same high culture that marked the opinion makers in the southern towns, had strived to speak correctly and stay informed and associate with educated people, with the genteel. But their ambivalence was always pronounced. True culture, my father would say, is a matter of the heart and conscience. For him, a cultured person was a thoughtful person, kind to other people, humane in the ethical, not the academic, sense of the term.

I had looked to education as a pathway to something better than what I knew growing up as a child, had thrown myself into it—at least by the time I entered college—with a passion that could almost be described as religious. I had viewed education as a means to transcend my own provinciality, of which I was, by my junior year in college, acutely aware. And so part of me could understand and sympathize with those urban southerners who wanted their ministers to be rational and genteel. I valued a sort of gentility myself.

In dwelling on the passion for education, however, I must also turn in another direction, toward social forces and impulses of which I was unaware but that formed my generation of scholars. Among the most important of those forces were economic ones. I entered college in 1959, toward the end of the Eisenhower years, when the economy was falling into a phase of stagnation, with high unemployment accompanied by an inflation that was also high by the standards of the time. By the time I was ready to graduate in 1963, however, the economy was in the middle of a five-year spurt that almost halved the unemployment rate and reduced the inflation rate to 1 percent a year. Real income increased, corporate profits doubled, and I was, without recognizing the reasons, one of the beneficiaries. Financial aid was plentiful, and for my seminary and graduate training, I received full and generous fellowships from the Danforth Foundation and the Woodrow Wilson Foundation. By the time I began my teaching career, the economy was more troubled, but I had nonetheless been among the winners who profited, often without having any awareness of the larger economic picture, from economic forces over which I had no control.

I enjoyed the benefits of some of the nation's political changes as well. In 1965 the United States Congress created the National Endowment for the Humanities (NEH). It was a tiny piece of Lyndon Johnson's Great Society, and I have no memory of even being aware of its creation. But a year-long fellowship from the NEH made it possible for me to complete the book, and the endowment continued to be a source of support for some of my later research. It taught me how a well-run government program can make a difference for someone.

And finally, I ended up, partly by sheer accident, teaching in a university that valued writing and research and gave its faculty members time to pursue both. As I was completing graduate school, I explored the possibility of returning to a small college in the South, the sort of place that I had attended. I was only vaguely aware that few of the teachers in those small colleges at that time ever had sabbaticals or research support that allowed them to engage in travel to distant libraries or in years of reading on a topic. For most of them, the teaching responsibilities alone were almost overwhelming, and if I had chanced to teach in one, I would not be writing this essay today. With the antebellum southern theologians, I share one conviction: we control much less of our lives than we think we do, and we depend far more than we sometimes realize on webs of relations that transcend our awareness.

Notes

1. E. Brooks Holifield, *The Gentlemen Theologians: American Theology in Southern Culture, 1795–1860* (Durham, N.C.: Duke University Press, 1978).

2. L. Billington, review of *The Gentlemen Theologians: American Theology in Southern Culture, 1795–1860,* by E. Brooks Holifield, *History* 64 (Oct. 1979): 409–10.

3. Paul Tillich, *The Courage to Be* (New Haven: Yale University Press, 1952).

4. Paul Tillich, *Systematic Theology,* 3 vols. (Chicago: University of Chicago Press, 1951–63).

5. John Calvin, *Institutes of the Christian Religion* (1559), ed. John McNeill (Philadelphia: Westminister Press, 1960); Friedrich Daniel Ernst Schleiermacher, *The Christian Faith,* ed. H. R. Mackintosh and J. S. Stewart (Edinburgh: T. and T. Clark, 1928).

6. H. Richard Niebuhr, *The Meaning of Revelation* (New York: Macmillan, 1941).

7. Willie Morris, *North toward Home* (Boston: Houghton Mifflin, 1967).

8. Sydney E. Ahlstrom, *A Religious History of the American People* (New Haven: Yale University Press, 1972).

9. Edmund S. Morgan, *American Slavery, American Freedom: The Ordeal of Colonial Virginia* (New York: Norton, 1975).

10. James R. Graves, *The Great Iron Wheel; or, Republicanism Backwards and Christianity Reversed* (Nashville: Graves and Marks, 1855); William G. Brownlow, *The Great Iron Wheel Examined; or, Its False Spokes Extracted* (Nashville: author, 1856).

11. H. Shelton Smith, *In His Image, But . . .: Racism in Southern Religion, 1780-1910* (Durham, N.C.: Duke University Press, 1972); Eugene D. Genovese, *Roll, Jordan, Roll: The World the Slaves Made* (New York: Pantheon, 1974); Charles A. Johnson, *Frontier Camp Meeting: Religious Harvest Time* (Dallas: Southern Methodist University Press, 1955); John B. Boles, *The Great Revival, 1787–1805: The Origins of the Southern Evangelical Mind* (Lexington: University Press of Kentucky, 1972); Arthur S. Link and Rembert W. Patrick, eds., *Writing Southern History: Essays in Historiography in Honor of Fletcher M. Green* (Baton Rouge: Louisiana State University Press, 1965).

12. Robert King Merton, *Social Theory and Social Structure* (Glencoe, Ill.: Free Press, 1949).

13. Herbert H. Hyman, "Reflections on Reference Groups," *Public Opinion Quarterly* 24 (fall 1960): 383–96.

14. Thomas Cochran, *Railroad Leaders, 1845–1890: The Business Mind in Action* (Cambridge: Harvard University Press, 1953).

15. J. H. Hexter, *The History Primer* (New York: Basic, 1971).

16. John Kent, "Review of *The Gentlemen Theologians,*" by E. Brooks Holifield, *Journal of Ecclesiastical History* 31 (1980): 238.

Among the Baptists: Reflections of an East Tennessee Episcopalian

John Shelton Reed

ately we seem to have entered the Age of the Memoir. All sorts of people are now committing their recollections to paper, despite the fact that many of them apparently do not have much of interest to recall. And those who do—well, I often find myself wishing they hadn't gone to the effort.

Old-fashioned writers of memoirs usually asked, implicitly, to be admired for what they had done, but these days a lot of folks seem to be asking to be admired for what has been done to them. (I think we may have Oprah to thank for that.) You may gather that I am not happy about this development, and you are right. I have read a lot of memoirs in the last few years, out of some warped sense of obligation, and nine times out of ten I have not wanted to thank the author for sharing.

So you will not be hearing much about my youthful suffering or indiscretions. I am not even saying that I had any. As Bill Bennett once said, when someone asked him about using drugs in college, "If I have any confessions to make I'll make them to a priest."

No, one of my role models—indeed, as we used to say, one of my heroes—is the great libertarian Albert Jay Nock, author of *Memoirs of a Superfluous Man,* one of the most reticent autobiographies of all time. Nock wrote that "whatever a man may do or say, the most significant thing about him is what he thinks; and significant also is how he came to think it, why he continued to think it, or if he did not continue, what the influences were which caused him to change his mind."[1] You may find that a desiccated, intellectual view, but it is my view, too, and I am sticking to it.

The question I address in this essay is how someone who has spent his adult life writing and teaching about the American South came to write a book about the Victorian Church of England. Oddly enough, there is a southern angle even to that.

I grew up as an Episcopalian in upper East Tennessee, surely one of the furthest-flung corners of the Anglican Communion. Where I come from, Episcopalians were—I reckon still are—a tiny minority, outnumbered not just by Baptists and Methodists but by Presbyterians and Campbellites and all manner of Pentecostals. In grade school, my teachers sometimes killed time by asking students to go around the room and say where they went to church. Invariably I was the only Episcopalian. (This was in the early 1950s—well before the Supreme Court started meddling with religious expression in the public schools.)

But please do not think I am complaining. I know some children do not like feeling different, but I rather enjoyed it, at least in this respect. I was cocky enough to feel that being the only Episcopalian made me special. And, of course, there was no stigma attached to it. I do not think my churchmanship was actually an advantage (although, looking back, I can see that it was a *sign* of advantage), but it was not a drawback or a handicap. I was not like the poor Jehovah's Witness who had to leave the room when the class had a Halloween party, or the Jewish boy who sat outside during the weekly visit of the Bible teacher, or even the few Catholic kids, who had their own grade school and lived in a sort of parallel universe as far as we were concerned.

True, other southerners sometimes call my people "whiskey-palians," referring to our noncompliance with the Eleventh Commandment of Evangelical Protestantism, but I don't believe I ever heard that label in Kingsport. The one time I ran into anything other than matter-of-fact acceptance from my schoolmates, it was not a matter of hostility but of innocent curiosity. A boy who attended the Church of God, in the mill village down the hill, approached me once and said that his preacher said that we Episcopalians "worshipped the golden calf," and he wanted to know if that was true. I denied it more vigorously then than I would now that I understand what the preacher meant.

To explain how I wound up with this peculiar affiliation requires an excursion into genealogy, but southerners tend to confuse biography and genealogy anyway. Briefly: my mother made me what I am.

There were a lot of other possibilities. Like many southern highlanders, my father's people were mostly Germans and Scotch-Irish who came down the Great Wagon Road from Pennsylvania in the eighteenth century. They settled in the hills of southwest Virginia, near the Kentucky and Tennessee lines. (My grandfather used to joke that they were looking for the Cumberland Pass but couldn't find it.) These folks were teachers, preachers, and small farmers. Most were Unionists in the 1860s, but there were enough Confederates to spice things up. Their churches were ethnic ones—Lutheran and Reformed and Brethren for the Germans, Presbyterian for the Ulstermen. Despite his Scotch-Irish name, my Grandfather Reed was born into the Church of the Brethren, a German pietist sect whose practice of baptizing by triple immersion gave them the nickname "Dunkards." Somewhere along the line a Reed had evidently married a Dunkard *frau*, and the children had taken their mother's religion.

My grandmother's ancestors were much the same—in fact, many were the same people, since she and my grandfather were second cousins. (There's a point at which my family tree doesn't branch.)

Granddad's first job was as a schoolteacher, but Grandmom, who was also a teacher, taught in the girl's reformatory in Richmond to put him through medical school. (He worked part-time as medical officer for the Confederate veterans' home.) After medical school they went back home to Dickinson County, but when George Eastman founded the Tennessee Eastman Corporation in 1920, to make film base for his cameras, Granddad saw his chance and took it. He moved fifty miles or so, across the state line, to the new town of Kingsport and set up the first hospital there.

At some point (I am not sure when) he marked his upward mobility by becoming a Southern Baptist—albeit one with a marked taste for whiskey and poker—and my father was raised in Kingsport's First Baptist Church. If I had been brought up in his boyhood religion my story would be less unusual, but, as I said, I got my religion from my mother.

She is a Yankee girl, true blue, from Rochester, New York. My father met her when he went to the University of Rochester on an Eastman scholarship. After he finished medical school and became a doctor like his father, he married her and brought her back to Kingsport. Her maiden name was Greene, anglicized from Gruen, and she got it from a line of Alsatian millers, who may well have been Jewish in Alsace, although they got off the boat in the New World as Protestants. But her Grandfather Greene married a Griswold. That's old Yankee stock—none older. The Griswolds came to Connecticut in the early seventeenth century from Warwickshire, where they had been ever since the Angles and Saxons pushed out the Celts. In storage somewhere in the San Diego museum is a bust of my Griswold great-grandmother that was made for a turn-of-the-century anthropometric exhibit to illustrate the 100 percent pure Anglo-Saxon type. (No kidding.) Her son, my grandfather, was, like her, a Congregationalist.

But my mother's religion came from *her* mother. (Are you seeing a pattern here?) Grandma Greene came from the Anglo-Irish, that race of poets, soldiers, and rogues whose church was the established Protestant Church of Ireland, the Anglican church of "the ascendancy," the Irish version of Episcopalianism. My father adopted my mother's genteel religion early on, with (he says) a great sense of relief. He had never forgiven the Southern Baptists for some hellfire and damnation preaching that gave him nightmares as a boy. My brothers, sisters, and I were christened as Episcopalians before we were old enough to have an opinion in the matter, and although I have drifted away from the church now and again, I have never been tempted by any other variety of religious expression.

In the Kingsport of my youth, Episcopalians were rare, as I said, but there were enough of us to support the small church of St. Paul's. Many were transplants like my mother, the families of executives at Eastman or one of the other Yankee-owned industries that gave the so-called Model City its economic base. A few were from the old low-church tradition of Virginia, Carolina, and the Cotton South—the church that buried Robert E. Lee and Jefferson Davis and Booker T. Washington and William Faulkner. (How's that for a trivia question?) What we did not have at St. Paul's were many natives of East Tennessee or southwest Virginia, aside from a few converts like my father. And, of course, there was a class element to this, although I could not have articulated it at the time. Our congregation was made up mostly of the families of executives and professional men: its social range did not extend much below the upper-middle class.

The church was a small stone building, built to a self-consciously Olde English model. Before the big ungainly parish hall was added, it looked like something you might have found in the Cotswolds. It was on the edge of downtown, though not on Kingsport's imposing, central "church circle." That was reserved for the columned edifices of First Baptist, First Presbyterian, First Methodist, and Broad Street Methodist. (The two Methodist churches had been built before the 1939 reunion of the northern and southern denominations.)

St. Paul's was served by a remarkable priest, the man who baptized my father, me, and eventually my first child. No novelist could have invented a more English name than that of the Reverend Leicester Kent, although Mr. Kent was, in fact, from Ohio.

Before he came to Kingsport he had spent some years as archdeacon of the Yukon, traveling by dogsled to remote congregations of Indians and Inuit. He had a very distinctive voice: I can only describe it by saying that it was perfect for the role of Santa Claus, which he played every evening in December on the local radio station, reading children's letters and talking about his preparations for the big night. When his young parishioners asked how come Santa Claus sounded just like him, he said that living at the cold North Pole must have affected Santa's voice the same way living in the cold Yukon had affected his.

Mr. Kent was and still is to my mind the model of an Anglican parish clergyman. After his death I learned that he had corresponded for some years with Carl Jung, and I recall that he was an early reader and admirer of C. S. Lewis. Our little parish library stocked the Chronicles of Narnia and *The Screwtape Letters*, and, believe it or not, I remember learning as a teenager the words *agape* and *eros* from a sermon that must have been based on Lewis (although Lewis's book *Four Loves* was not published until several years later).

Mr. Kent was not on the rota of local clergymen who came, one a week, to our school assemblies. Someone told me later that he did not belong to the local ministerial association because black ministers were not allowed to join, and that may have been. It would have been in character. Although he did not preach any sort of Social Gospel that I recall, quiet witness was certainly his style. I remember the time when our small youth group, the House of Young Churchmen, met in the parish house with a group of black teenagers from Kingsport's A.M.E. church to make palm crosses for Palm Sunday. This was the first and only racially integrated social event I experienced until I went to college in Massachusetts. I believe it would still be unusual—and not just in the South. Certainly it was remarkable for Tennessee in 1956.

In Anglican terms, St. Paul's was characterized by low-church liturgy and broad-church theology, although I did not know that at the time. I was far more familiar with our differences from other Protestant denominations than with our differences from other Episcopalians. One summer, though, when I was about fourteen, I went to church camp at Monteagle, Tennessee. Not only was it a novel experience to be surrounded by several hundred teenaged Episcopalians, I distinctly remember some young people from Chattanooga who called their minister "Father Jim" (or something like that), distinguished themselves by what were to me unpredictable crossings and bowings in chapel, spoke of incense and other mysteries, and adopted a somewhat superior and pitying attitude toward the rest of us. This was my first encounter with "high-church" Episcopalianism, and I confess that I was jealous.

But back home in Kingsport I spent far more time worshipping with evangelical Protestants than with my fellow Episcopalians. Besides the ministers who addressed the school assembly each week, there was an itinerant lady Bible teacher who visited each grade-school class. Naturally each morning at school began with prayer on the public address system (student-led prayer, beginning in junior high), and our music program included a healthy dose of hymns and other more or less religious music. I remember in particular "The Old Rugged Cross" and "The Little Brown Church in the Vale." (The chorus of that last one used to crack up us nasty adolescent boys. In our weekly music assemblies we would *shout* it: "Oh-oh come! come! come! come!") One of my best friends when I went to college up north was an Arkansas boy, raised as a Christian Scientist. Among the many things we had in common, we discovered, was nostalgic attachment to the same Baptist and Methodist hymns.

I mentioned the House of Young Churchmen (most of whom were young churchwomen, actually). It was a valiant but ultimately rather sad affair: a half-dozen of us, a dozen at most. Nothing to compare to the legions of the Methodist Youth Fellowship (MYF) or the Baptists' Royal Ambassadors. For some reason most of my best friends were Methodists—including eventually my girlfriend, now my wife—and I often went to MYF, just to be with them. I even went with them one summer to the Methodist church camp at Buffalo Mountain, Tennessee. I remember distinctly that it was the summer of the Everly Brothers' "Bye Bye Love," which makes it 1957. MYF piety was very much what the Brits call "happy-clappy," so there was a lot of singing and sharing on the agenda at Buffalo Mountain, but it was not oppressive: better than school, actually. The last night of camp we sat in the big outdoor amphitheater, sang and prayed, and concluded by signing cards pledging that we would not drink or smoke. For most of us—fifteen years old, with no driver's license in a dry county—drinking was only an aspiration, but a good many had already taken up with Lady Nicotine. I remember walking down the hill from the service, feeling solemn and committed as only a sentimental teenager can, when a semi-hoodlum friend named Ritchie pulled a Marlboro pack from the rolled-up sleeve of his T-shirt and threw it into the woods. Amazed, I asked him if he had taken the pledge. "Naw," he said. "Damn pack's empty." That certainly shattered the solemnity.

Not too much later, I confess, I lost my youthful faith. It was a gradual process, proceeding through a sort of deism to agnosticism, helped along by books like Thomas Paine's *Age of Reason* and Bertrand Russell's *Why I Am Not a Christian*. (I was a bookish lad, and those books could be found even in Kingsport.) There was no anguish about this, no dark night of the soul. Quite the contrary: after all, being a freethinker was even more different—more special—than being an Episcopalian. I flaunted my new opinions, scandalizing some earnest young people, annoying some older ones (including my parents), and no doubt amusing some others. I think Mr. Kent knew the score: he asked me once if I had any doubts that I wanted to discuss, but I was, oddly, reluctant to tell him. For once I kept my opinions to myself—somehow I felt that he would be disappointed in me. (I am certain now that I was wrong about that.)

In 1959, when I was seventeen, my involvement with southern religion took a different turn, a commercial one. I got a summer job at a thousand-watt "daytimer" radio station in the little community of Church Hill, a few miles out of Kingsport. On weekdays I ran the "Noontime All-Hymn Program" for two hours, followed by three hours of top-40 rock and roll, then an hour and forty-five minutes of "Sunset Hymn Time." I dropped my voice an octave to read "the Obituary Column of the Air, brought to you by Bruton snuff. Sure as shootin', you'll like Bruton. Bruton Scotch and Bruton Sweet, Bruton snuff just can't be beat."

On Sundays I signed the station on at 7:00 A.M. and worked for thirteen hours straight. Aside from patching in a broadcast of the 11:00 service at Church Hill's First Baptist Church (the station owner's church), my job was to ride herd on an all-day parade of preachers and their flocks who bought time by the half hour to worship in our studio and to spread the gospel throughout radioland. I took their money—$15.00 for thirty minutes, $25.00 for a full hour—and sat at a control board behind the glass to introduce them and to close them out with something like: "You've been listening to the Four-Square Gospel Hour, with the Reverend T. H. Phipps. This ministry needs your support. Please send your free-will love offering to Reverend Phipps at Box 24, Route 17, Surgoinsville, Tennessee."

Most of these folks were Baptists of one kind or another, but a few were tongue-talking Pentecostals who could be difficult to cut off when their time was up. (I never saw any serpents in the radio station, but my dad sometimes treated folks from up around Big Stone Gap whose faith had been insufficient.) All of the patrons of the station were white, but occasionally a black preacher would show up and ask to announce a revival or something. Invariably he would be greeted warmly and introduced on the air as "Brother" so-and-so, and at least one was asked to lead a prayer, which he did. I have to say that these occasions were among the very few times I saw "separate but equal" actually work out that way.

I also remember in particular one preacher, a brawny countryman who drove a truck during the week and who often came into the control room after his hour was over. We talked and joked and gradually became friends. One day, out of the blue, he asked me quietly if I knew Jesus. Even a callow youth had to recognize that he was offering me, his friend, something very important to him. As with Mr. Kent, though, I did not want to tell him the truth. I did not want him to think less of me, so I lied.

I worked at WMCH, "your good neighbor station in Church Hill," three summers altogether. For my fifty-three-hour week I received $40.00, the glory of being what was not yet called a "media personality," and an acquaintance with white gospel music that is unusual, I believe, for an Episcopalian. I must say that I also came away with a lasting respect and sympathy for the more downhome varieties of southern religious experience. As an advanced thinker myself, of course, I held the primitive beliefs of these people in contempt, but I could not help noticing that they were good and decent folks—better Christians, by and large, than I was used to associating with. Nearly forty years later, when I saw Robert Duval's remarkable movie *The Apostle*, it brought it all back.

But much as I admired my preacher friend's commitment to his faith, I was not drawn to it myself, any more than I was to the more saccharine piety of the Methodists and downtown Baptists. Like many southerners who don't go to church, I always knew which church I wasn't going to.

I didn't go to it for a long time. I left Kingsport for college smug in a sort of nineteenth-century scientism, and nothing I encountered in college at MIT or graduate school at Columbia did anything to undermine that. For ten years in Massachusetts and New York I lived in an almost entirely secular world. Nearly all of my friends were irreligious or soon became so. Religion was something we rarely thought or talked about. Going to church was an odd thing that a very few among us unaccountably did—like rock climbing.

For sentimental and diplomatic reasons I did go to St. Paul's when I was back home in Tennessee. In particular, I went every Christmas Eve with Dale, my girlfriend, who midway through that decade became my wife. We were married in the mammoth sanctuary of Broad Street Methodist, her church, but Dale's minister was conveniently on vacation that week, so we were married by Mr. Kent, in a Prayer Book service (so it counts). Except for a couple of other weddings, though, I literally never went to church in Massachusetts or New York.

Finally, with a dissertation half written and a child on the way, I took a job in Chapel Hill, and we shook the dust of New York City off our shoes. Not long after we returned to the South, I returned to the church. I was ready, but it helped that the Episcopal church in Chapel Hill had splendid music and, in Peter Lee (subsequently the bishop of Virginia), an intelligent and amusing rector. Once again, a lot of reading was involved—some apologetics and theology, of course, but even more church history and liturgiology.

I always knew that much of what I had missed about the Episcopal Church was precisely what set it apart from evangelical Protestantism: the brocaded vestments of priest and deacon; the choral processions; the glittering brass of candlesticks and crosses; the dark, carved wood of the pews and stalls; hymns by Christina Rossetti, William Alexander Percy, and John Mason Neale; the calm, instructive sermons; and especially the stately and sonorous cadences of Thomas Cranmer's *Book of Common Prayer*.

When I returned to the church I was baffled and irritated to find it in the process of junking the old Prayer Book, and I read everything I could find that might shed light on why anyone would want to do that. Although there were good historical, theological, or structural reasons for a few of the changes, most had been made for reasons that struck me (and still do) as fatuous. I have ever since regarded the new book as penance imposed for my time away—although why my poor ex-Methodist wife should have to suffer, too, is a mystery.

But I learned a lot from this course of reading. In particular, I slowly came to realize that much of what I loved about Anglican worship, the actual words of the Prayer Book aside, was not unbroken tradition from before the Reformation, as I had supposed, but Victorian innovation—the result of a conscious effort to turn back the clock, an effort that began with John Henry Newman and his friends in the Oxford Movement of the 1830s and culminated in the so-called Ritualism of the 1860s and '70s. Today's Anglo-Catholics, like those high-church teenagers from Chattanooga I had met at Monteagle, were the Ritualists' direct descendants, but over the years Anglo-Catholics had moved the entire Anglican Communion in their direction. Even the ceremonial and decoration and architecture of our little low-church parish in East Tennessee looked like that of an early Oxford Movement church, not an Anglican church of, say, 1800.

Well, now. How did this happen? Smarting over the changes to the Prayer Book, I had reasons to be interested in successful reactionary movements. As a sociologist, I knew "the literature" on social movements and knew what questions to ask—most obviously, who took up the movement, who opposed it, and why? But the more I read, the more I came to realize the truth of a remark by the ecclesiastical historian John Kent: "Somehow, the central problem remains untouched: why did a section of the nineteenth-century Anglican Church move so dogmatically and successfully back to a style of religious behaviour that had seemed so entirely abandoned in England?"[2] There was a vast literature on and of Anglo-Catholicism, but no one had really asked that question—or rather, those who had, put it down to the operation of the Holy Spirit. That is an answer I would not dismiss out of hand, but it is not one that would satisfy the readers of the *American Journal of Sociology*.

I laid out the problem in a research proposal for the Guggenheim Foundation and was lucky enough to receive a fellowship. (Maybe the Holy Ghost at work again—who knows?) It let me spend a delightful year reading Victorian pamphlets and newspapers in London and Oxford, church-crawling in the towns and countryside of England, and exploring the amazing variety of Anglican worship—choral evensong at Christ Church, Oxford; morning prayer and sermon in little Norman village churches; high mass at All Saints Margaret Street; benediction and exposition in the chapel of Pusey House, Oxford, . . . but we are getting pretty far from East Tennessee. The product of this year was a suitcase full of notes and, nearly twenty years later, that book I mentioned, a volume called *Glorious Battle: The Cultural Politics of Victorian Anglo-Catholicism*.[3]

Irony is cheap these days—almost as devalued as memoir—but it is a central theme in that book. The ironies that are relevant here, though, have less to do with the story of Anglo-Catholicism than with the story of my writing about it. Let me close with a few words about that.

One reason it took me so long is that I could not tell the story I had expected to tell. As I read my way into the nineteenth century, my sympathies became less one-sidedly with the Anglo-Catholics. I had originally seen them as they saw themselves, as sturdy defenders of the historic faith, rolling back the obnoxious innovations of their Protestant foes. But I came to understand that their opponents saw *them* as the obnoxious innovators, imposing strange new practices on congregations that were content with their accustomed forms of worship—rather like the advocates of the new Prayer Book, in fact.

And there's another irony. In my account I tried to do justice to the many prominent Anglo-Catholics who were saintly men and women, but in the early days many enthusiasts for the movement were the kind of pert and insufferable young people who like to be different because it makes them feel special. This often makes for an amusing story, but I didn't find it entirely amusing because, in short, in some of the movement's less attractive followers I recognized myself.

Mea culpa.

Notes

This essay is adapted from a paper presented at the Conference on Southern Autobiography held at the University of Tennessee—Chattanooga, 6–8 April 2000. Thanks to Bill Berry, who organized the conference and gave me permission to publish my paper here.

1. Albert J. Nock, *The Memoirs of a Superfluous Man* (1943; rpt., Chicago: Henry Regnery, 1969), xi–xii.

2. John Kent, "The Study of Modern Ecclesiastical History since 1930," in J. Daniélou, A. H. Couratin, and John Kent, *Historical Theology*, Pelican Guide to Modern Theology, vol. 2 (Harmondsworth, U.K.: Penguin Books, 1969), 324.

3. John Shelton Reed, *Glorious Battle: The Cultural Politics of Victorian Anglo-Catholicism* (Nashville: Vanderbilt University Press, 1996).

I Just Can't Get Out of Virginia: A Personal Journey into Southern Religious History

Thomas E. Buckley, S.J.

When I was growing up, my mother taught me not to discuss politics or religion outside our home. We were an army family, and army people were apolitical. My parents did not even vote until my father retired to civilian life. Army families went to various churches or none at all, so one did not argue about religious faith either. Religion belonged to the private sphere. Yet despite such sensible family rules, an interest in religiously based politics has preoccupied much of my adult life and focused my research in southern religious history. Three diverse aspects of my development fostered this research interest: the varied experiences of an "army brat's" upbringing, a strong Catholic family environment, and, after I joined the Jesuits, the ecumenism of the post–Vatican II Catholic Church.

Army life for me started in the South. I was born at Fort Bragg, North Carolina, where my father, an army captain, served on the Field Artillery Board and tested weapons, ammunition, and communications equipment. Nazi Germany had just invaded Poland, beginning World War II in Europe. I was the fifth child. Perhaps my affinity for the South began then, though within two years my father was reassigned to Camp Roberts in California. We moved to San Jose, where my mother's relatives lived. That was our "hometown," more or less.

Mostly less. Growing up in the army meant continually changing homes and schools—from San Jose to Washington, D.C., for most of the war years and then back to San Jose until we joined my dad in Japan in 1947; then Fort Monmouth in New Jersey, the Presidio of San Francisco, and Arlington, Virginia, where my father worked at the Pentagon during the Korean War. Family, not place, furnished the roots. We were a big—six children, plus Brownie, our dog—rollicking, mostly Irish, all Catholic family. Bushels of aunts, uncles, and cousins inhabited California, which we periodically invaded for clan reunions and summers at the Capitola beach near Santa Cruz.

So far as I know, people still argue about whether such a nomadic life is a good way to raise children. Certainly stability possesses obvious advantages. But the army offered a breadth of formative experiences for which I have always been grateful. Postwar Japan, for example, displayed the appalling aftermath of warfare. Driving from our home in Yokohama to the center of Tokyo, roughly the distance between Washington and Baltimore, we passed mile after mile of gutted ruins, fire-bombed buildings with scarcely a structure standing. I can still visualize the destruction and the gangs of half-starved Japanese children outside the commissary and PX begging food from the GIs. Visits to Japan's shrines such as the Great Buddha at Kamakura and the Temple of the Three Monkeys exposed me to the variety of religious experience. At a very early age, I learned that people believe and express faith in strikingly different ways.

The experience that formed my outlook toward African Americans occurred while we lived at Fort Monmouth. The nun in charge of the fourth grade at St. James's School in Red Bank already had sixty-eight children in her classroom and simply could not teach one more, so my parents found a place for me at Holy Names in Rumson. This meant riding a school bus into Red Bank and then transferring to a city bus that took the maids, gardeners, and chauffeurs out to the posh residences on New Jersey's gold coast. I was the only white person on the Rumson bus. For a year and a half I traveled each school day with the same people. We became friends. Ordinarily I sat with the same one or two, but I got to know everyone on the bus. We would laugh and joke; they would ask about my school or quiz me on my homework; and each day they would give me so much candy that by the time I got to school my lunch bag was filled with Mounds bars, peanut brittle, and chocolates. When I inadvertently mentioned this to my mother, she told me never to take candy from strangers. But these women and men became closer friends than the affluent children who attended my school. The post dentist got a mouth full of cavities to work on, but I learned that race made no difference in friendship.

Moving about the country enhanced my love for its history, as did my parents. My father had graduated from West Point, and my mother, a school teacher before she married, had majored in history at Berkeley. Usually we changed army posts by driving across the country. My parents loved to visit the national parks and tour historic sites. I remember stopping at Fort Necessity, which George Washington had defended in the French and Indian War, and later that same trip being mightily impressed at Fort Bridger, Wyoming, when I learned that someone had dug an Indian arrowhead out of Jim Bridger's back. Weekends on the East Coast meant touring the battlefield where Molly Pitcher manned her husband's cannon in the Revolution, inspecting Independence Hall and Betsy Ross's house, and consuming whole days at the castle building of the Smithsonian Institution. Washington, D.C., held the most attractions. While dad safeguarded the nation from his Pentagon office, mother would trot me around the capitol beat. Curious memories still linger from those days. I can still recall Felix Frankfurter's pointed nose sticking up in the air from behind the Supreme Court bench. Perhaps that trip sparked my interest in church and state.

Religious faith was part of the atmosphere we breathed. No trip to California was complete without special visits to our "sainted aunts," mother's older sister, a contemplative Carmelite nun in a monastery at Carmel, and dad's youngest sister, a Sister of Notre Dame de Namur who taught in various parochial schools along the West Coast. Educated and devout, our parents subscribed to religious magazines and newspapers and filled our home with Catholic books. As a boy I devoured the appealing biographies of the North American martyrs, Isaac Jogues and Jean de Brebeuf, and then in high school I read the autobiography of Thomas Merton, *The Seven Storey Mountain*, and his further journals and spiritual writings.[1] We listened to the *Catholic Hour* on the radio and watched Bishop Fulton Sheen on TV. Our parents made enormous sacrifices on a slender army salary to give their children a Catholic education.

But the Buckleys were not gullible consumers. At breakfast on Sunday mornings after mass, my father would comment on the priest's sermon, often critically. From dad's perspective, the fidelity with which Catholics attended mass despite the poor preaching offered stunning proof for the divine foundation of the church. We never skipped a Sunday. Saturday afternoons usually found us lined up outside the confessional. Invariably, mother was the last one to finish her penance, much to dad's amusement. Evenings, particularly during Advent and Lent or when my father was away with troops, mother would gather us children together to say the rosary. My older brothers loved to recall the time when I happened upon this scene at the tender age of about four. It was wartime, dad was absent, and mother had assembled my older siblings for family prayers when I toddled into the room. "Tommy," she suggested, "why don't you go upstairs, put on your pajamas, get into bed, and surprise mommy?" "Mommy," I purred, "Go to hell." So much for the influence of those neighbor kids. While I got hustled upstairs, my brothers rolled on the floor with laughter.

Catholicism in the 1950s was fervent, militant, and triumphant; but unlike many others of my generation, I grew up outside the Catholic ghetto. Army life guaranteed the religious diversity while simultaneously enhancing the identities Will Herberg explained in *Protestant-Catholic-Jew*.[2] Except for a year and a half in Yokohama, I went to parochial schools, five in all, but every neighborhood we lived in contained a mix of religious faiths. My playmates came in all varieties. For three years of grammar school in Virginia, our neighbors were Episcopalian on one side and Congregational on the other. Across the street lived Methodist, Baptist, and Presbyterian families. We kids played softball in backyards and kick-the-can in the street. Summer days we spent exploring the homes being built in the nearby woods, turning ditches, foundations, and walls into forts for war games. We were buddies, but very occasionally, when an argument arose or a fight broke out, the parting retort might be something like, "You're nothing but a dirty Catholic." I wondered what that meant and where it came from. Paul Blanshard's writings were not on our bookshelves at home.[3]

High school enhanced my interest in religion. After retiring from the army in California in 1954, my father taught mathematics at the Jesuits' Santa Clara University, my mother returned to teaching at a public high school, and I attended Bellarmine, a Jesuit prep school in San Jose. History was my favorite subject, but next to a good party I loved religious apologetics. Debating a passing Jehovah's Witness for a couple of hours always beat mowing the lawn. One older brother became a Jesuit, and the other graduated from West Point. For a time I considered Georgetown and the foreign service. But instead, much to the skepticism of some friends who laid bets on how long I would last, I entered the Jesuit novitiate of the California province at Los Gatos in 1957.

Becoming a priest had been in my head for several years. I admired the Jesuits I knew, and with its extensive foreign missions, apostolates in secondary and higher education, and varied parish, retreat, and writing ministries, the Society of Jesus presented multiple options for good work. During my early years as a Jesuit, pre–Vatican II Catholicism was in full bloom. As novices and then young scholastics, we lived apart from "the world," with outside contacts restricted mainly to family members. Life was regimented and rigorous, with a 5:00 A.M. rise bell and specified times for prayer, study, and recreation. Vows of poverty, chastity, and obedience focused our energies. But community life was familial and supportive, and the men shared a strong esprit de corps. Nor did the absence of newspapers and TV keep a couple of us from avidly following John F. Kennedy's campaign for the presidency. That election made for a perfect mixture of politics and religion, in which I reveled.

After four years at Los Gatos, the first two spent in religious formation and two more devoted to classical studies with a heavy emphasis on Latin and Greek, I was sent to study philosophy for three years at Mount St. Michael's, the Jesuit house of studies outside Spokane, Washington. Academic life there sometimes participated in the unreal. Imagine trying to grasp Einstein's general theory of relativity when both teacher and text used Latin. In Psychologia Rationalis, which we dubbed "rat psych," the syllogism to prove the existence of the soul translated into something like this: "Every man has what he ought to have; and he ought to have a soul; therefore he's got one." The ethics courses with Clifford G. Kossel, a superb pedagogue who taught in English, proved far more intellectually compelling. Three afternoons a week I bused to nearby Gonzaga University to pursue a second undergraduate major in history. I emerged from the first seven years in the Society of Jesus with a double A.B. in history and philosophy, a licentiate (ecclesiastical license) in philosophy, and enough credits to gag a horse.

The period in Jesuit formation known as regency followed. From the abstruse heights of philosophy, I dropped into the real world of high school boys. Teaching, counseling, and moderating student activities, while physically exhausting at times, proved exhilarating. At different periods over the next three years, 1964 to 1967, I happily taught world history, American history, Latin, and civics at St. Ignatius High School in San Francisco. The grace of this experience cemented my vocation as a Jesuit and confirmed my desire to pursue graduate studies in history. In addition, because the school was located on the edge of the Haight-Ashbury district, the haven of hippies and flower children, one could observe at close hand the sixties take hold of America.

Meanwhile, the Second Vatican Council had already begun the transformation of the Catholic Church. In multiple ways we Jesuits became caught up in that process, almost from the coronation (the term used then) of John XXIII in 1958. This roly-poly Italian peasant did not look papal—which is to say he did not look like Pius XII. As Pope John opened the church's windows, the air freshened. Xavier Rynne's revealing articles in the *New Yorker* helped us follow the progress of the council.[4] Liturgical alterations in Jesuit houses kept pace with Rome's mandates, and theological and ecumenical opportunities proved intriguing. While on summer vacation at Priest Lake in Northern Idaho, several of us received permission to attend the first Protestant Sunday worship I had ever witnessed. Afterward we introduced ourselves to the minister and thanked him. The singing and sense of community appealed to us, though the communion service seemed truncated. But I thought then that getting to know our "separated brethren," as Pope John called them, could become a vital part of my life. An interest in ecumenism would further focus my studies in religious history. A few years later the first book I ever reviewed was entitled *The Anglican Eucharist in Ecumenical Perspective.*[5]

Regency ended in the summer of 1967, and instead of an assignment to Alma College, the California theologate (school of theology), I was sent to study theology and prepare for the priesthood at Weston College (today Weston Jesuit School of Theology), the theologate of the New England province. Located in a suburb of Boston, on an extensive wooded tract of land with a shallow lake and ragtag golf course, the huge cold brick and stone building made a classic ecclesiastical fortress. But the administration and faculty were lowering the drawbridge, and we students were the fortunate beneficiaries. In those immediately postconciliar years, ecumenism blossomed. Just that spring Weston had helped found the Boston Theological Institute (BTI), a consortium of seven graduate and professional theology schools including the Episcopal Theological School (today the Episcopal Divinity School) and Harvard Divinity School.

The BTI policy of complete cross-registration provided an instant benefit, which I seized by enrolling that first semester in John E. Booty's superb course on the English Reformation at the Episcopal school. I had studied Tudor England from one perspective; now I got another. From an academic point of view, these next years proved the most satisfying of my Jesuit studies thus far. I loved scripture and theology, and the Weston faculty included some fine Jesuit scholars and teachers. I took another course on Anglican history from Professor Booty, and over at Harvard Divinity School, C. Conrad Wright introduced me to American church history with a rigorous exactitude for which I have always been grateful. I believe I was the first Jesuit to take his class, but he still remembered vividly the alarming presence of another Jesuit who had lived and worked in Cambridge.

Father Leonard Feeney headed the Saint Benedict Catholic Center at Harvard in the late 1940s. A powerful street preacher and vigorous religious presence, he had influenced a number of Harvard students toward Catholicism, including Avery Dulles, the future Jesuit theologian, and a young Jewish woman who later became the prioress of a Carmelite monastery in Vermont. She and I became friends while I was studying theology. Feeney had gone too far, however, when he proclaimed that the theological formula *extra ecclesiam nulla sallus* should be taken literally and absolutely; in other words, that those who were not baptized Catholics were destined for hell. Working through Archbishop Richard J. Cushing of Boston, Rome insisted that the Jesuit priest renounce this position. When he refused to retract, Feeney was expelled from the Jesuits after an ecclesiastical trial and then excommunicated from the church. While these procedures were taking place and for the next several years, Feeney regularly assembled his followers, the "Slaves of Mary," for processions and prayer services on Cambridge Commons. Professor Wright recalled those events all too well, and after our first seminar meeting in his office, he showed me his copy of *The Loyolas and the Cabots*, Catherine Goddard Clarke's account of Feeney's heresy trial.[6]

When the time came a few years later to formulate a proposal for doctoral studies, I seriously considered asking to pursue twentieth-century American religion with a eye on Feeney as a dissertation subject. What he taught, although heresy, many Catholics believed; even more important, most Protestants thought the Catholic Church agreed with Feeney. Thus it seemed to me that Rome's condemnation of his position held enormous importance for the development of ecumenism and interfaith dialogue, and several of Vatican II's documents on those subjects. One of my Jesuit professors at Weston had served as a lawyer at Feeney's trial and offered me his file cabinet of materials on the case. But when I approached the New England provincial for access to the province's materials on the Feeney case, he advised that the issues remained too fresh and controversial. Feeney himself was still alive—he would be reconciled to the church only shortly before he died—and oral interviews had been taped with other figures that could not be released until after their deaths. But the career of Leonard Feeney remains a significant subject for the history of American Catholicism and ecumenism.

Most older Jesuits shied away from discussing Feeney; obviously, he offered no model for Ignatian obedience. They found him an embarrassment, I think. But we were a different breed of Jesuits—"the new breed," some called us. The Vatican Council had transformed Catholic concepts of the church and attitudes toward Protestants. For students of theology, ecumenical dialogue was the order of the day. In classes and as a member of the student coordinating committee of the BTI, I met men and women preparing for ministry in various denominations. Some, particularly at the Episcopal school, became good friends during those years. Relationships became even easier when Weston College left the woods to share academic quarters with the Episcopalians in Cambridge, and we gave up our semi-monastic existence. By the winter of 1968, I was living in a small community of Jesuits in a house a few blocks from Harvard Square. There among ourselves and with Protestant friends, we talked ecumenism and church unity. For me the path toward those goals lay through understanding the histories of our multiple religious traditions. The diversity and appeal of Protestantism to so many people as well as its formative political role in defining national goals and values fascinated me.

By the mid-1960s, national politics appeared more conflicted than at any time since the Civil War. As my regency ended and theological studies began, American society became unglued. I was still teaching in San Francisco when the civil rights movement collapsed in the summer of 1965, and the struggle against the Vietnam War began. The justice in ending segregation and guaranteeing complete racial equality appeared obvious and long overdue, but at first the opposition to the war troubled me. I was, after all, an army brat born and bred. West Point's motto, "Duty, Honor, Country," weighed heavily in my upbringing. Anticommunism belonged to the Catholic ethos of the time. Only very gradually did American involvement in Vietnam appear as the colossal blunder of an overreaching imperialist power. But that lesson came not from street demonstrations but through the study of history and politics. My only direct involvement in protest during those years came when a group of us wore our Roman collars to Boston Common in 1968 to rally against George C. Wallace's racist appeal. A number of his Irish Catholic supporters did not appreciate our presence and let us know it.

The Alabama governor had been expanding his base that year into the urban North, feeding on racial antagonisms and conflicted emotions over Vietnam. Meanwhile, I took advantage of new opportunities for travel to reacquaint myself with the South. On several occasions I visited family and friends in Virginia and the Carolinas, and over a long Christmas break two Jesuit friends and I drove a deadhead car though the South. Enroute we stopped to inspect Robert E. Lee's shrine at Washington and Lee University. Later that evening in Cookeville, Tennessee, we learned how a dry county operated. While my companions pushed on to Texas to deliver the car, I dropped off in Vicksburg, Mississippi, to spend almost two weeks with my oldest sister and her husband, an army officer in charge of the Waterways Experiment Station. They introduced me to a South newly emerging from segregation and under assault from a North that was only beginning to discover its own racial problems. I will never forget an encounter at a holiday party, when, after the routine queries about my impressions of Mississippi, a slightly inebriated woman asked, "We're not as bad as they say we are, are we?"

I returned to Boston fascinated by the South. Unlike so much of the America I knew, it was neither prosperous nor self-assured. The race problem appeared overt, not hidden. Catholics did not form a substantial portion of the population there, and religion was worn on the sleeve. The following year, as I prepared for ordination to the priesthood, I asked my superiors for permission to apply for doctoral studies. With the Feeney materials inaccessible, I decided to emphasize the history of American Protestantism and the South. The hunt for appropriate schools had already begun. Years before in Spokane, I had started an M.A. in history at Gonzaga University. I transferred to Loyola University in Los Angeles during regency summers and finally completed the degree there in 1969. Professor Anthony F. Turhollow, the longtime department chair at Loyola, became my mentor, and he recommended several schools, including the University of California at Santa Barbara.

I knew what I wanted: a doctorate in history from a secular institution that would permit me to utilize the work I had already completed in religious history. I also wanted to live in a Jesuit community beyond New England's snow. In addition to its glorious weather, Santa Barbara possessed distinct advantages in having strong departments in both history and religious studies. I could live nearby at our Jesuit novitiate. On a summer visit to the university before I formally applied, Professor Morton Borden took time out from his own work to explain the program. A year later, following ordination as a priest, I began the Ph.D. program in the fall quarter of 1970.

The choice of Santa Barbara proved excellent, and I was blessed in the professors who guided my studies. Borden taught the early national period and shared my interest in religion and politics. When I explained that I wanted to combine these with a southern topic, he proposed that I explore the efforts to pass Thomas Jefferson's Statute for Religious Freedom in post-Revolutionary Virginia. My paper for his seminar became the basis for the dissertation that he later guided with masterly direction and great kindness. Meanwhile in Wilbur R. Jacobs's colonial seminar I wrote an essay on early Baptist struggles for religious liberty in New England.[7] While these papers were in progress, I met Carl V. Harris, who had only recently joined the faculty to teach southern history. He introduced me to the complexities and ironies that make the South so intriguing a subject for historians.

The university required doctoral students to take one field in a department outside their concentration. When other secular institutions across the country were just beginning to develop religious studies programs, Santa Barbara already possessed an exceptional department. Although most history students gravitated toward sociology or anthropology, I moved easily into religious studies, where Professor Robert S. Michaelsen acquainted me with the recent historiography and new approaches to the study of religion in America.

After advancement to candidacy, dissertation research took me from Boston down the coast to North Carolina. With its bevy of archives and libraries, Richmond provided an excellent base. For almost a semester I enjoyed the hospitality of a community of Benedictine monks—long known for taking in wandering Jesuits—across the street from Battle Abbey, home of the Virginia Historical Society. The building contained only a third of the space it enjoys today but held superb collections for my area. William M. E. Rachel, editor of the *Virginia Magazine of History and Biography* and the epitome of a southern gentle-

man, explained the Old Dominion to me while gently correcting my pronun-
ciation of words like Botetourt and Fauquier. The Virginia State Library and
Archives (today the Library of Virginia), the Baptist Historical Society at the
University of Richmond, and the Union Theological Seminary library all held
rich deposits for southern religious history, as did the Earl Gregg Swem Library
at William and Mary, where Margaret Cook was forever digging out manuscripts
for me to inspect. I also spent weeks in the Library of Congress archives, as well
as those at the University of North Carolina, Duke University, and, of course,
the University of Virginia. Everywhere I went I found the South a delightful
place to work and southerners unfailingly gracious and helpful.

How could I not return? After completing the degree and accepting a position at newly renamed Loyola Marymount University (LMU) in Los Angeles,
I spent the summer of 1974 in Virginia, mainly in Williamsburg, turning the
dissertation into a book. At LMU I was engulfed in teaching—twelve hours a
semester with multiple and varied preparations. A senior professor already owned
the colonial through early national period courses. So, concentrating on the
nineteenth century, I taught Jacksonian and Civil War courses as well as courses
on the South, American religious history, American peace movements, and
politics and religion in the United States. The administration expected close,
regular faculty-student contact; scholarship was not a priority in the 1970s. Later
that would change, and the course load would be reduced, but in my early teaching years virtually no time was available for research and writing during academic semesters. I loved teaching and the students, but I was committed to
keeping at least a finger in the scholarly pie.

After completing *Church and State in Revolutionary Virginia, 1776–1787* in
1977, my interests in religion and politics focused on further study of church
and state.[8] My research on the Statute for Religious Freedom demonstrated
that southern evangelicals deserved far more credit for the passage of that law
than Jefferson, Madison, the Supreme Court, and historians generally had
awarded them. But the ways in which Baptists and Presbyterians embraced the
statute for their own purposes intrigued me. The future belonged to them, at
least in religious terms. I wondered how they negotiated the law. How could
they at once urge strict church-state separation and yet build the Christian
America they envisioned? My research indicated that when the Supreme Court
in the 1940s reached back to the Virginia statute to explain the meaning of the

First Amendment and adjudicate contemporary church-state issues, the justices (or their clerks) had misunderstood the history of the statute's passage. They also ignored how Virginians later used that law. This omission was understandable, however, because little or nothing had been written about its application. I determined to pursue that subject.

Initially I projected a study of the statute from its passage to Jefferson's death, a forty-year period during which evangelicals captured the Old Dominion from the rationalists, converting some and vanquishing others. I began with the long but ultimately successful Baptist-led struggle to seize the former established church's property, and particularly the glebes (farm lands), from the Episcopalians. Cliometrics was the rage in the 1970s, so I learned SPSS (the Statistical Package for the Social Sciences). The published legislative *Journals* contained the roll call votes, and a Graves Research Award in 1980 provided a free semester in Richmond to dig up the backgrounds of the members of the House of Delegates for the crucial sessions of 1797 and 1798. Jon Kukla, Brent Tarter, and Sandy Treadway of the publications staff at the Virginia State Library offered liberal encouragement and sound advice and became lasting friends. Back home I taught a full load and punched computer cards. I returned to Virginia for a sabbatical two years later to complete this project and explore other aspects of the statute's use.[9]

While I moved into the nineteenth century to mull over various church-state issues, a committee planning the bicentennial celebration of the Virginia Statute for Religious Freedom at the University of Virginia in 1985 invited me to present a paper on Jefferson for the occasion. The result, entitled "The Political Theology of Thomas Jefferson," gave me an opportunity to return to Jefferson's thought from an angle I had never pursued.[10] In rereading his writings, I found that his most important political testaments relied on theological arguments. That applied, of course, to documents he drafted in the struggle for independence, but he had also based his case for religious freedom on the nature of the relationship between God and the human person. And throughout his political career, Jefferson repeatedly invoked religious symbols and language drawn especially from the Hebrew Scriptures to bind the nation together. I thought he came off as a notable public theologian and a major craftsman of American civil religion, no matter what his private beliefs may have been.

The interlude with Jefferson's political theology dragged me away from southern evangelicals and the statute. Such interruptions have occurred regularly over the past twenty years—the present essay is a case in point—and brought some extremely interesting projects involving related interests, particularly ecumenism. For example, when Pope John Paul II visited New Orleans in 1987, I was invited to warm up his audience, a group of Catholic school administrators. My talk, "The Promise of American Catholicism," compared the transformation in Catholic culture in the United States after Vatican II with the experience of religious freedom enjoyed by Protestants after the American Revolution. That fall I happened to be a visiting professor at the Pontifical Gregorian University in Rome, teaching the history of American Protestantism and U.S. church-state relations. *La Civiltà Cattolica*, a semi-official Vatican journal, published an Italian version of this talk.[11] I was told at the time that some in the Roman curia found the essay helpful in understanding the Catholic Church in the United States.

American Catholics need to explain themselves to one another as well as to the larger church of which they are a part. Early on this became a major reason for focusing my attention on American Protestantism. The history that has shaped Catholics in the United States is unalterably bound up with that of America's Protestants. I find an analogy drawn from Wilbur J. Cash's *Mind of the South* particularly apt.[12] In his search for southern distinctiveness, Cash argued for the interrelationship of black and white southerners. Over the centuries, beginning with slavery and, ironically, intensifying in segregation, blacks and whites mutually affected and formed one another. Grasping this relationship is critically important for understanding the southerner and the South. So also it seems to me that we cannot comprehend the distinctive character and qualities of Christianity in America without considering the historic presence of both Protestants and Catholics and their influence on one another, for good and ill. Regional differences further complicate the picture. Southern Catholics differ in significant respects from their northern and western religious confreres, just as southern Protestants possess certain attributes that set them apart.

An even bigger tangent from my research into the application of the Statute for Religious Freedom developed after I started collecting divorce petitions. The vast petition collection at the Library of Virginia contains treasures for virtually every conceivable subject. I mined it extensively for the church-state controversies in Revolutionary and post-Revolutionary Virginia. While thus engaged, I discovered divorce as a subject for religiously based moral legislation. First in haphazard fashion and then systematically over more summers than I care to remember, I sifted through the entire petition collection, culling out all divorce petitions as well as any touching on church-state concerns. What was originally projected as a chapter on moral legislation in the church-state book has developed into a book-length manuscript entitled "'The Great Catastrophe of My Life': Divorce in the Old South."

Although this research and writing took me away from arguments over the statute's usage, I thought the excursion worthwhile. Divorce became a prism through which to study the evolution of southern culture, including its religious perspectives, from the 1790s through the antebellum era. Two particularly intriguing divorce petitions developed into separate articles. The first petition, a massive document over fifty typed pages in length, described a year and a half of a battered woman's hell with the man she married. While editing it for publication, I found the process of tracking down Evelina Gregory Roane's life all engrossing.[13] Divorced by the age of twenty-one, this extraordinary woman married three more times and died at the age of eighty-two. I located her Tidewater homes, found bundles of papers under her descendants' beds, and visited her grave. Another, much shorter divorce petition riveted my attention when I first read it. In 1816 Robert Wright, a free African American, asked the legislature for a divorce from his "free white wife."[14] The lawmakers trashed his petition because Virginia law forbade marriages across the color line. But related memorials and four sets of county court papers involving the Wright relatives, black and white, exposed the complexity of antebellum race relations and an acceptance of interracial sex that historians such as Martha Hodes have publicized.[15] Both of these projects sharpened my abilities as a historical sleuth and helped me understand cultural aspects of the South that are important in studying its church-state arrangements.

The study of divorce produced an even bigger tangent from church and state when I began reading the McDowell papers at the University of Virginia. I had been searching for materials on the experience of divorce, looking for something more intimate than the legislative petitions, when I came across the letters of Sally Campbell Preston McDowell and John Miller. McDowell, the daughter of the governor of Virginia in the mid-1840s, had been divorced from

Governor Francis Thomas of Maryland in 1846. Eight years later, Miller, a Presbyterian minister from Philadelphia, met her while on summer vacation at Virginia's springs and proposed marriage. Following a courtship by mail of twenty-six months, they wed in 1856. In order to grasp McDowell's experience of her first marriage and divorce, I had to read the entire correspondence. These almost five hundred letters provide such an extraordinarily personal view of nineteenth-century life and values on the eve of the Civil War that, with the vigorous encouragement of Brent Tarter, I decided to edit them for publication.[16]

Invitations to present papers in the 1990s offered the opportunity to return again to the application of the Virginia statute. As my research deepened, the chronological scope of a book once projected to end at Jefferson's death expanded into the twentieth century. The glebe business with which I had begun the investigation proved to be only the first bucket from an abundant well. Multiple issues surfaced, ranging from state control over church property and legal incorporation for religious groups to the rights of conscientious objectors, Bible reading in the public schools, and government funding of sectarian institutions. The Old Dominion faced all these concerns in rich complexity, long before the Supreme Court applied the First Amendment to the states. The research surfaced some peculiar anomalies. I found, for example, that antebellum Virginia, while claiming fidelity to Jefferson's vision, exercised more oversight over the churches than any other state in the union.[17] As nineteenth-century Virginians read their Statute for Religious Freedom, it committed them to strict separation of church and state. Yet as evangelical Christians concerned for a religiously based morality, they understood separation to mean, at least in some respects, something quite different from the Supreme Court's present interpretation.[18]

The divergences, as well as the agreements, are instructive. Church-state relations remain obviously complex today; battle lines over politico-religious issues are drawn to an extent we have not seen for many decades, if ever before in our history. At times we appear to be at an impasse. What kind of people are we? Are we a "people" at all? Or merely a collection of individuals bound together only for specified limited purposes? In striking contrast to interpretive trends that dominated historiography for most of the last century, historians today—and especially those of the South—find the key to much of our past in a deeper understanding of the religious beliefs and values that drove our history as a people.

My personal interests are larger, however, than simply the exploration of a history on which to base a coherent policy on church and state. An appreciative knowledge of our diverse religious experiences as churches can also draw Christians closer together in ecumenical cooperation and understanding. The vision of Pope John, the pastoral approach of Vatican II, and the leadership of Pope Paul VI and the American bishops committed Catholics to that enterprise a generation ago. Although perhaps not so evident today on the local church level, ecumenism continues, most notably in the doctrinal conversations of theological commissions and at consortia of divinity schools such as the one at which I teach today. In 1996 I left Loyola Marymount University after more than twenty very enjoyable, productive years to join the faculty at the Jesuit School of Theology at Berkeley, one of nine divinity schools (six Protestant, three Catholic) that comprise the Graduate Theological Union. These institutions are helping to prepare women and men for ministry in the Christian churches as well as for careers as teachers and scholars.

In several important ways I have come full circle, returning to an environment like the one in which I studied theology over thirty years ago while exploring religious history with John Booty and Conrad Wright. By the time my doctoral studies ended, a commitment to the history of church-state relations, which grew out of personal interests in religion, politics, and history, joined with a fascination for the South that has never abated. Morton Borden surely pointed me in the right direction. Curiously, Mr. Jefferson's state has produced more than its fair share of politico-religious types, almost from the outset. As I write this, my research into Bishop James Cannon's role in the Old Dominion's Bible wars has scarcely begun, and already I look forward to delving into the backgrounds of Jerry Falwell and Pat Robertson. As I told my friend Frances Pollard, director of library services at the Virginia Historical Society, a few years ago, "I just can't get out of Virginia."

Notes

1. Thomas Merton, *The Seven Storey Mountain* (1941; rpt., San Diego: Harcourt Brace, 1990).

2. Will Herberg, *Protestant-Catholic-Jew: An Essay in American Religious Sociology* (1960; rpt., Chicago: University of Chicago Press, 1983).

3. See, for example, Paul Blanshard, *American Freedom and Catholic Power* (Boston: Beacon Press, 1949).

4. These were later collected, expanded, and published as Xavier Rynne, *Letters from Vatican City* (New York: Farrar, Straus and Giroux, 1963); *The Second Session* (1964); *The Third Session* (1965); and *The Fourth Session* (1966).

5. Edward P. Echlin, *The Anglican Eucharist in Ecumenical Perspective: Doctrine and Rite from Cranmer to Seabury* (New York: Seabury Press, 1968).

6. Catherine Goddard Clarke, *The Loyolas and the Cabots* (Boston: Ravengate Press, 1950).

7. Later published as Thomas E. Buckley, S.J., "Church and State in Massachusetts Bay: A Case Study of Baptist Dissenters, 1651," *Journal of Church and State* 23 (1981): 309–22.

8. Thomas E. Buckley, S.J., *Church and State in Revolutionary Virginia, 1776–1787* (Charlottesville: University Press of Virginia, 1977).

9. This first project became Thomas E. Buckley, S.J., "Evangelicals Triumphant: The Baptists' Assault on the Virginia Glebes, 1786–1801," *William and Mary Quarterly*, 3d ser., 45 (1988): 33–69.

10. Thomas E. Buckley, S.J., "The Political Theology of Thomas Jefferson," in Merrill D. Peterson and Robert C. Vaughan, eds., *The Virginia Statute of Religious Freedom: Its Evolution and Consequences in American History*, Cambridge Studies in Religion and American Public Life (Cambridge: Cambridge University Press, 1988), 75–108 .

11. Thomas E. Buckley, S.J., "Le promesse del cattolicesimo americano," *La Civiltà Cattolica* 138 (3 Oct. 1987): 16–29.

12. Wilbur Joseph [W. J.] Cash, *The Mind of the South* (New York: Knopf, 1941).

13. Thomas E. Buckley, S.J., "'Placed in the Power of Violence': The Divorce Petition of Evelina Gregory Roane, 1824," *Virginia Magazine of History and Biography* 100 (1992): 29–78.

14. Thomas E. Buckley, S.J., "Unfixing Race: Class, Power, and Identity in an Interracial Family," *Virginia Magazine of History and Biography* 102 (1994): 349–80, reprinted in Martha Hodes, ed., *Sex, Love, Race: Crossing Boundaries in North American History* (New York: New York University Press, 1999).

15. Martha Hodes, *White Women, Black Men: Illicit Sex in the Nineteenth-Century South* (New Haven: Yale University Press, 1997).

16. Thomas E. Buckley, S.J., ed. *"If You Love That Lady Don't Marry Her": The Courtship Letters of Sally McDowell and John Miller, 1854–1856* (Columbia: University of Missouri Press, 2000).

17. Thomas E. Buckley, S.J., "After Disestablishment: Thomas Jefferson's Wall of Separation in Antebellum Virginia," *Journal of Southern History* 61 (1995): 445–80.

18. I explored this in a paper at a Library of Congress symposium in 1998, later pub-

lished as Thomas E. Buckley, S.J., "The Use and Abuse of Jefferson's Statute: Separating Church and State in Nineteenth-Century Virginia," in James H. Hutson, ed. *Religion and the New Republic: Faith in the Founding of America* (Lanham, Md.: Rowman and Littlefield, 2000), 41–63; and in "Virginia's Bible Wars: Separating Church and State in the Twentieth Century," a paper delivered at a meeting of the Southern Historical Association in 1999.

Personal Reflections on Community and the Writing of American Religious History

Jean E. Friedman

river divided my town, but I was drawn to the bridge that connected North and South Bethlehem, Pennsylvania. The Lehigh River crests on both shores of North and South Bethlehem, but it bisects two different histories, cultures, destinies. The iron bridge opened an avenue across the river, across the canal, across history, and brought me home, to an undivided self.

I was raised on the industrialized South Side of town, the immigrant, Catholic, working-class section. The discovery of anthracite coal in the mountains upstate had led to the organization of the Lehigh Coal Company in 1792. By 1820 the Lehigh Coal Company and the Navigation Company that built a system of canals made Bethlehem an important transportation and service center. In the decade before the Civil War the Lehigh Valley Railroad supplanted the old canal system in transporting the coal from upstate Pennsylvania to the ports of New York and Philadelphia. The railroads laid the groundwork for industry. The Lehigh Zinc Company (1855) and the Bethlehem Iron Company (1861) took advantage of nearby Saucon Valley zinc and iron deposits and the railroad transportation system to make South Bethlehem a competitive industrial center.

Industry drew scores of European immigrant laborers into the area at the turn of the century. By 1899 the Bethlehem Iron Company emerged as the Bethlehem Steel Company and absorbed the Lehigh Zinc Company in 1911. Bethlehem Steel needed even greater sources of cheap labor and so attracted numbers of Eastern European immigrants. Proud of its unique ethnic and industrial character, the borough of South Bethlehem, founded in 1855, the same year the railroads established their transportation system, incorporated itself as a city in 1865 and did not merge with North Bethlehem until 1916.[1]

Within this industrial complex, however, the Lehigh University Campus on South Mountain sprawls like an enchanted forest surrounded by village-like national enclaves. My family lived near the university in a German neighborhood. Austrians, Hungarians, Wends, Slovenes, and Pennsylvania Dutch recreated the neat cultivated European fields in their backyards and fostered the close ties of German folkways. Nothing impersonal existed in our neighborhood—stepping outside the door meant greeting a half-block of good-natured, curious people.

The German Catholic church and school at the bottom of South Mountain preserved the language, ritual, and heritage of the German-speaking Catholics. By the mid-1940s when I attended Holy Ghost Church, hymns, prayers, and an occasional sermon were in German. For German Catholics, preservation of the language preserved the faith.[2] But as a third-generation German Catholic, I did not learn the language; I was part of the transitional generation that received the German Catholic heritage but translated it into strategies for social mobility. Germans valued integrity, hard work, cleanliness, efficiency, and humor, characteristics designed to aid accommodation to the secular world. However, above all, ethnic Catholics esteemed piety.

A Latin mass with some German prayers made church a mysterious, frightening place. And so awesome was the cathedral-like splendor that it made me ill, literally. I spent as much time outside that mighty fortress dealing with nausea as inside praying. God and the saints seemed remote, powerful figures much like the pastor, Monsignor Scott A. Fasig. He was a dignified, educated man who appeared rather quaint; he wore pince-nez glasses on the bridge of his nose and was rarely seen without his biretta.[3] His full priestly authority and crankiness in the confessional only distanced him from children. In church I felt small, swallowed up in larger forces I did not understand. On the periphery of the church, however, on the side aisles and in the back, sat the women who saved me from my abstraction, that is, my terrible awe. Pious German women wearing old-fashioned, high-crowned hats rocked in prayer with their rosary beads or, deeply attentive, prayed from their German prayer books. I held onto the sight of them; even as a child I recognized their devotion, their holiness. They embodied spirituality; their strong, vital natures survived, even throve on their encounter with the Divine. Trusting them, I trusted God as I would my grand-mother. My paternal grandmother had a deep devotion to the saints. She kept an "altar" on top of her bureau with statues of St. Theresa, St. Joseph, and the Blessed Mother. Those German grandmothers possessed an intensity that out-stripped even the nuns who taught at the school.

Pre–Vatican II parochial schools deserve their reputation as formidable dis-ciplinary institutions, but they dispensed social justice along with justice by the paddle. We were taught that as Catholics in a hostile world we had to stand up and fight for values, truth, and faith, no matter the cost. The church's martyr-ology was especially cogent in teaching stamina, courage, persistence. I was particularly drawn to Joan of Arc, who evoked visions of women in battle. The Second World War appeared romantic and noble to me; I regretted not being a part of it. One day in class I claimed Jeanne d'Arc as my patron saint. My fourth-grade teacher blanched and refused to recognize such an outlaw as a saintly model. The more genteel interpretation of the Blessed Virgin dominated parochial classrooms in those days.

The traditional church views of male and female roles may be traced to nineteenth-century moral theology, taught in the seminaries of the 1930s and influential in the pastoral attitudes of the 1940s. According to the teaching, women, in particular, and the shame and scandal attached to sexuality outside of marriage presented a sexual threat to the moral purity of men.[4] As a child I once stood in the church sanctuary, the leader of the May procession. Father Reginald S. Billinger, the associate pastor, otherwise a generous and compas-sionate man, announced to the girls assembled there that our presence in the sanctuary was an exception—that females went beyond the sanctuary gate only on their wedding day and the day of their funeral. Even as a child I deeply re-sented that pronouncement, the implication that somehow females are by nature shameful and not spiritually worthy. The priest implanted a gender con-sciousness that day that prompted me to distrust clergy and challenge any fur-ther clerical condescension toward women.

In truth, we lived in a ghetto; we experienced no political or racial conscious-ness, yet somehow we understood that geography, history, and science revealed broader parameters of vision. I still remember our geography book—the story of a boy, excused from school (an envious predicament), who accompanied his parents on an around-the-world trip. Taught from a fourth-grade perspective, geography became personal. I imagined how I might travel around the world and what the reactions of a ten-year-old girl would be. In first grade, Sister Emerentia explained the solar system using a bell, an apple, and an orange. She used a primitive method, perhaps, but we glimpsed the universe. We gathered that school prepared us for a world beyond our world.

Parochial schools in the early 1950s radiated various kinds of wonders. Anti-communist hysteria and fear of the bomb encouraged a kind of Catholic millennialism—the doom of Fatima's secret prophecies intimated an end to our short lives—so we longed for visions or we hoped to see a statue move. In our neighborhood a woman hosted a visionary who predicted that the world would end in the summer of 1950. As children we formed rosary societies: prayer groups designed to express our piety, impress our elders, define our friendship groups, and stave off disaster. We imagined a world of wonders as the no-nonsense nuns attempted vainly to curb the wilder reaches of our imagination. Miraculously, we did not slip off the edge into hysteria or superstition because silence—silence in the classroom, silence on the street as we walked two by two, silence in prayer, silence in the church—shaped awareness of an interior life, a life not bounded by fear. Silence made a space; how wide we did not yet know. Yet within the space we felt a closeness, the presence of God in the presence of family, church, kin. A Christmas Star burned on South Mountain celebrating Bethlehem as "The Christmas City," but for the close-knit working-class neighborhoods, God dwelt on that mountain.

From the heights of South Mountain you could see Central Moravian Church and the historic Moravian College buildings that stood gracefully, peacefully, by the river. Central Moravian Church with its plain belfry, seemed distant—Protestant, comfortable, and austere. For my family, with few means for education, Moravian College offered the only choice. However, my Catholic high school withheld the records of all students applying to non-Catholic colleges. Since mine was a hardship case, an exception was made, although Allentown Central Catholic High School believed I proceeded at peril to my soul. After twelve years of a parochial education, Moravian presented unknown territory—so I walked across the bridge to the North Side. The New Street Bridge made of a wrought-iron grid design delighted the walker—if you walked fast and looked down at the river through the tiny spaces, it was as if you walked on the river. Quickly, quickly you walked so that you were one with the river. The river then was not a divide but a connector with familiar shores.

The Moravian community known as the Unitas Fratrum of Moravia (Bohemia) emigrated to Bethlehem, Pennsylvania, and established their settlement on Christmas Eve 1741. A pietist sect that traced its origin to the fifteenth-century Hussite Movement, the Moravians established a closed community that excluded nonbelievers until 1844. In order to support a growing missionary movement, the church organized communicants into what were called Choirs, segregated by sex and marital status. The unmarried brothers and sisters lived in communal housing. Children also lived apart from parents as a measure to reinforce communal rather than nuclear family values. Relieved of family duties, women assumed positions of influence and authority in the community.[5]

Industry supported the communal venture; the enterprising Moravians invested in the coal and transportation companies and created a business center that served them—a tanning mill, grist mill, apothecary, shops, and an inn. In order to connect with the outside world they built a wooden bridge across the Lehigh River. In addition, the community established boarding schools for girls and boys in the colonies, which later evolved into Moravian College and Theological Seminary and Moravian Seminary and College for Women. The Moravian Men's and Women's Colleges remained separated by sex until their unification in 1954.[6] I attended a coed school in 1959.

The former Women's College is situated in a complex of historic buildings that included the church, the Single Sisters' Home, and the house of the eighteenth-century Moravian Indian missionary John Heckewelder. The history of that place evoked in me a new wonder and respect for Protestant devotion and missionary work. Moreover, the Moravian faculty exemplified Christian dedication and commitment. Mary Kennedy in particular stands out as an eccentric, tough-minded professor of history. She wore a wig and a straw hat; when she lectured, she sniffed at the things of which she disapproved, such as machine politics and corruption. Under her direction I wrote an honors project on the decline of Bethlehem's South Side Democratic machine politics in the early 1960s. When Dr. Kennedy retired in 1963, she then became a missionary to Latin America. I solemnly announced to her, "I will follow you." Years later when I read Thomas Merton's *Seven Storey Mountain*, I recognized the callow grandiosity of my discipleship. The day the soon-to-be celebrated monk Thomas Merton entered the monastery, he met a man and beseeched him, melodramatically, "Pray for me."

The Moravians taught a more practical spirituality. The Moravian faculty stressed the value of community. I understood that term in the context of a caring faculty, a socially aware church, a multinational missionary effort, the Moravian history of community building, and community regard for women's talents. The faculty encouraged my leadership role as president of the student body. Also in my senior year at the college I won an award for "community service." I was especially proud to receive recognition for work esteemed by Protestants. Community values had instilled purpose within me and confidence as a woman.

In 1963 Moravian College established an ecumenical lecture series that provided a dialogue between Jesuit theologian Gustave Weigel and Protestant theologians Robert McAfee Brown and Barry Ulanov. I introduced Professor Ulanov. It was revelatory for me to see a Catholic and Protestants engage in critical but polite public dialogue. At the time I was less aware of Vatican II than I was of the sincerity of Protestant conciliation. The dialogue bridged the two separate parts of my religious life. A stint at a Catholic law school upon graduation from Moravian made me uncomfortable with any narrow sectarian institution.

When I returned to Bethlehem's South Side in 1965 to earn my master's degree at Lehigh University, I reentered the ethnic community. This time, however, I used the South Side as a laboratory for my concentration upon nineteenth-century political studies. I investigated the Chamber of Commerce during the Progressive era and rediscovered my Hungarian-Jewish grandfather's role in the ethnic politics of the period. My grandfather spoke seven languages, a talent not uncommon in the national mix of Eastern Europe. With his facility for languages, he helped Bethlehem immigrants through American bureaucratic and cultural mazes. His biographer notes that William Friedman "worked with great devotion toward the unity of the Hungarian community."[7] Despite the high regard with which he was held in the ethnic community, the local press, controlled by business elites, ridiculed my grandfather, for what they interpreted as his pretension to leadership. When he gave a public address, the paper covered the event in a special-interest column and jeered, "Call CBS, call ABC! Willy Friedman gave a speech!" The raw ethnic politics of the early twentieth century suggested that no community is without its bitter tensions and divisions.

My newly discovered tie to my grandfather reinforced my growing interest in politics. My grandfather, after all, took a public stand on behalf of immigrants, especially Hungarians. At an all-male engineering college, Lehigh University, feminist politics seemed natural.[8] I helped organize a "consciousness-raising" group, supported women employees in their labor dispute with the telephone company, and joined in feminist advocacy of the antiwar movement. In 1970 I marched down Fifth Avenue in New York City with "Women for Peace" in the first neofeminist parade of this generation. Meanwhile, I remained a faithful Catholic and attended mass at Holy Ghost Church. The American Catholic bishops' antiwar stance maintained my loyalty to the church and to its regard for social justice.

Eager to participate in the civil rights movement, I applied to the Southern Christian Leadership Conference and was recruited to teach in a southern black college. In 1967 I went south and taught at Benedict College, in Columbia, South Carolina. I arrived just as the civil rights movement turned its attention northward and began to concentrate upon the Vietnam War. Conditions in the South, however, remained dangerous, even volatile. Upon arrival on campus I experienced the novelty of being a racial minority—a white woman in a black community. My introduction to the campus was an introduction to Congressman Adam Clayton Powell, the guest speaker at the college's opening events. Powell, at the time much maligned in the press for his financial and sexual misadventures, appeared heroic, even humble as he took time out to encourage students living through a racial crisis. "Turnabout" described my situation. In a new community I had to assume a different set of values and assumptions, and the students were the teachers.

Benedict College existed literally as a walled-in community. A high wall surrounded the college complex, and a security guard stood at the entrance. But the wall could not guarantee safety in that precarious year of assassinations and violence. The question of safety raised a new pedagogical issue for me as a novice teacher: how to protect students. I encountered my first test in the classroom the morning after the Orangeburg Massacre. On 8 February 1968, local police and the South Carolina National Guard opened fire on a group of African American students at the predominately black Orangeburg State College campus. The students were protesting a segregated bowling alley in the town of Orangeburg, South Carolina. The city police and state patrolmen—with the militia standing by—killed three students and injured twenty-eight.[9] Benedict students lost friends and knew those injured in the shootings. On 9 February 1968, I entered a traumatized classroom. Students grieved over their personal losses and feared for their own lives. Above all, they doubted the future of the civil rights movement. Outsider or not, I had to calm the deepest fears of these African American students. First, we simply talked through the events as some students either cried in anguish, angrily denounced the police, or remained silent, attentive, ready to spring. At that moment they were the civil rights movement, battered and at a turning point. My only resource was history, so I offered them the long view—that black civil protest and civil rights remained alive through Reconstruction and the Second World War just as Benedict College survived all the terrible forces of prejudice. But how could I give them faith, when some of the younger generation of African Americans had lost confidence in nonviolent resistance and had split from civil rights leader Martin Luther King Jr.?

Only a fighter with the toughmindedness of a lawyer and the sensitivity of a poet could challenge obdurate racial oppression and express the hidden pain that numbed young black women and men. Pauli Murray, the distinguished lawyer, poet, and civil rights activist who served the college as vice-president in that fateful year, gave students their lives back with a promise, her own promissory note, called *Proud Shoes*.[10] Her book, an autobiography, documents Pauli Murray's determination to overcome racial prejudice and reveals her public and private triumphs. At Benedict she told her history plainly: her slave grandmother being raped by the master's twin sons, her happiness on the family farm, her struggle for an education, her involvement with the *Brown v. Board of Education* decision, her friendship with Eleanor Roosevelt, and her role in the founding of the National Organization for Women. But it was her poetry that she most wanted to express, as if by her own will and expectation she could lift those students out of their fear. She read her poetry, later published in *Dark Testament and Other Poems*, at a student gathering.[11] One poem written in 1944 presaged the vision of Dr. King. Her words challenged students soon to be tested by King's assassination:

> Then let the dream linger on.
> Let it be the test of nations,
> Let it be the quest of all our days,
> The fevered pounding of our blood,
> The measure of our souls—[12]

Yet Pauli herself vowed never to walk outside the walls of the college. Her terror shocked me. Nonetheless, her courage, which sprang from a silence, an unknowableness within her, prompted her to venture forth into the city and backcountry of South Carolina.[13] Only when she returned to New York in 1968 would she talk about her love of St. Mark's-in-the-Bowery, her neighborhood church from which she drew her inner resources. She did not mention to her white Benedict friends her battle with the Episcopalian clergy over the treatment of women. She joined increasing congregational criticism of unequal treatment of women in the church and won her point in an unexpected way when she felt called and was ordained to the priesthood in 1977. Pauli Murray was an example of how to survive in an embattled community. She used gentleness and curiosity to teach and build networks of friendships. Those friendships sustained her in the critical moments when she challenged oppressive social structures, southern segregation, episcopal hierarchy, and male-dominated employment systems. Above all, she loved to teach with a message. When Pauli Murray talked about nineteenth-century slavery, my classroom became a forum exploring each student's concerns about their own civil oppression.

In the late 1960s color and class roiled the enclosed African American community and made Pauli, a light-skinned, brilliant, and highly educated African American, a target of prejudice. Pauli simply ignored the sloe-eyed envy of her darker female peers. She was a stranger in her own land. So the black community existed as a world within a world, with its own divisions and prejudices. The assassination of Martin Luther King Jr. increased fear and racial tensions within Benedict College. Students, agitated after a gathering, began shooting at whites on the campus. The spree shut down the college for spring break. A charismatic white radical exacerbated tensions within the college. He was a faculty member who, when reprimanded for seducing coeds, desecrated a former Benedict College president's grave and then threatened the current president, Benjamin F. Peyton, with violence. Instantly, the black faculty armed themselves and surrounded the building into which the young radical fled. The arrival of the police ended the crisis. Within this tiny community I witnessed racial strife; the walls could not prevent the violent epidemic from reaching faculty and students. In 1967–68, *community* did not mean stability, safety, or harmony.

My return to Lehigh University in 1968 and the study of political history and feminist politics took me far away from any consideration of religion, family, or community. Only a reentry into the South awakened that interest. In the fall of 1977 I began to teach at the University of Georgia. I wanted to write about southern women; my question was, why did the women's reform movement organize so late in the South? Scholars brushed off the question because the answer to southerners was so obvious—slavery. Yet, I wanted to know more about how the system worked. Before I left for the South an African anthropologist warned me, "You do not understand the culture you are moving into; it's a family culture like Africa. It's different." Upon arrival in Georgia, I noticed that the social cues were indeed different. In the North acquaintances asked, "What do you do?" In the South people wanted to know if I had family in the South and to what church I belonged.

I settled into a semirural neighborhood and observed that I had moved into the middle of a family network. Sons, granddaughters, and parents all lived as neighbors in this small town. On a visit to Augusta with my friend Ann Berrigan, we visited her old neighborhood, and I noted the same pattern repeated itself. The tightly knit Augusta neighborhood encompassed family and treated neighbor as family. In the southern town where I lived, the churches formed the center of the neighborhood. Yet, Christian identity proved a protection for whites only. When an interracial couple moved into the neighborhood and the young woman wished to open a beauty salon, "Sampson and Delilah," white neighbor women fumed. To allay fear, the beautician went about the neighborhood handing out business cards with Scripture on the reverse side. A short time later the couple moved out.

In my own church, the Catholic Center at the University of Georgia, the pastor, Father Joe Hollahan, had been an activist in the 1960s. His deep humanity and spirituality, his friendship with women as well as men, went far toward healing my distrust of clergy. A Franciscan priest, Father Joe emphasized community as the primary goal of his church. Community, integrity, and freedom had been the values of the antiwar movement, and yet this priest had integrated them into the church in his own unique way. In the late '70s we truly were a Catholic community, dedicated to social justice and sensitive to the needs of the parish and university community. It worked because Father Joe could be all things to all people. He talked physics to physicists and history to historians, and he was a vulnerable man. He once openly wept among his

parishioners that he did not have a family. Yet, he said, speaking of the priesthood, "where else would I go?" Community meant shared vulnerability, a conscious purpose, and the collective will to sustain religious and social bonds. In
those years community was very real to me; I felt part of something I had not
known as an adult, a Catholic community.

My experience did not dictate but rather confirmed what I learned in my
research. Frank Owsley, Robert Kenzer, Michael Anderson, and Ronald F.
Anspach explored the primacy of kin relations in the rural South and in urban
environments. My project sought to understand how family connections affected
nineteenth-century southern women. On the first day of research I encountered a very unusual but compelling source, Anna Maria Akehurst's dream, on
31 March 1871, of death and redemption. In her dream Anna Maria, riding in a
railway car, falls off a bridge to her death and enters a harmonious heaven where
she is transformed.[14] Here lay the enigma of southern women's spiritual life, an
interior life unexplored by historians. From that day I pursued the dual thread
of narrative: text and subtext, conscious and unconscious, mind and spirit. Southern souls wrapped in culture lived for redemption; what that meant I had to
know. Anna Maria's dream crossing of a bridge opened new spiritual possibilities for me.

Anna Maria Akehurst took risks in her life; a northerner, she came south,
married several times, but always lived on the edge of poverty. In her dream
she grasped onto the bridge's timbers before she "fell." When she "let go," her
risks carried her beyond her terrible struggles to a peaceful conversion, an accommodation of faith.

My own experience paralleled the historical lives I studied. In fact, the southern women's lives became models for my own. My bridge of faith began to give
way. Within the Catholic community that I cherished, I experienced the
breakup of relationships. One especially, an intimate relationship with a
wounded former priest, shattered the foundations of my life. This led to a religious conversion.

I had read so many conversion stories in my research, it was as if I had attended an archival revival. Perhaps unconsciously, the narratives had placed
me on the "anxious seat." At least my intellectual work prepared me to recognize the conversion process and the experience itself. Fortunately, I had a
mentor, a wise and funny nun, Ellen Nolan, who conveyed me through the

shoals and over the falls of the spiritual tempest. At one with the divine river of grace, I felt connected at last to the source of intimacy. I renewed my activity at the Catholic Center, this time as a spiritual director trained by Ellen Nolan and the Jesuits of Guelph, Ontario, Canada.

It would be inaccurate to claim that my life experience shaped the thesis in *The Enclosed Garden: Women and Community in the Evangelical South, 1830– 1900.* The book concentrated upon the development of evangelical community and the obstacles to women's reform. However, my religious experience enlivened the passages about conversion and formed a sympathetic bond with women in the past who faced their limited autonomy with ambivalence and hope. *Enclosed Garden* expresses a certain historical coherence, a community drawn together in religious righteousness, fragmented in the Civil War, and realigned in the postwar period. Nonetheless, the work depicts the church trials that dispensed justice with a double standard according to gender. Churches held women responsible for serious or sexual transgressions more often than men. Furthermore, the reader can almost hear the din of evangelical exhortation that engulfed the uninitiated in every letter written and dialogue spoken in an evangelical household. The evangelical community, so sure of its permanence before the war, experienced decline and indifference after the war. I am struck by how fragile community is and yet how resilient; communities, like rivers, are never the same; they exist in many incarnations and change their populations and directions. As a historian, I build the bridgework over the river of change, attempt a oneness with the past, but remain above, an observant risk taker.

Catholics believe conversion is a life-long process. My "fortunate fall" during the writing of *Enclosed Garden* did not end my search to become more inclusive in my religious understanding. After the completion of *Enclosed Garden* I wished to expand my knowledge of how community systems operated during the Civil War. I was several years into the research on a topic whose working title was "Families at War: Northern and Southern Communities in the Civil War," when I decided that my sources were not sufficiently diverse.

While researching at the Virginia Historical Society I remembered the Moses Myers house that I had visited many times when I lived in Norfolk.[15] I asked the senior librarian, Frances Pollard, if the Historical Society had any Jewish Civil War family papers, specifically the Myers family. She directed me to the

Mordecai and Myers Papers, and again I fell in love with the sources. The first manuscript delivered to me was Jacob Hays's will, drawn up with numerous official wax seals and written in a direct, intimate style. Who and why some individuals would inherit and others would not is expressly stated in fascinating detail. In addition, the papers included the family's anguished correspondence with Alfred Mordecai, a U.S. Army colonel who headed the Watervliet Arsenal in New York State, attempting to persuade him to join the Confederate cause. Emma Mordecai's harrowing eyewitness account of the fall of Richmond is also found among the papers. Finally, I read the absorbing diary of Rachel Mordecai Lazarus.

The diary is a record (1816–21) of Rachel's attempt to teach her seven-year-old stepsister, Eliza, according to an enlightened pedagogical guide, *Practical Education*, written by Anglo-Irish educators Richard Lovell Edgeworth and his daughter, Maria Edgeworth. The method demonstrates Lockean premises through family anecdotes. Rationality and natural values are imposed with gentle firmness that leads to a contractual, non-authoritarian relationship between mentors and children. Impressed by the narrative, its style, story, and depth of self-analysis, Nelson Lankford, editor of the *Virginia Magazine of History and Biography*, asked me to edit the manuscript for the Virginia Historical Society's document series.

The diary revealed such exciting possibilities for an exploration of enlightened pedagogy, or "character training," gender conflicts between generations, and ethno-religious responses to dominant southern evangelical culture that I decided to publish the diary with contextual and analytic chapters, a plan not conducive to the documentary series. Curiosity about my grandfather's Judaism and the desire to understand Jewish life and culture formed the impetus for the expanded project. William Friedman, the gambler and later policeman in Bethlehem, married my Catholic grandmother Theresa Stangle, settled into domesticity, and converted to Catholicism. Except for one "cousin," William's family cut him off, and we never knew my grandfather's Jewish relatives. The sense of loss and the desire for reconciliation permeated my research.

Working on *Ways of Wisdom: Moral Education in the Early National Period* led me to new interests in moral behavior.[16] Rachel's diary explains her failure to mold Eliza into a "good girl," or a prototype of one of Maria Edgeworth's fictional heroines. Eliza, an enlightened child open to moral questioning, sought a deeper level of moral integrity. Eliza's resistance to rational training opens the way to holiness for both teacher and pupil. For Rachel, the spiritual journey leads to a conversion to Christianity, and for Eliza, a committed and active acceptance of Orthodox Judaism. The Enlightenment, therefore, did not necessarily lead to secularism, but in the case of Orthodox Jews, enlightened critical method challenged foundational religious assumptions and authority.

The Jacob Mordecai family, isolated in a small town, managed a distinguished boarding school for girls, the Warrenton Academy. Rachel taught in the school and learned about the enlightened Continental pedagogy from her father, the principal. In her diary and in her correspondence with Maria Edgeworth, Rachel insisted that the Mordecais suffered no prejudice living in a majority Christian culture. The evidence, however, demonstrates otherwise. Systematic and even secret proselytization attempts forced the family into a defensive posture. Jacob Mordecai, the father of Rachel and Eliza, wrote stunning defenses of Judaism against the dogged challenges of the Reverend Adam Empie, an evangelical Episcopalian priest. Furthermore, the family removed the caretaker for Harriet Myers, a cousin of the Mordecais, because the woman secretly sought to baptize the mentally deranged Harriet.

The Mordecai study revealed the pain of the marginalized religious. Jews, even those who held prominent roles in the villages and towns of the early national period, suffered anti-Semitism and cultural isolation. Ethnicity and religion divided early American communities. My own background experience of religious, ethnic, and gender differences served to incline my sympathies toward the Jewish minority.

The more I read of Jewish faith and historic experience, the more deeply I perceived the practice of the presence of God. Rachel's diary is marked by prayer. She begins her experiment with an enlightened prayer, a plea for knowledge in the service of God. She prays: "[M]ay I be rendered capable of forming the materials which nature has bountifully placed in my hands; may reason, combined with virtue, and nourished by education, form a character eminently fitted to discharge every duty of this life, and when called from this transitory state of being, worthy to repose eternally in the presence of its Creator."[17]

These prayer-filled lives made moral training a highly meaningful practice. The most important issue in the Mordecai household was knowledge in the service of others and self. Yet Eliza learned her moral lessons in conflict that only enriched the lives of teacher and pupil and illustrated the new cultural paradigm, the romantic, expressive character.

The proof of moral depth lay in the sisters' lives. Rachel's tragic and sincere deathbed conversion served as a point of departure. Eliza's life of service and her heroic death, tending to a nephew wounded in the Civil War, proved equally compelling. To the salvation history that I once traced in the lives of African American and white evangelical southerners, I now added the work of southern Jews whose salvific mission is best described in the work of Jewish theologian and philosopher Emmanuel Levinas as a movement out into the world.[18]

The fact that I am a Catholic with faith in an all-embracing salvation, a Catholic with experience as part of an ethnic minority, a Catholic woman with the onus of a prejudicial magisterial authority, suggests that I tend to look for bridges, preferably those that expand vision and imagination toward unity.

It takes courage to cross bridges; no matter the energy or empathy expended in the crossing, the other shore may prove inhospitable. Communities exist only if they change and expand toward greater inclusiveness as the Moravian community did. It is a theme I continue to pursue.

Notes

1. M. Mark Stolarik, *Growing Up on the South Side: Three Generations of Slovaks in Bethlehem, Pennsylvania, 1880–1976* (Lewisburg, Pa.: Bucknell University Press, 1985), 22, 99; Beverly Prior Smaby, *The Transformation of Moravian Bethlehem: From Communal Mission to Family Economy* (Philadelphia: University of Pennsylvania Press, 1988), 44.

2. James S. Olson, *Catholic Immigrants in America* (Chicago: Nelson-Hall, 1987), 56.

3. A biretta is a stiff, square cap, divided by three or four material buttresses that join in the center, worn by Roman Catholic and Episcopal clergy.

4. For a discussion of the history of Catholic moral theology see Charles E. Curran, *The Origins of Moral Theology in the United States: Three Different Approaches* (Washington, D.C.: Georgetown University Press, 1997), 77, 135–42.

5. Smaby, *Transformation*, 3–4, 10, 26–27.

6. W. Ross Yates, chair of Editorial Committee, *Bethlehem of Pennsylvania: The First One Hundred Years* (Bethlehem, Pa.: Bethlehem Book Committee, 1968), 58, 99, 142, 182; Smaby, *Transformation*, 44.

7. Koroly Castelli, *Az American Windish and Hungarian Publishing Co. Fennallasanak,*

Tiz Eves Emlekere [*In Memory of the Tenth Anniversary of the Formation of the American Windish and Hungarian Publishing Company, 1919–1929*] (Bethlehem, Pa.: American Windish and Hungarian Press, 1930), 44–45.

8. Founded in 1865, Lehigh University began to accept women in its graduate program in 1918. The university did not admit women to its undergraduate program until 1971. Both men and women have attended Lehigh University's summer school since 1929. See W. Ross Yates, *Lehigh University: A History of Education in Engineering, Business and the Human Condition* (Bethlehem, Pa.: Lehigh University Press, 1992), 261, 269.

9. Pat Watters and Weldon Rougeau, "Events at Orangeburg: A Report Based on Study and Interviews in Orangeburg, South Carolina, in the Aftermath of Tragedy" (Atlanta: Southern Regional Council, 25 Feb. 1968), 11–16; Jack Bass and Jack Nelson, *The Orangeburg Massacre*, 2d ed. (Macon, Ga.: Mercer University Press, 1984), 61–78.

10. Pauli Murray, *Proud Shoes: The Story of an American Family* (New York: Harper Row, 1956).

11. Pauli Murray, *Dark Testament and Other Poems* (Norwalk, Conn.: Silvermine, 1970).

12. Pauli Murray, *Song in a Weary Throat: An American Pilgrimage* (New York: Harper and Row, 1987), 378.

13. Ibid., 375.

14. See Jean E. Friedman, *The Enclosed Garden: Women and Community in the Evangelical South, 1830–1900* (Chapel Hill: University of North Carolina Press, 1985), 45–46.

15. I taught at Old Dominion University in Norfolk, Virginia, from 1971 to 1974. The Moses Myers house held particular fascination for me because it demonstrated the diversity of early American merchants.

16. Jean E. Friedman, *Ways of Wisdom: Moral Education in the Early National Period* (Athens: University of Georgia Press, 2001).

17. Rachel Mordecai, Diary, 1816–21, p. 1, Myers Family Papers, Virginia Historical Society, Richmond, Virginia.

18. Emmanuel Levinas, *Time and the Other*, Richard A. Cohen, trans. (Pittsburgh: Duquesne University Press, 1987), 7.

A Fire in the Bones

Albert J. Raboteau

W hen I was ten years old, I went to sing in Europe with five other choirboys from my parish church, St. Thomas the Apostle, in Ann Arbor, Michigan. We six were selected to sing in Rome at an international congress of boys' choirs. After singing at St. Peter's Basilica, we would travel to Paris to spend a week at the headquarters of the sponsoring organization, the Singers of the Wooden Cross. I was the only African American in our group, and as we mingled with other choirs from around the world in St. Peter's square, European singers, who had rarely, if ever, seen a black person, routinely asked me to pose for a picture with them. I agreed, rejecting the advice of one of my fellow Americans to "charge them a buck a picture." In Paris we were greeted by the director of the French Singers of the Wooden Cross, a jovial monsignor, who asked me to sing a "Negro spiritual," which, he claimed, "we love." Embarrassed, I refused his request to sing "Swing Low, Sweet Chariot" or "Go Down, Moses" and was surprised to learn that he, and apparently other foreigners, knew of these songs, which my mother sometimes sang while doing dishes or when worries saddened her spirit. Already singled out, I was reluctant to draw any more attention to myself. I also felt a vague unease about exhibiting something of my people for the enjoyment of white folks. I was troubled by his request, my uneasiness enhanced by a sense that spirituals belonged, not to our Roman Catholic choir's public repertoire, but to a more private and meditative place, reflecting my people's distinctive identity, an identity that I already felt uncomfortable about exposing so far from home and family. I had never before felt so American and so un-American at the same time.

My bewilderment about the complex relationship of race, religion, and national identity was shared, I would learn later, by many Americans, white and black. Within months of my European trip, the United States Supreme Court delivered its decision in *Brown v. Board of Education*, catalyzing forces that would soon push the nation into a period of sustained and tumultuous struggle over the meaning of race and the legality of racial discrimination. In retrospect, I realize that my interest in African American history and religion, an interest that has dominated my teaching, research, and writing over the past two decades, originated in the issues that erupted for me and for the nation in those years. In subsequent years I have attempted to understand the religious history of black Americans and to ascertain what that particular history means for the nation as a whole.

Heading for the library late one summer afternoon more than thirty years ago, when I was a student at Loyola University (now Loyola Marymount) in Los Angeles, I noticed a tall Jesuit walking toward me. We both glanced up at the same moment. Our eyes met, and I nodded a "Good afternoon, Father." "Good afternoon," he responded as we passed. I suddenly realized I had just greeted John Courtney Murray. I had seen his picture on the cover of *Time*. I had struggled through part of his celebrated and demanding book *We Hold These Truths*. I was impressed that day by his stately bearing, the liveliness of his eyes, and most of all by the fact that this brilliant intellectual, walking slowly across campus in the late-afternoon light, was saying the rosary.

Fire in the Bones

"The old meeting house caught on fire. The spirit was there. Every heart was beating in unison as we turned our minds to God to tell him of our sorrows here below. God saw our need and came to us. I used to wonder what made people shout, but now I don't. There is a joy on the inside, and it wells up so strong that we can't keep still. It is fire in the bones. Any time that fire touches a man, he will jump."[1] These are the words of a former slave, describing the religious services of his people just after Emancipation. I was first arrested by these words twenty-five years ago, when I began to research and write about the religious history of African Americans. The paradoxical conjunction of "sorrows here below" and "joy welling up on the inside" puzzled me. Over the years, the image of "fire in the bones" stuck in my memory and eventually became for me a metaphor of the distinctive character of African American Christianity, a mood of joyful sorrow, sorrowful joy, or, more accurately, sorrow merging into joy. The paradox resonated within me, stirring memories of forgotten ancestors whose stories I needed to learn, stories with important lessons not only for me but for others as well.

What does this "fire in the bones" have to do with John Courtney Murray? One of the central concerns of Murray's intellectual life was the problem of pluralism: What truths do we Americans hold in common? Upon what basic principles can our nation, made up of people of diverse religious and moral values, reach consensus? In the essays published in that book I found so difficult in my freshman year of college, *We Hold These Truths: Catholic Reflections on the American Proposition* (1960), Murray elegantly argued that such a set of principles, a "tradition of rational truth," could be derived from natural law. Taking up Murray's interest in the question of pluralism, an issue even more hotly debated now than in his day, I would like to reflect upon truths we hold in common from the perspective of African American Christians, a people excluded for much of their history from full participation in their nation and their church because of race.

The issue of race did not figure in Murray's discussion of American pluralism, nor did he take sufficient account, I think, of the symbolic value of history to bind a people together (or conversely, to keep them apart). Beyond allegiance to a set of shared principles, a prime source of identity for a nation is history, construed as a set of interlocking stories that we tell one another about our origins and our past. I mean the mythic history that establishes our sense of national identity, destiny, and purpose (Lincoln's "mystic chords of memory"). It is important to note that our sense of common history can change over time to accommodate our expanding awareness of the variety of who we are ethnically, racially, and religiously. The expansion of our historical vision usually occurs in response to social pressure from some group whose story has been left out of the national story. This was precisely the impetus for the black studies movement of the late 1960s and early 1970s, the period when I came to intellectual and academic maturity. That cultural movement—mirroring the social and political movement to guarantee civil rights for blacks—effectively demonstrated that African Americans, despite their absence from the dominant academic and popular versions of American history, had been of central importance to the development of the nation. Moreover, the neglect of black history distorted not only American history but also both white and black Americans' perceptions of who they were. For a people to "lose" their history, to have their story deni-

grated as insignificant, is a devastating blow, an exclusion tantamount to deny-
ing their full humanity. To ignore the history of another people whose fate has
been intimately bound up with your own is to forgo self-understanding. Thus
for many of us, the attempt to recover African American history had more than
academic significance. I felt that in the recovery of this history lay the restoration of my past, my self, my people.

*I was born in 1943, during the second war in this century to rack the world with
death and destruction and untold misery—a war that demonstrated the horrors
that doctrines of racial supremacy can effect. I was born into a county and a part
of the country burdened by racism and racial oppression. I was born black in the
American South, in the state of Mississippi. I was born into a family of Indian,
French, German, and African ancestry in a small town on the Gulf of Mexico
named after a king of France, Bay St. Louis. I was born three months after my
father was shot and killed by another man, a white man, in Mississippi, in 1943.*

Intending to help develop a new African American historiography, I chose to
write a history of the religious life of slaves in the United States. As I sought
sources for my study, I became fascinated by the voices of former slaves preserved in narrative accounts of their lives under slavery, not just as historical
evidence but as voices that seemed to be speaking directly to me. These voices
were special: they rang with the authenticity that comes from those who have
endured brutal suffering and triumphed over it. In my historical writing, I tried
to capture the tenor of these voices, their rhythms, and especially the wisdom
that they conveyed.

What did they say, these voices of elderly black Americans who had lived
part of their lives under slavery and all their lives under discrimination? They
spoke of slavery as a central religious and moral fact in the history of our nation, a fact that could not be excused as an exception to the "real" American
story. Their voices contradicted the proposition that America is the story of the
gradual expansion of freedom and opportunity to a wider and wider group of
people. The national story has to include the ongoing rejection and degrada-
tion of others because of race. Those versions of the American story, therefore,
that tend to be triumphalist, smug, or celebratory fail the truth. What's more,
they are dangerous because they facilitate our tendency to ignore the terrible
urgency of those who still live in the long shadow of the plantation, trapped in

poverty and despair. The moral claim laid upon us by our ancestors' insistent voices is continual awareness that racial inequity has been woven into the fabric of our society from the start and is still very much a part of its social and economic pattern.

I was born into a family that was Roman Catholic as far back as we knew. I was baptized in St. Rose de Lima, a black church, and given the name Albert Jordy, after my dead father. When I was two, my mother, my sisters, and I moved to the North, partly because of what had happened to my father. But we returned during summers to visit relatives down home. One summer down South I remember especially well; I remember one Sunday when we had missed mass at St. Rose, so we went to the white church, Our Lady of the Gulf. We sat in back, I remember, squeezed together in a half pew. I remember going to receive Holy Communion. I remember the priest carrying the host; I remember him passing me by, and again passing me by, carrying the host in his hands, passing me by until he had given communion to all the white people; I remember, I was seven years old.

As I continued to teach and to write about the religious history of African Americans, I encountered time and again the charge that Christianity, as a compensatory and otherworldly religion, distracted black people from their situation and encouraged them to accept their lot as the will of God. "Take this world but give me Jesus." On the contrary, the voices that I heard spoke, in the main, with righteous anger and prophetic certainty about the destruction awaiting this nation unless it repented the evil of racism. Their God was a God of justice, they asserted, the Lord of history, who intervened in human affairs to cast down the mighty and uplift the lowly. And a whole cloud of biblical witnesses supported their case: the children of Israel freed from Egyptian bondage, Daniel standing unscathed in the lions' den, Shadrach, Meshach, and Abednego safe in the fiery furnace, and so on and on down the litany of prophets, apostles, and martyrs whose lineage they claimed as their own. Slavery and racial exclusion contradicted the essence of Christianity. "Bear ye one another's burdens. How can the master claim to bear my burdens, when he burdens me down with the heavy chains of oppression?" demanded a group of slaves in 1774.[2] Any form of Christianity that condones slavery or racial discrimination is to that extent false and will be punished. "Ain't everybody talking 'bout heaven, gonna go to heaven." Slaveholding and segregating Christians practiced a perversion of

Christianity. The segregation of black and white churches signified the existence of two Christianities in this nation, and the deep chasm that divided them
demonstrated the failure of the nation's predominant religious institution, the
major source of its common symbols, images, and values, to achieve meaningful, sustained community across racial lines.

*In my hometown there was a Roman Catholic seminary. It was founded in 1920
to train black men to be priests, because most other seminaries would not accept
them. It was named for St. Augustine, since he was from Africa. My stepfather
studied there. He was ordained a priest, but in 1947 he left. He left disillusioned
and angry because of the racial prejudice he encountered in the church, even
among fellow priests.* Ad introibo ad altare Dei, ad Deum qui laetificat juven-
tutem meum. *When I was ten I became an altar boy. The sound of Latin, the
glow of candles, the fragrance of incense, the splendor of the altar, the solemnity
of the saints' statues surrounded me with sacred mystery. May processions, bene-
dictions, daily school masses, music, chants, the liturgical seasons, the sacraments,
all supported within me a profound sense of the tangible presence of God. Despite my stepfather's experience, and my own, of racism in the church, I believed,
as did he, that the sacraments worked* (ex opere operato). *From the age of ten, I
wanted to be a priest. I wanted to stand at the altar and offer God in my hands.*

So it was that when I came to investigate the religions that enslaved Africans
brought to the Americas, I encountered something that seemed very familiar, a
correspondence that Africans themselves had discovered centuries ago between
their religions and Roman Catholic Christianity. The most obvious of these
correspondences was the identification of Catholic saints with African spirits,
so characteristic of African American religions like Voodoo and Santería.
Though my family has Louisiana roots, none of us, as far as I know, served the
lwa (practiced Voodoo). No, African religions seemed familiar because they
shared with Catholicism a sacramental vision of the world in which another
world, a spiritual world, coinheres with this one. Behind its flat surface, our
day-to-day world opens onto depths full of meaning, pattern, and spiritual presence. Ritual, like a doorway, gives access to this spiritual world. Through ritual
we step into a kingdom of divine light, mystery, and wonder. The material ob-
jects of ritual not only symbolize spiritual realities but make them present: in-

cense becomes the fragrance of prayer; the light of the candles becomes the flame of devotion; the images of the saints enable the power of ancestors to help the living. Liturgical ritual in African religions, as well as Catholicism, culminates in moments of transparency between worlds when the Divine and the human touch and life is transformed. From this perspective, our society, in general, seems ritually and symbolically impoverished. (The national civic symbols and rituals that do exist are weak and shallow sources of identity and community.) Societies need ritual to transmit meaning and value from one generation to another. Without effective and affective shared rituals, our sense of community atrophies. We are left with the symbols manufactured by mass culture for ceremonies of common consumption.

There were correspondences that obtained between African religions and Protestantism as well, though more subtle than those associated with Catholicism. In the emotional preaching and ecstatic behavior of Baptist and Methodist revival services, African American slaves encountered a ritual equivalent to the spirit possession ceremonies of Africa. The crucial factor linking the two traditions was a conviction that authentic worship required an observable experience of the divine presence. "It ain't enough to talk about God, you've got to feel Him moving on the altar of your heart," as one former slave explained.[3] Ritual, in this liturgical perspective, is supposed to bring the Divine tangibly into this world. The presence of God becomes manifest in the words, the gestures, and the bodies of the believers. Their praying, singing, preaching, and dancing occasion as well as signal the Spirit's arrival. In this form of African and African American ritual, the Divine is embodied in the faithful. The emotional ecstasy of black Protestant worship symbolizes a profound religious truth: the preeminent place of God's presence in this world is the person. His altar is the human heart. Moreover, it is the whole person, body as well as spirit, that makes God present. In a society chronically split between body and spirit, African American ritual exemplifies embodied spirit and inspired body in gesture, dance, song, and performed word. In worship the human becomes an icon of God. A radically personal vision of life flows from this liturgical sensibility. Contrary to the depersonalizing pressures of slavery and racial oppression, the person is of ultimate value as image of the Divine. Anything, then, that defaces that image is sacrilegious.

As I wrote and taught about African religions, their transmission and transformation in America, I realized that they represented a legacy of wisdom about the nature of the world and people in the world from which we all could benefit. Contemporary perspectives might be complemented and enhanced by the traditions of these ancient societies, unknown to most of us. For example, in the personalized world of traditional African religion, the self is conceived as relational. Each person is constituted by a web of interpersonal relationships. Our health, our fortunes, our very lives depend upon the state of our relationships with others, including those who have gone before, our ancestors, who continue to figure prominently in the progress of our lives. By contrast, the tendency of American culture to overemphasize the individualized self empties the life of the communal presence that gives depth and background to our existence. Similarly, a greater appreciation of the self as relational might help us perceive the selfish desire for aggrandizement hiding behind many of our images of success. To achieve at the expense of others, from the perspective of traditional African religions, is witchcraft, pure and simple. And if you choose to move too far outside or too far above your community, you risk becoming bewitched.

In Bay St. Louis, unlike the North, there always seemed to be time and space enough for the long-time love. In the evening twilight, we gathered for supper. The table was heavy with food, laughter, and stories, stories about the old people that went on long into the night, until the last warm sweet sip of anisette placed a benediction on the evening. I heard stories about my great-grandmother, who'd been a slave. She had to flee New Orleans with her son, my grandfather, because his father, a merchant mariner, wanted to take the boy with him when he returned to Germany. They remembered my great-grandmother starching and ironing white shirtwaists while singing snatches of opera she had heard in New Orleans. Her grandchildren used to laugh behind her back and call her "Black Patty" after the famous Fisk Jubilee singer. There was no rush about them, as with the people up North. They attended carefully to the daily tasks of community. Graciousness with others, gentleness, generosity, care, kindness, politeness—these were the virtues of down home. Being known, because my grandparents were known, I glimpsed the deep patterns of my people, patterns that healed. These were my people. They had an ease about them that put others at ease, like a warm embrace. Up North, black Catholics were few. I was one of a handful of black stu-

dents in St. Thomas School. I didn't say it, but I felt different, alone, far from my
people, far from home.

A peculiar people, Americans have always thought of themselves as a chosen
people, specially blessed by God with freedom, liberty, and prosperity. At best,
this national myth of chosenness has supported ideals of service, tolerance, and
freedom; at worst, attitudes of chauvinism, materialism, and militarism. African American Christianity has continuously confronted the nation with troubling questions about the myth of chosenness. After all, if Americans are the
New Israel, and America the Promised Land, what are we to make of the pe-
rennial claims of black Christians that they are the children of Israel, at last
freed from slavery but still far from crossing into the Promised Land? Election,
moreover, brings not only preeminence, elevation, and glory but also, as black
Christians knew all too well, humiliation, suffering, and rejection. Chosenness,
as reflected in the life of Jesus, led to a Cross. The lives of his disciples have
been signed with that Cross. To be chosen, in this perspective, means joining
company not with the powerful but with those who suffer, the outcast, the poor.
Being chosen means entering the mystery of suffering in the sure hope of coming through to the other side.

African American Christians believed they were a chosen people, not because they were black, nor because they suffered, but because their history fit
the pattern of salvation revealed to them in the Bible. They saw themselves in
Christ, the suffering servant. Their lives modeled the paradoxes of the gospel:
in weakness lies strength; in loss, gain; in death, life. "Blessed are the poor, for
theirs is the kingdom of heaven. Blessed are the meek, for they shall inherit the
earth. Blessed are those who hunger and thirst after righteousness, for they shall
be filled."

The problem of suffering was complicated for black Christians by racism. In
accepting their suffering, black Christians were not accepting the racist argument that God intended them to suffer; they were asserting that chosenness
empowers people to make something out of suffering. In the end, suffering is a
fact of life. We can try to ignore it, evade it, deaden it, overpower it, but only at
the cost of our humanity. To recognize that life brings suffering does not mean
we have to succumb to fatalism. Suffering and injustice must be challenged at
the deepest existential level, the level of defeat and despair that Christ over-

came through his passion, death, and resurrection. In this sense, African American Christianity is a paradigm of the central mystery of the gospel, sorrow becomes joy, death yields life.

We should not underestimate the difficulty of living such beliefs. The temptations to despair, to reject Christianity as white man's religion, to abandon belief in a God who permits the innocent to suffer, were, by all accounts, very real. Like Job, black Christians received no logical answer to the question of why they suffered, but only the command to trust in God. Like Jacob, they wrestled all night and instead of achieving victory gained only a blessing. Two sources sustained them in their struggle against despair, the personal experience of conversion and the communal experience of worship. The conversion experiences of black Christians grounded their identity in the knowledge that they were accepted by God, indeed, were of ultimate value in the eyes of God, no matter what white men thought.

I travel to the low country of Georgia and the South Carolina coastal islands to talk to elderly black Christians about their experience of conversion, about a process called seeking, which they underwent many years ago. Led by the Spirit into the wilderness to pray, each had a spiritual father or mother to examine dreams and visions and to serve as a guide in the way of salvation. Now in their eighties and nineties, these are hard-pressed people who have been poor all their lives. They have been through the fire and refined like gold. When they speak about their conversion experiences of sixty and seventy years ago, their faces light up with joy. I ask one ninety-five-year-old man what the difference is between his time and mine. "Love," he replied. "Too much love has gone out of the world. We didn't have nothing, and we helped one another. Now it seems like all everybody is interested in is making the dollar."

From black people like these came a music that constitutes one of this nation's most significant contributions to world culture. And many around the world have been moved by their songs, songs that transform the particular suffering of one people into a parable of human experience. What is the meaning in all this sorrow? What good is it? Simply this. It must be lived through; it cannot be evaded by any of the subterfuges of power or spurious means of escape devised by people to distract one another from reality. Life in a minor key is life as it is, bittersweet, joyful sadness. Unless we are mature enough, realistic enough, to accept sorrow, we will never be able to truly laugh, to be genuinely creative, to authentically love. Instead, we succumb to illusion, becoming preoccupied by an ever-spiraling cycle of needs, in a vain attempt to deny suffering and death. We become bewitched by the illusion that we have no needs that we ourselves cannot meet, that we are omnipotent, that we control our own lives. Illusions of power become dangerous when we try to live them out by controlling others. This deformation of our humanity takes on exceptional force because it is driven by a deep, inchoate fear. The spirituals speak of an alternative. They reveal the capability of the human spirit to transcend bitter sorrow and to resist the persistent attempts of evil to strike it down.

One Sunday, last December, at the start of a very bleak winter, I stood in the front of Saints Peter and Paul Orthodox Church to receive the sacrament of Chrismation. The priest anointed my head, eyes, nostrils, ears, lips, chest, hands, and feet with holy oil and gave me a lit candle to hold as I stood for Divine Liturgy. After the anointing I thought about the last step in the process of icon painting, which is the application of warm oil. The oil serves to bind together the colors of the icon and to bring out their depth. At the beginning of the liturgy we sing the words of Psalm 103, "Bless the Lord, O my soul, and all that is within me, bless his holy name." And I am moved once again by the sad joyfulness of the chant tones. Once again I feel the prayers of the congregation as if their hands hold me up. I think back to the night of Pascha when we had proceeded around the church with lit candles and then stood at the doors of the church chanting "Christ is risen!" When the doors opened and we all moved into the church, I felt the presence of generations of Christians standing with us, generations moving into the church with us, present with us on Pascha, our ancestors in the faith.

Our nation, too, has ancestors. Now, as much as ever, we stand in need of their presence. We, the American people, need to hear and to listen to the stories of all our forefathers and foremothers. We need to be informed by the memories of their lives. Can these bones live, these dry bones? If we allow them to be reknit, re-membered. Memory, story, ritual—these are all ways of re-membering a community broken by hate, rage, injustice, fear. Not to avenge, nor to make up for, not undoing what cannot be undone, but perhaps to heal. There are those who fear that the stories will not cohere, that they will remain a disparate set of unrelated or conflict-ridden experiences that only confirm our feelings of divisiveness, of us against them. Perhaps. But I am convinced that if we listen, truly listen, to the stories of others, something else will happen. We will find ourselves intrigued by the drama of these stories, moved by their poignancy, and, finally, surprised at the common humanity that lies beneath their distinctive details. In the end, what we hold in common is a set of shared stories. If we seek commonality, we will discover it in the telling and listening to each other's stories, confident that an adequate history of the varied races and religions who came to dwell in this land will reflect our continually expanding American identity. Because of our habitual tendency to repeat the congratulatory story, excluding others that do not fit a celebratory mood, we must resist the collective pressure to abandon, deny, or forget the particular stories of all our people and our connection to them.

I grew up without knowing the full story of my father's death. My mother and my stepfather decided not to tell me until I started college because they did not want me to grow up hating white folks. As a result, I wondered if the story were shameful—otherwise they would have told me. I never knew my father. I had no memories of him. I had no stories of him—only one blurry picture. I knew only his absence. Several months ago, I went back to Mississippi in search of my father. I didn't know what I would find after all this time, only that I needed to go. I talked to aunts and uncles, cousins, and close family friends. I found two newspaper accounts of his death. I spoke with the son of the man who killed my father. On the last day of my trip, I went to visit my father's grave. I had been there many times before, but for the first time, I suddenly began to cry. I cried for him, for my mother, for my sisters, for a father and son who never met. Then, as if in memory, I saw him. I saw him laughing; I saw him raging; I saw him shot, and falling, falling into my arms, into my life. After all these years of waiting, my father and I have finally met. I bend down, pick up some dirt from his grave and rub it on my head. All the sorrow wells up inside me and merges with the joy of meeting him, finally, for the first time . . .

It is fire in the bones.

Notes

From *A Fire in the Bones* by Albert J. Raboteau. © 1993 by Albert J. Raboteau. Reprinted by permission of Beacon Press, Boston.

1. Clifton H. Johnson, ed., *God Struck Me Dead: Religious Conversion Experiences and Autobiographies of Ex-Slaves* (Philadelphia: Pilgrim Press, 1969), 74.

2. Appeal to Governor Thomas Gage and the Massachusetts General Court, 25 May 1774, *Collections of the Massachusetts Historical Society*, 5th ser., 3 (1877): 432–33.

3. Johnson, *God Struck Me Dead*, 144.

A Journey to Southern
Religious Studies

Charles Reagan Wilson

My journey to the study of southern religion began as a child in Nashville, Tennessee, took me to Texas, and brought me to Mississippi. It began in the Church of Christ, led to years outside any church orbit, and has brought me now to Episcopalianism. I am a historian but easily see ways to use the theories and methods of other disciplines to illuminate the study of southern religion in context. I have had many mentors, both actual teachers and intellectual figures whose works have shaped me. Looking back on my life, I see how spiritual issues have been enduring influences, if sometimes oblique, on my academic work.

My roots and raising were in Tennessee, as part of a very close-knit southern family. My parents were from small towns in middle Tennessee, tobacco-growing country north of Nashville. My folks were what historians would call the "plain folk"—not wealthy, not the stereotypical "poor whites," but, in my father's case at least, poor in worldly goods. My father's people were burdened with a hardscrabble life as sharecroppers who had lost family land in the early twentieth century. My mother's life was more sheltered in the small town of Springfield, though again life was not extravagant for her as the daughter of a barber. Their spiritual lives may have been constrained, as with so many others, because of the austere context of their material lives.

I inherited from my parents pronounced churchly orientations. My mother was a Southern Baptist, my father a member of the Church of Christ. My father's parents were, it seemed to me, faithful members of the Coopertown church, and my memories of church there are of hard pews, lean preachers, and the groaning tables of fine dinners on the grounds. My grandparents on my mother's side were religious but less churchly. My grandmother betrayed an insecurity, perhaps, in judging weekly services as too much a social occasion, with the congregation more interested in what she was wearing than in her soul. Perhaps this showed insecurity, but perhaps it showed that her religious beliefs were more important to her than her appearance. My grandfather Charlie Ward, for whom I am named, was a gentle man, a model Christian to me, although not in church that often. I do remember going with him to the Ebenezer Baptist Church, in Greenbrier, Tennessee, and sitting through innumerable invitation calls.

My father would not attend any church but the Church of Christ, so my mother switched to that church when she married, even being rebaptized as this demanding new faith required. She reserved the right, nonetheless, to give an occasional Baptist critique of the Sunday sermon on the way home from services. I attended the Church of Christ regularly as a child, along with my brother, Martin, who was two years younger than I. In visiting relatives, though, we might attend Baptist or Methodist services as well as those of the Church of Christ. I thought of them as interchangeable experiences at the time, which suggests that preachers were not fully communicating the complexities of the differing theological traditions of those churches to the young. The Church of Christ is a Restorationist church that strives to re-create the early Christian church, based on the books of the New Testament. Growing up in it gave me a thorough grounding in the Scriptures, the stories and characters and wisdom of, in fact, the Old Testament as well as the New. I recall reading the King James Version around the kitchen table with my mother, father, and brother, and I can still see in my mind the graphic, sometimes gory illustrations of our edition. I absorbed more lessons in Sunday school and vacation Bible school, that southern summer ritual of childhood. Familiarity with the Bible surely has benefited my studies of southern religion, grounding me in specific biblical incidents to recall in reading historical texts and also providing tropes for my own conceptualization of southern sacred experiences.

The Church of Christ, I would later discover, is not an evangelical church, as it remains grounded in theological inheritances from its early influences in Presbyterianism and Scottish Common Sense Realism. It shares much with its southern evangelical neighbors, though, as I remember from childhood—not only the familiarity with the Bible that one would expect in a fundamentalist faith but also that wide body of hymns and gospel songs that unite believers across denominational lines. My mother was surely a character from rural folk tradition in knowing by heart innumerable songs and keeping the church hymnal around for others, as she sang to my brother and me throughout our youth and beyond. I learned from her and from those songs, more than from ministers, about the grace of Jesus. "I come to the garden alone, while the dew is still on the roses," says one of the most comforting of those songs, portraying what a friend we have in Jesus, as another of my favorites says. The singing in the Church of Christ is without musical accompaniment, though, which sounds odd to nonmembers, but I remember the compelling quality of the spare sounds. The bass voices coming in on "Up from the Grave He Arose," which we sang each Easter morning, still electrifies my memory. I consciously weave references to these religious songs into anything I write.

When I was nine years old, in 1957, we left Tennessee to move to El Paso, Texas, a move occasioned by my mother's worsening health in the wet and humid Southeast. The uprooting severed me from an extended kin of grandparents, aunts and uncles, and cousins, but it bound me even closer to my nuclear family. I grew up in a very cosmopolitan, suburban place, in El Paso, a city with a mobile military population, strong cultural influences from southern California (we watched the Los Angeles Dodgers on cable TV), and the intriguing Anglo-Hispanic culture of a Mexican border town. One of my strongest memories is of walking past a church not long after moving to Texas and seeing men dressed in long robes and white collars sprinkling water on animals, a menagerie of cats and dogs and birds and others—the blessing of the animals on St. Francis Day, although I did not realize what I had observed until much later. At the time, I simply realized I was not in Tennessee anymore, or at least the Tennessee in which I had grown up as part of a Protestant family little exposed to other religious traditions. In any event, I now was in a spot to observe a bright world of Hispanic Catholicism, living in a borderland that exposed me in ways I did not even realize to the sights and sounds of a multireligious culture.

Every summer after we moved to Texas, my brother and I, with our mother and father when he could get away from work, would return to small-town Tennessee, spending it with grandparents in Greenbrier. I loved much of that life, but my high school years were more preoccupied with the Beatles and fear of the Vietnam War than of any icons of the South. I positively repudiated the ugliness in the South's resistance to social change as I was coming of age in the early 1960s. For me, religion was about the brotherhood of man, and I did not see much of it in the South of my roots and raising.

The death of my grandfather, my mother's father, was a jolting event that led to a loss of faith. He was a sweet, funny, endearing man, who played old-time tunes on his fiddle—as perfect a grandfather as one could have created. True, by the time he died, I had heard his stories one too many times, and as a teenager part of me rebelled against him as a symbol of the traditional South I could not embrace in the 1960s. My grandfather remained, though, a powerful embodiment for me of a good, decent man, and his death shook my faith. Unresolved questions about suffering and death focused emotional and intellectual doubts I had developed about my fundamentalist faith. His death came in the summer of 1966, the same year that I began college at the University of Texas at El Paso (UTEP), which until that year had been called Texas Western College. There I learned new ideas and viewpoints, many of which challenged my inherited Church of Christ beliefs, and my inability to come to terms with what I then saw as the injustice of my grandfather's death added to my spiritual turmoil. I drifted away from the church, from religion, with intellectual activity replacing it. I had as a young teenager even aspired to preach, although I feared I could never achieve the moral level I had heard sketched endlessly from the pulpit. Now, a secular aspiration replaced the ministerial one—I would be a professor, a historian.

In college I discovered my fascination with ideas and with history in particular. I remember taking a course entitled the Philosophy of Civilization, during which we read and reread only one book, Alfred North Whitehead's *Adventures of Ideas*, which led me to Whitehead's other books that intimated a very individualistic vision of spirituality requiring no institutional church. I worked with Carl T. Jackson, a scholar of Asian religions in the United States, on my M.A. thesis at UTEP, flirting at first with a topic involving Asian religions in America before writing about the portrayal of Native Americans in American popular magazines. I included a long chapter on Indian spirituality, which became one of my first published articles and reflected my interest in writing about religious issues in history.[1]

I pursued my doctorate at the University of Texas at Austin, where I discovered what I wanted my life's work to be—studying the South and its religious history. UTEP had first set me on this path because I worked there with another outstanding mentor, Kenneth K. Bailey, one of the first scholars to publish a major work on southern Protestantism. From him, I learned rigorous standards of scholarship and how to take religion seriously as a subject of historical research. I now immersed myself in studying the South's complex history, which raised issues that seemed to call forth to me religious understandings. I had absorbed Reinhold Niebuhr's work and, like others, found his use of historical irony most applicable to the southern story I wanted to tell. C. Vann Woodward's "The Irony of Southern History" pointed me to the theme, and I saw a chance to explore its religious meanings, which Woodward did not develop. What interested me was the post–Civil War period, where spiritual issues relating to defeat, poverty, a mean-spirited moralism and racism, and an uncritical longing for the past nurtured the Lost Cause.

I then discovered the seminal work of Samuel H. Hill, and I still work within his intellectual orbit. *Southern Churches in Crisis* (1966) had a profound influence upon me. It defined a distinctive interdenominational southern religious system that gave coherence to my other readings on the South and resonated with my experiences as a native southerner. His work made me see that southern religion had intellectual substance and cultural meaning, that its complexities were worth grappling with. His insights about southern Protestant worship services made me see in new ways what I had lived through. The tone of moral outrage over religious racism hit the deepest chord in me. The book was simultaneously an objective study, bringing a wide perspective of European theological and church historical understanding to southern religion, and also a passionate subjective treatise calling the southern churches to task for moral failures.[2]

I had not gone to Austin intending to study southern religion, though. I worked with William H. Goetzmann in American intellectual and cultural history. Those areas were clearly my main interests, and I was surely already a regionalist, but I went to Austin expecting to study the West with this Pulitzer Prize–winning historian of western exploration. Goetzmann himself had studied with a preeminent Yale southernist, David M. Potter, and he reacted positively when I told him of my desire to study the South instead of the West. He gave me my original dissertation topic, which was "Fundamentalist Attitudes toward the Civil

War." When I investigated, I discovered that the early-twentieth-century Fundamentalist movement had little to say about the Civil War, but when I looked at southern religious life after the Civil War I refined my topic to that subject. The University of Texas library is one of the nation's best for studying the South, thanks to the Littlefield Fund, and I happily researched church records, the files of *Confederate Veteran* magazine, annual meetings of denominational assemblies, ministerial memoirs, and other primary sources. I traveled elsewhere, to the Presbyterian archives at Montreat, North Carolina, discovering there a genteel researcher's world where nice ladies not only brought you church records but also served tea and cakes in the afternoon. I visited the United Daughters of the Confederacy Museum in Austin and was welcomed as, in the words of my elderly hostess, the only "gentleman caller" of the day.

Out of my research came my dissertation and eventual first book, *Baptized in Blood: The Religion of the Lost Cause* (1980). At the heart of its conceptualization was the idea of the civil religion, a still debated but useful idea that sees spiritual significance in nationalism or, in my case, regionalism. G. Howard Miller, who taught American religious history at Texas, introduced me to the concept and directed my reading about it, although he himself was skeptical of it. Robert N. Bellah's seminal article in 1969 argued that religion existed not just in churches but in cultural institutions and in such social rituals as holiday celebrations, patriotic commemorations, and political ceremonies. Bellah suggested that the civil religion had prophetic as well as celebratory features, citing figures such as Lincoln, who brought the nation under divine judgment.[3]

The idea of the civil religion was an odd one for me to embrace. Growing up in the Church of Christ gave me no sense of the history of religion in general and certainly not an understanding of how religion could exist away from the sanctuary. As a Restorationist church, the Church of Christ skipped over centuries, millennia, to reach back to the original communities of Christianity as models to re-create. Alexander and Thomas Campbell were iconic figures in the church but disembodied for me as actual historical actors associated with any time or place. I grew up also without a sense of the church's wider role in society. I mainly recall hearing preaching on individual sin, moral standards, individual redemption, and the necessity of contending for the faith. Yet in graduate school, I was fascinated with civil religion's positing that society, not just the individual, could have religious significance. Bellah saw American democratic ideals as embodying for Americans a sacred cause throughout history.

My understanding of how religion fits more broadly into southern culture was deepened when I worked as a fellow with John Shelton Reed in his 1980 National Endowment for the Humanities Summer Seminar on Continuity and Change in Southern Culture. Reed exposed me to interdisciplinary study of the South in new ways, especially showing me how social science research could be useful. I began thinking how my historical studies of southern religion related to his findings of much continuity of southern religion into the contemporary era. His own engaging lecturing and writing style also made me realize the value and pleasure of academic essays, where one could even use a phrase that might make one smile in reading it.

I conceived in his seminar, nonetheless, a still ongoing, somber research project, "The Southern Way of Death." Anthropologist Christopher Crocker had used that title for a case study in the 1970s, but I am studying how death beliefs, rituals, symbols, and customs can be a window into the larger issues of the behavioral and ideological dimensions of the southern way of life. This study of such cheerful topics as funerals, cemeteries, and mortality rates undoubtedly revealed my continuing interest in the suffering side of life. When I told my mother that I was following up my study of the South's Lost Cause of defeat with a study of death, she looked at me and said, "Can't you find something happy to write about?"

I came to the University of Mississippi in the fall of 1981 to coedit the *Encyclopedia of Southern Culture* with William Ferris and to teach in the department of history.[4] I have lived in Mississippi eighteen years now, teaching, among other things, courses on American religious history and southern religion. When my course enrollments were very high the first time I taught the latter course, my departmental chair, Robert J. Haws, suggested students thought they were signing up for a devotional hour. Often, though, the biggest challenge in teaching religious history courses is to persuade students to take all religions seriously. Most of my students are middle class, and anything too emotional or unorthodox simply will not do. I show them films of Appalachian snake handlers but try to make the students see how they are part of the same religious culture as snake handlers, those exaggerated fundamentalist believers who take biblical passages literally.

Teaching at the Center for the Study of Southern Culture enabled me to see the folk and popular dimensions of the southern evangelical culture that has so long dominated the region. Bill Ferris, our founding director, documented African American religious and musical traditions in the Mississippi Delta of the late 1960s and 1970s, and his films have a timeless, primitive quality that still gives an intimate view of those traditions. Lisa Howorth taught a folk arts course in the Southern Studies curriculum, and I learned much from her about the images and styles of rural folk art. Tom Rankin's documentary fieldwork and photography similarly opened my mind to new visual perspectives on southern religiosity. While working single-mindedly during the 1980s on the *Encyclopedia of Southern Culture*, I found myself still reflecting on southern religion, gravitating toward interest in the South's popular religion and its relationship to the larger evangelical culture.

My intellectual interest in the symbols, rituals, imagery, and icons of popular religion emerged at the same time as I began attending the Episcopal Church in the mid-1980s. Friends had invited me to attend St. Peter's Episcopal Church in Oxford, and I had been drawn to its liturgical ceremony, the beauty of its services, the sense of community in the small church, and, the more I studied it, the middle way of Anglican theology, drawing from both Protestantism and Roman Catholicism. This was a dramatic departure, of course, from my religious raising. As I had known it, the Church of Christ had been an austere visual and liturgical experience, but I now discovered that those dimensions would be important in any new spiritual commitments I made. Episcopal aestheticism is far from popular religion, of course, but I sensed that my academic and spiritual aspirations were somehow converging, with the need for both experiential and intellectual understanding of the mythic and ritual.

I had the good sense to marry a Mississippi woman, Marie Antoon, in 1985, at the Episcopal Chapel of the Cross, north of Jackson, Mississippi. Marie is Roman Catholic, not always a churchly one but one in spirit. The ancient church grabs hold of its young early and leaves its mark, or at least that is so in the case of Catholics I have known. She is introspective and sometimes intense, my temperamental opposite. Our marital separation in the early 1990s became a metaphor in my self-understanding of the divided life I had often led. I had worked hard on teaching and scholarship, sometimes to the detriment of both my marriage and my spiritual life. Through my renewed relationship with

Marie, seen in our marital reconciliation, I discovered the need to bring more closely together the intellectual and emotional sides of my personality, a realization that is far from achieved but that has contributed in turn to my increasing personal interest in spirituality and my continuing academic fascination with the mythic and ritual.

Out of all of these developments and reflections in the late 1980s and early 1990s came *Judgment and Grace in Dixie: Southern Faiths from Faulkner to Elvis* (1995). A collection of essays that had been previously published, the book summarized my thinking on southern popular religion and its relationship to broader regional culture. Some of the essays extended my thinking on the civil religion concept as it related to the South. In particular, I argued that the seemingly unrelated agrarian literary movement of the early twentieth century and the civil rights movement in the late twentieth century both saw the South as having a transcendent meaning, still under divine judgment and expectation. I was countering the idea that the South no longer had distinctive regional meanings, showing that different southerners had invested different meanings in it. Despite the extraordinary social changes in the recent South, I believe southern culture still is associated with a worldview rooted in the past and specifically in religion. While the social and economic foundations of the South have surely shifted, southern cultural forms are yet adjusting, with religion itself an anchor as the South continues modernizing. I also suggested that the civil religion was not only seen in ideology but also bubbled up from below, in such modern southern rituals as beauty contests and college football games. The book looks at the recent South in the long perspective of southern history, and I made conscious comparisons between the Lost Cause I had studied and the recent commemoration of the civil rights movement.[5]

My academic work had begun with *Baptized in Blood*, a study of the white southern cultural identity rooted in religion. *Judgment and Grace in Dixie*, on the other hand, explored the biracial context of southern identity. I had long before discovered James McBride Dabbs, a white South Carolina farmer and social activist, whose mid-twentieth-century writings, such as *Haunted by God* (1972), had analyzed the complexities of black-white relations in the South and their deeper spiritual significance for people of faith, and his work has deeply influenced my conceptualization of southern culture. Folk art, literature, and music especially seemed to embody this theme, and my examination of those topics in *Judgment and Grace* enabled me to look at biracial cultural interaction and at similarities and differences in cultural styles. The essays in the book came out of lectures I had given that often related to broader monographic studies on which I am working, analyzing the relationships between the socially constructed, racially exclusive identity of white southerners and the biracial, behavioral features of a southern culture that represented an alternate regional identity. Religion has been crucial to each, sacralizing the white southern identity yet providing the shared evangelical culture that has nurtured blacks and whites throughout hard southern times.[6]

Oxford, Mississippi, was a stimulating community context for me in the early 1990s as I pondered these matters. I joined St. Peter's Episcopal Church in 1992, entering into educational, spiritual, and outreach activities of the church. I went through an Education for Ministry program that deepened my understanding of church history and theology; I began contemplative prayer sessions each Tuesday morning and have continued with them for some seven years. Again, I am constantly struck by these departures from my religious raisings. Contemplative prayer, especially, rests in the profound legacy of Roman Catholic mysticism and such modern exemplars of it as Father Thomas Keating. The Church of Christ has an intellectually activist tradition, contending sharply for points of belief, but with little sense of the need for meditation. The church aspires to consensus, although it has often been forced to deal with schism and controversy because points of faith do not always turn out to be so obvious when interpreted. The assertive, and argumentative, Paul of New Testament letters would be the patron saint of the church, if it had saints. Yet I find that in meditating, I do draw from less contentious scenes, evoked from the southern gospel music I grew up with—the peaceful garden, the friend of Jesus, even the green pastures of heaven. My earlier church tradition did include prayerful devotionalism, with which I find continuities now, even though the disciplines and conventions of contemplative prayer and Protestant devotionalism remain so distinct.

St. Peter's has been significant during the last decade for its involvement in a biracial religious effort, which is still unusual for a small southern town. Duncan Gray III, rector of St. Peter's, and Leroy Wadlington, pastor of Second Baptist Church, grew up in Oxford, coming of age in the 1960s and both living through the turbulent violence and social instability in Oxford during James Meredith's entrance as the first African American student at the University of

Mississippi. Yet, as part of racially segregated communities, they never knew each other growing up. In 1992 the two began intentionally bringing their churches together for carefully planned activities, both religious and social. The two preached at each other's churches, with their congregations hospitably listening to the very different styles than what they were used to hearing. After Wadlington's lively Baptist sermon, the associate rector, representing the congregation, thanked him, noting that even though he was an Episcopalian, he had almost yelled out "Amen." Several of us met afterward in small groups at neighborhood houses to reflect on the experience. No one had prepared the Baptists to rely on the Episcopal Book of Common Prayer to guide them through the service. Some members of Second Baptist had been surprised, moreover, to taste real wine in the Episcopal communion, rather than the grape juice they were accustomed to taking. Since then, the congregations have had joint summer picnics in the town park, visited each other's services, sponsored youth retreats, and even tailgated together before a football game in the once all-white Grove at the University of Mississippi.

I played a minor role as a supporter of this exchange, participating in its activities and in a racial self-awareness workshop the church sponsored and also chronicling the story in an article for *Christian Century*—all of which represented the latest way that my own grappling with religious issues has influenced my study of religion. My mentor here has been Duncan Gray III, rector at St. Peter's since 1985, who has articulated for me a model of the Christian faith that I find shaping my intellectual and spiritual life. The son of Episcopal bishop Duncan Gray II, who achieved renown for his courage as a racial moderate in Mississippi during the 1960s, Gray leads the contemplative prayer sessions in which I participate but also insists that spirituality is not a phenomenon disengaged from society. He understands the challenge of nurturing a just society that overcomes the continuing racial divide, which still symbolizes a division in the human psyche, rather than the wholeness that his Christian faith represents in ideal. As a native Mississippian, he understands the special burden and opportunity his home state possesses in addressing this concern.[7]

Although not a native of Mississippi, I, too, understand the special responsibilities on race relations facing the state in which I live and especially my home institution, the University of Mississippi. I am working with a new institute on campus, the Institute on Race Relations and Civic Renewal, to help shape public policy, provide service and research opportunities for faculty and students, and generally address the continuing American social crisis of race relations. In my own work, I am increasingly drawn to the issue of civic society and what the South may have to offer in the growing national discussion of that concept. I see the concept growing out of the idea of the civil religion. Southern conservatives have long articulated a regional tradition of community concern, a belief that laissez-faire economics and the ruthless individualism of capitalism are insufficient bases for the good society. White southerners interpreted their Confederate and agrarian heritages as foundations for spiritual meanings to "southernness." Social progressives in the South have had a similar belief that American individualism is inadequate for civic life. Since the 1960s, southern progressives have esteemed the cultural values and achievements of traditional southern rural society while at the same time urging reform in economic and social institutions, often motivated themselves by the Judeo-Christian ethic of brotherhood. The shared value placed on religious sentiments and a religious worldview in the South may provide a common ground for new ideals of civic renewal. Certainly, regional belief in the value of civility in social discourse seems a contribution the nation desperately needs at this point in its political life.

Students of southern religion have represented a distinct field for several decades now. My first book followed shortly after early works by Kenneth K. Bailey, Samuel H. Hill, John Lee Eighmy, and others gave legitimacy to the field. One of the most promising signs of its continued vitality is the appearance of insightful new studies by such young scholars as Paul Harvey, Beth Schweiger, Daniel Stowell, and others. Back in 1984, I directed a symposium entitled "Religion in the South," which brought together Bailey, Hill, John B. Boles, Wayne Flynt, C. Eric Lincoln, Edwin S. Gaustad, and David E. Harrell Jr. For Bailey, it was a return to the Mississippi in which he had grown up, and amidst his scholarly observations he had perhaps the best line of the symposium. In the old days, he said, southern ministers had known not only their church traditions but also "how to thump a watermelon." That evocative image neatly conveyed how important the regional context had been in understanding religion in the South. I am old enough to have a memory of the rural religion of my grandparents, a religion that surely connected them to generations of earlier southern worshippers. My own life since then has moved me through personal experiences linking the academic world with broader southern society. I have moved away from the fundamentalist church of my childhood, but I know it planted in me a seriousness with which I take religion, both personally and in my apprehension of its role in southern society. The Episcopal Church in Mississippi, in which I now make my spiritual life, remains also, of course, a very southern church albeit far from the "southern" church of Mississippi Episcopalianism half a century ago. It has been the institution through which I have glimpsed possibilities of combining personal and societal spirituality, which I believe will continue to form the backdrop to my scholarly work.

Notes

1. Alfred North Whitehead, *Adventures of Ideas* (New York: Macmillan, 1933); Charles Reagan Wilson, "Attitudes toward the American Indian in Popular American Magazines, 1865–1900" (master's thesis, University of Texas at El Paso, 1972).

2. Samuel H. Hill, *Southern Churches in Crisis* (New York: Holt, Rinehart and Winston, 1967).

3. Charles Reagan Wilson, *Baptized in Blood: The Religion of the Lost Cause, 1865–1920* (Athens: University of Georgia Press, 1980); Robert N. Bellah, "Civil Religion in America," in Russell E. Richey and Donald G. Jones, eds., *American Civil Religion* (New York: Harper and Row, 1974), 21–44.

4. Charles Reagan Wilson and William Ferris, eds., *Encyclopedia of Southern Culture* (Chapel Hill: University of North Carolina Press, 1989).

5. Charles Reagan Wilson, *Judgment and Grace in Dixie: Southern Faiths from Faulkner to Elvis* (Athens: University of Georgia Press, 1995).

6. James McBride Dabbs, *Haunted by God: The Cultural and Religious Experience of the South* (Richmond, Va.: John Knox Press, 1972).

7. Charles Reagan Wilson, "Church Burnings and Christian Community," *Christian Century* 113 (25 Sept.–2 Oct. 1996), 890–95.

Greek, Southern, and Baptist: A Southerner's Experience of Race, Religion, and Ethnicity

Andrew M. Manis

Dig deeply enough and you can almost always find autobiographical reasons why historians are drawn to the subjects about which they teach and write. The same is true, I suspect, for anyone who writes. Maya Angelou writes of and out of her experience as a southern black woman. Nobel Prize–winner Elie Wiesel writes of and out of his experience of surviving the Holocaust. This phenomenon is common enough to require little comment. For southerners who write about their region and its religion, however, the tendency is perhaps stronger. The southerner, white or black, is given to storytelling, and southern evangelical traditions have traditionally emphasized the role of "giving one's testimony." This collection of essays seeks to test the hypothesis that being southern and being religious powerfully affect those professional historians who focus their work on the religious history of the South. This particular contribution makes that connection very clear.

There is at least one day a year that I reflect on the difference it makes that I am a white, ethnic, religious southerner from Birmingham, Alabama. Oddly enough, it is the Monday in January that Americans are bidden to remember the life and death of an African American preacher from Georgia. Martin Luther King Jr.'s birthday always reminds me of the role King and the civil rights movement played in liberating southern whites from the racial universe in which we found ourselves. What the movement did in my hometown somehow made a difference in the way I looked at the world and ensured that I would look at it through a historian's eyes. Being a practicing religionist also makes a great difference. In fact, the combination of the these elements — being a white Birminghamian and being a religious one — more than anything else shapes what I study, as well as how and why I study it.

In 1986, the first year King's birthday was celebrated as a federal holiday, I sat in the Louisiana Superdome waiting for Jesse Jackson to address the crowd gathered for the occasion. Ordinarily I would have been teaching my religion classes at Xavier University of Louisiana, but on this particular Monday we had the day off. Xavier is the only predominantly black Catholic university in America, and as I waited for the birthday party to begin, I found myself wondering, "What's a white, southern boy like me doing in a place like Xavier?" It was a long way from Miss Hamil's eighth-grade class in Birmingham, where I apprehensively and, I must admit, disgustedly learned my first lessons with three black classmates, to my own classroom in New Orleans. I laughed to myself thinking that my Uncle John, who complained about African Americans every chance he got and once took my mother to a White Citizens Council meeting, was having a seizure in his grave knowing where his godson worked. It was also a long pilgrimage from the old country of Greece, where the grownups in my life were born.

Much later I used to salve my tender southern conscience by joking that none of my ancestors owned slaves or even lived in the South until 1925 or so. My forebears spent their time hanging around the Greek island village of Aperi or the Parthenon (not the one in Nashville, mind you) rather than the ol' plantation. Yet as I matured I discovered that my Greek and Orthodox family had imbibed almost as much American and southern racism as the Joneses next door. More than one African American comic has joked that the "N-word" was the first English word immigrants were taught when they got off the boat in America.

Apparently it had been an early lesson for my mother, who though born in Greece grew up mostly in Birmingham. One morning when I was a boy she angrily woke me up with the news that I had left the back door open all night. She scolded me agitatedly, asking, "What if we had found a *mavro* standing over us with a knife when we got up this morning?" Literally, *mavro* is Greek for "black," but in the context it meant "nigger." The word came into play again one day in 1963 when King entered a Birmingham jail. A few miles away Mama called me in from a Birmingham playground with the warning, "Don't go out today; it's too dangerous. The *mavrous* are causing trouble again."

I do not know whether these anecdotes reveal more about the power of south-ern culture to shape the attitudes of foreigners who came to live within it or the seemingly intrinsic racism of whites who live in all regions of the nation. I do know that they keep me from exonerating my own people from the race con-sciousness about which King and the other civil rights ministers preached. I cannot fault my mother completely, however. Despite her occasional racist comments, she voted for Lyndon Johnson in 1964, when racial issues led most white southern voters into the Goldwater camp, and she *never* voted for George Wallace. At least until I got to college, she was the only white person I ever heard say anything positive about King—she acknowledged that he was a great speaker. Most everyone else seemed to agree with my baseball coach, who made a few pointed, not to say inhumane, comments when King was assassinated. I wish I could say his words disgusted me as much then as they do now, but the truth is that I was as caught up in racial ambivalence as was my mother.

That ambivalence comes from the immigrant experience in America, and especially in the South, where since antebellum times the keepers of the status quo were especially wary of foreign ideas infiltrating the region. Had my uncle asked around, he might have been reminded that his Citizens Council col-leagues—often called "Klansmen without the sheets"—were almost as likely to burn a cross in his yard as that of blacks. He might have recalled the family lore about "Bull" Connor, more famous for his police dogs and fire hoses, making nasty remarks to another relative about "you damned Greeks."

So on the one hand, my people grew up being lumped with other less than "one hundred percent Americans." The kids with whom I played ball in Southside Birmingham were not, for the most part, WASPs. Their names and ethnicities were varied: Shunnarah and Ajlouny (Syrian), Schilleci and Verciglio (Italian), Tebsherani (Lebanese), Tofel (French). One of the more American sounding names among my pals was Miller, but even he was Jewish. The preju-dice was there, though experienced more directly by my older sister than by me personally. One of the traumas of her adolescence was being "blackballed" from a high school sorority, she still believes, because she was Greek.

On the other hand, like most immigrants, we were still seen and seeing our-selves as above the status of the African Americans who were gradually moving into our neighborhood. To varying degrees, we shared the stereotypes, laughed at the same jokes, and complained just as loudly when integration finally came to Glen Iris School. My brother and I were incensed when blacks moved in next door, and we were all but paralyzed with fear the day my foul tip sent our baseball over the back fence and through their window. If it had not been for my eighth-grade teacher, the imperious Miss Hamil, who looked for all the world like Martha Washington and ruled her domain with iron-fisted dignity, the arrival of our first three black classmates would likely have been greeted with intimidation and perhaps violence instead of merely internalized disdain.

Thus one Sunday morning at the Holy Trinity–Holy Cross Greek Orthodox Church my family felt great ambivalence when we heard our priest announce with trembling voice: "Today a part of Christ's Body suffers. The Sixteenth Street Baptist Church has been bombed, and four young girls were killed as they sat in Sunday school." Father Soterios Gouvellis was a Yankee, having come to Birmingham from Michigan. In January 1963 he joined a group of Birmingham ministers who publicly called upon newly inaugurated Governor Wallace to cool his "Segregation today, segregation tomorrow, segregation forever" rhetoric. In April that same year, after racial demonstrations began in the city, the same group of ministers publicly criticized King and called the demonstrations "untimely." Their open letter became the occasion for King's epistolary response, which of course later came to be known as his *Letter from Birmingham Jail*. One of the ministers, however, saw matters a bit differently and refused to sign the open letter to King. The clerical dissenter was our own Father Gouvellis. It was not terribly long after this that we had a new priest. Although there were other extenuating circumstances leading to his departure, one of the factors was the same race consciousness that pressured Protestant ministers to avoid challenging the accepted racial arrangements. Greek Americans, often as "other" as the *mavrous*, but hoping desperately to prosper in a new land, could ill afford a troublemaking priest.

My own exodus from such ambivalence began as a high school junior, when I experienced an evangelical conversion. My transition from the Divine Liturgy of Greek Orthodoxy to Southern Baptist Bible-thumping is long and circuitous. So, too, is my gradual exodus to the place where I claim with southern prophet Will Campbell to be a "Baptist from the South" but not a Southern Baptist. But that is another story. Neither story needs to be told here. Suffice it to say that within two years I was studying for the ministry at Alabama Baptists' Samford University in Birmingham. In one of my classes, a political science professor forced me to read the letter King wrote when he was in jail and I was on the playground in Birmingham. A fledgling Baptist minister read another Baptist minister's words: "I have looked at the South's beautiful churches with their lofty spires pointing heavenward. I have beheld the impressive outlines of her massive religious-education buildings. Over and over I have found myself asking: 'What kind of people worship here? Who is their God? . . . Where were they when Governor Wallace gave a clarion call for defiance and hatred?'"[1]

In the early 1970s, while I was in college, I first began to be embarrassed by the southern churches' reactions to the civil rights movement and their reactionary hatred of King and other ministerial proponents of integration. Still more embarrassment arose when I learned that the particular group of Baptists to whom I had become attached had come into denominational existence in 1845 because of their defense of slavery. That fact alone probably would not have bothered me if, more than one hundred years later, my fellow Baptists (and other denominations as well) had not remained quite unreconstructed. In my naive view of the world, I was baffled by otherwise kindhearted Christian folk who continued to use the N-word. Nor could I fathom why deacons stood guard in church vestibules lest any African Americans ventured to attempt to desegregate a white worship service.

My initial attempts at preaching were highly moralistic events, filled with prophetic fervor against drinking and smoking. On those issues it did not take long for a former Greek Orthodox who never heard such jeremiads in church to be influenced by the southern homiletic style, both in terms of delivery and content. Still, the zeal of a new convert slipped racism onto its list of sins against which to inveigh. Once, while concluding a sermon in a Baptist church in Tuscaloosa, I mentioned King's name. Before I could finish my remarks, a man left his pew and stormed out of the sanctuary, slamming the door behind him. Eventually, King's question about the kind of people who worshiped and the sort of religion found in the southern white churches became my own. Reading King's *Why We Can't Wait* convinced me that King's life and words had to be understood in and of themselves, rather than through the misinterpretations of fundamentalist segregationists.

Moving from college to the Southern Baptist Theological Seminary (SBTS) in Louisville, Kentucky, I found myself among a different sort of Southern Baptists, for whom King was a hero. King had spoken in the chapel there in 1961 and was met with a standing ovation when he concluded his address. Southern Baptists out in the hinterlands raised a chorus of protests about his being invited to speak, and with a view to the constituency, seminary president Duke K. McCall publicly apologized for King's appearance. McCall was in reality a racial moderate who I suspect had no real objection to King's speaking on his campus. Like most Southern Baptist administrators, however, he could ill afford to get too far ahead of the folk whose offerings funded their institutions. By 1977, when I began my student days there, the seminary was dominated by progressives on theological and social issues.

Over the course of my higher education I had developed an interest in history, majoring in that discipline as well as religious studies. Wayne Flynt, noted southern historian and author of another essay in this volume, became a significant mentor in college. I was not his best student and was still more "preacher boy" than young historian. Still, he was the first professor to sit across from me and say, "You're a good student, Mr. Manis," and inspire me with his knowledge and his interest in me as a person. He and other professors nurtured my growing interest in church history. Once in the seminary I encountered E. Glenn Hinson, Walter B. Shurden, and Bill J. Leonard, who approached American religious history as classical church historians but, like Flynt, taught me the interactions of church and culture. Implicitly they agreed with James Baldwin's comment that "[white people] are, in effect, still trapped in a history which they do not understand; and until they understand it, they cannot be released from it."[2]

By the end of my first year in the seminary, I had decided that I would pursue a Ph.D. in church history. At that point I had not yet determined whether my "calling" would take me into the church or the academy. I was clear, however, that I would be a historian regardless of the direction I ultimately chose or which eventually chose me. That spring NBC broadcast a television movie on the life of King. Mesmerized by images of the infamous police dogs and fire hoses, I decided on a topic for a research paper for a course in Baptist history: Southern Baptist responses to King's assassination. The result was a rather preachy essay, full of a good deal of self-righteous denunciation of my racist co-religionists. Still, my professor encouraged me to revise it and submit the piece for publication. To my great joy, the work was accepted and appeared in the Southern Baptist historical journal *Baptist History and Heritage.*[3]

While I worked on that paper I had an experience that would affect my scholarship for several years to come. I happened to visit my uncle who was an architect and building contractor in Cincinnati, Ohio. As we talked, I offhandedly mentioned my research topic, and he asked if I had ever heard of Fred Shuttlesworth. In his construction business, it turned out, my uncle had only recently built the sanctuary of the Greater New Light Baptist Church, where Shuttlesworth was pastor. Shuttlesworth had earlier been pastor of Birmingham's Bethel Baptist Church and president of the Alabama Christian Movement for Human Rights, the city's indigenous civil rights organization. His tooth and nail conflict with "Bull" Connor had led Martin Luther King's Southern Christian Leadership Conference to join forces with Shuttlesworth for the protests of 1963. Having recently read *Why We Can't Wait*, I answered that I did indeed know of Shuttlesworth. After a quick call and an hour's wait, Shuttlesworth appeared in my uncle's living room, where we began the first of many conversations about his life and experiences in the civil rights movement. I would later interview him while researching my dissertation.

At that point a wrenching personal experience would affect my scholarly interests. In January 1979, during my second year in seminary, my mother was diagnosed with terminal cancer. The disease had metastasized by the time it was discovered, and we all knew she would not live long. Almost immediately she left her home in Birmingham to be cared for by her sister in Tuscaloosa. For six weeks I commuted between Louisville and Tuscaloosa to be with her on weekends. One can have some rather important conversations with a mother who knows she is going to die, and those six weekends were important for what I learned about my family. In those times I was often alone with my mother and her sisters and brother. As grown siblings often do when they are together, they lapsed into long talks about their childhoods. They all venerated their father, who had died before I was born. The stories about him fascinated me, along with their tales about their own growing up in Birmingham.

Being Greek but no longer Greek Orthodox is an odd reality. To take this step was in large measure to lay aside a central element of my ethnic heritage. At times I had done so with a sense of good riddance. Leaving behind my family's religion and also marrying an "American" girl (as my parents called her) meant that retaining some semblance of my Greek heritage would be very difficult, particularly since my pilgrimage into southern (Baptist) religion had led me to devalue that heritage. Though there was great sadness in those weekends of watching my mother die, the result of those long family reminiscences was that I reconnected. Not too long before this I, like millions of others, had been moved by ABC television's broadcast of Alex Haley's *Roots*. Now I was powerfully reminded of the importance of my own roots.

At the same time, when my mother and I spoke of spiritual matters, I found in her an attachment to her Greek Orthodoxy that I had never seen before. Planning funerals, I have since learned, can do that to a person. I also found, however, traces of religious expression in her that I recognized as coming more from southern evangelicalism than from the classic Orthodox faith. I began to wonder about the ways being in the Bible Belt influenced the religiosity of Greek southerners. I wondered about relations between Orthodox priests and Protestant clergy. About Greek converts to southern Protestantism and American converts to Orthodoxy. About the many ways Greek Orthodox people adjusted not only to America but to the South and its religious ways, and what they shared with the accommodations of Catholics and Jews in the South. Thus, while part of my intellectual curiosity focused on the interactions of race and religion in the South, another more personal part of me vowed to spend part of my time learning about the immigrant experience of Greeks in the Bible Belt.

By then I had decided to extend my education into Ph.D. studies in the field of church history, with a specialization in American religious history. At the time, however, I still had not determined whether my vocational goal would be the pastorate or to land a teaching position. Neither did I know whether to pursue doctoral studies at Southern Seminary or to apply to other schools. Rather late in my senior year, having already been accepted into the program at the seminary, I began to understand more clearly how seminary Ph.D.s were less highly regarded in academe and thus much less attractive on the job market than doctorates earned in universities.

Most of the upper-echelon Baptist schools such as the University of Richmond or Wake Forest were loath to hire Ph.D.s from any of the Baptist seminaries, particularly since by that time the Fundamentalist takeover of the Southern Baptist Convention was well under way. Hoping to outgrow their own Southern Baptist roots, schools such as these were as hungry for Ivy League or University of Chicago Divinity School graduates, as were most religious studies departments at state universities. At the same time, the smaller Baptist schools were increasingly fearful of hiring graduates of the "liberal" Southern Seminary. I realized all this rather late in the game, so other than the program at SBTS, where I had already been accepted, I applied for entry in only one other program—at Emory University to work with southern religious historian Brooks Holifield, who had recently made a name for himself with the publication of *The Gentlemen Theologians*.[4] Unfortunately, Professor Holifield had only one spot available, and either my record did not measure up or he was more interested in students with interests in Puritanism. I did not get accepted at Emory but still was happy to be studying with Bill Leonard at SBTS.

Being a southerner significantly affected my interests and eventually my methodology as I began my graduate work. A distinctive element in my program at SBTS was a component known as University Work. Earlier, in the mid-1970s, when the seminary changed its Th.D. program to a Ph.D., some professors suggested adding a requirement that doctoral students take at least six graduate school hours of study in a Ph.D.-granting university, along with the course work required by the seminary. Ostensibly, this was designed in part to help counter the impression that seminary Ph.D.s were inferior to those earned at universities, though the effort never really worked. Still, I determined to try to make the system work for me by doing my work at the best program in American religion I could find. So in the fall of 1980 I left Louisville for a semester and enrolled as a special student at the University of Chicago Divinity School. I took two courses, one with famed American church historian Martin Marty and the other with one of his highly respected mentors, Jerald Brauer.

I entered into this adventure with great hopes and even greater insecurities. For the first time in my life, I spent time outside the South, at one of the great universities in the nation. There were a few southerners enrolled in the divinity school, but they were mostly past their graduate exams, and I rarely had opportunity to interact with them. To their credit, they encouraged me and hoped I would do well. Nevertheless, I struggled with my intellectual and regional identity. For the first time in my life, I was self-conscious of my southern accent and my pedigree from Southern Baptist schools.

Interestingly enough, the course I took with Brauer, Regionalism in American Religious History, played into this consciousness. As a southerner studying the influence of regionalism on American religion, I wrote for Brauer a paper that investigated the impact of Jeffersonianism on the perspective of Baptist evangelist John Leland. I argued that Leland, originally a New Englander, had been influenced by Jefferson during his fourteen-year sojourn in Virginia. There his views of church-state separation became more radical than the views of his fellow New England Baptist Isaac Backus. This paper became my second publication, which appeared the following year in the *American Baptist Quarterly*.[5]

That course and publication had more long-term effects on my interest and methodology by focusing my historical interests on southern religion. I decided that whatever dissertation topic I ultimately chose, it would be related to the southern experience. This decision came partly because of the specific concerns of Brauer's course and, just as significantly, partly from my own experience of wrestling with my southernness in a place like Chicago. Soon I hit on what I thought would be an important contribution to American and southern religious history. Coming from Chicago, where Americanists often wrote on the subject of civil religion and did so with the insights of sociology of religion and the history of religions approach of Mircea Eliade, I excitedly returned to Louisville prepared to apply that methodology to southern and Southern Baptist historiography. I would write a dissertation on civil religion in the American South.

About a month later, while browsing through a bookstore, my heart fell as I discovered that I had been scooped. The University of Georgia Press had just brought out Charles Reagan Wilson's now classic study *Baptized in Blood: The Religion of the Lost Cause, 1865–1920*. At least my instincts were right about how important a contribution such a work might be, but I would have to look elsewhere for my own dissertation topic. The next year, however, I reviewed the book for our American religion colloquium. About the same time, I attended my first meeting of the Southern Historical Association (SHA), which by chance met in Louisville that year.

None of my professors or grad school classmates attended the meeting, an indication that they were less interested in doing Southern Baptist history within the context of southern historiography. Up until that time, most such historiography tended to be focused on denominational sources. This did not mean my Southern Seminary mentors were uncritical interpreters of American or Baptist church history. It did mean that they were not secularly trained historians, in touch with those historians who studied the South in places like Chapel Hill or Vanderbilt. This would soon change, as my doctoral adviser Bill Leonard, trained as a church historian at Boston University, would be quickly converted and would encourage me to branch out into the methodology more representative of the SHA and to move away from that of the purely Baptist historians.

At the SHA that year, my college mentor Wayne Flynt introduced me to the godfather of southern religious history, Samuel S. Hill Jr., and a younger professor from the University of Mississippi named Charles Reagan Wilson. After a friendly conversation with Wilson, I ventured to tell him I had recently reviewed his book. He graciously asked me to send him a copy of my review, which I did. I quibbled with certain details of his argument but, more important, asked him where I might focus another study of civil religion in the South. He suggested that someone might do well to see how the themes he discussed in the aftermath of Reconstruction were revisited and reformed during the Second Reconstruction, during the 1950s and '60s. Trying this idea out on my graduate committee, I was encouraged to pursue it as a dissertation that was entitled "Civil Religion in the South: Desegregation and Southern Images of America."

At first, like Wilson, I intended to survey the views of the big three white denominations in the South, the Methodists, the Presbyterians, and, of course, the Baptists. At the crucial point, however, when I had to have my prospectus approved, a faculty change put a new professor on my committee. Ethicist Glen Stassen, the son of frequent Republican presidential candidate Harold Stassen, suggested I could get his support for my topic more easily if I looked at black Baptist perspectives as well, contrasting them with those of their white co-religionists. My other professors agreed, and we settled on contrasting the images of America's role in the world as held by white Southern Baptists and black National Baptists.

As a result, I leaned heavily on the sociological and historical literature that had evaluated the American civil religion and applied it to what Wilson had called the southern civil religion. I argued that during the civil rights movement the South had to a great extent become a battleground of conflicting civil religions with competing understandings of America's divine mission to the world. Though they had a strong minority view, represented by what I called the Southern Baptist Convention's "progressive elite," most white Baptists saw America as God's chosen nation destined to embody the values and beliefs of white Protestant Christianity. By contrast, African American Baptists much more uniformly saw America as a chosen nation, but one whose divine calling was to enable the world to come to terms with racial and religious diversity. Looking back on that modest argument, I still see significant connections between the conflict of civil faiths fought out in the South during the civil rights movement and what came to be called the "culture wars" of the 1980s and '90s.[6]

After finishing my dissertation, I hit the job market fully expecting that I would wind up in the pastorate. Hoping against hope that I might land a teaching position, I put myself in the academic meat market known as the placement service of the American Academy of Religion, meeting that year in Chicago. I was interviewed for a three-year replacement position at Xavier University in New Orleans. A black Catholic university was the last place I expected would hire a Greek Southern Baptist with a seminary Ph.D. Ordinarily that would have been accurate. But in this case, luck (or providence, if you will) would have it that the person to be replaced at Xavier was taking a leave of absence to earn a Th.D. at, of all places, the New Orleans Baptist Theological Seminary. That made the rest of the department more open to my candidacy, along with the fact that I had written on the civil rights movement and taught part-time at the African American Baptist Simmons Bible College in Louisville.

Teaching in an African American context, and hoping to convince Xavier to offer me a tenure-track position, I decided to concentrate on African American religion and thus began casting about for a new research topic. Spending the summer of 1986 studying that subject at Princeton University with Albert Raboteau, David Wills of Amherst College, Preston Williams of Harvard Divinity School, and the late James M. Washington of Union Theological Seminary, I asked them if they thought a biography of Fred Shuttlesworth might be a worthy project. Williams said Shuttlesworth had been one of his boyhood heroes, and along with the others, he encouraged me to pursue the idea.

Because Shuttlesworth had been, in his words, "a fighter, not a writer," the "Shuttlesworth corpus" was very small. He wrote fairly little, so studying him would require significant amounts of oral history research. Many interviews with him would be necessary, which would dictate that the interviewer had to be someone he trusted. Having developed an entrée with him while in the seminary, I was well positioned to do the research. In addition, I think it interested him that a white Southern Baptist minister from Birmingham would write his story. He thus encouraged me to proceed, gave me permission to investigate FBI files on him, spent some seventy hours with me in interviews, and even asked me to preach in his pulpit.

More significant, perhaps, I wanted this book to reflect a balance between his life as an African American Baptist pastor and his role as a civil rights leader. It would be easy to let his civil rights life completely overshadow his pastoral role, and to some extent I succumbed to the temptation. His exploits in the civil rights movement are, at least to surviving participants, legendary. Almost to a person, they will say that no one in the movement showed more courage than Fred Shuttlesworth. But he still must be interpreted in the context of his rural southern upbringing and his context within African American religion. He thus is an unalloyed representative of southern black folk religion. Theologian James H. Evans Jr. has written of the "heavenly fire" of black Christianity, even as philosopher and social critic Cornel West has drawn attention to what he calls a "combative spirituality," by which he means a joyful eagerness to foment and capitalize on opportunities for liberation. Fred Shuttlesworth clearly embodied both these elements—"heavenly fire" and "combative spirituality."[7]

The work was fascinating largely because of Shuttlesworth's charisma. One could easily see how his persona would captivate his followers in Birmingham. But the work was very slow and painstaking. Interviewing Shuttlesworth, his family, his church members, his followers in the movement, along with a few of his opponents, was exceedingly time consuming, as was the task of researching the relevant primary and secondary sources. In addition, teaching in a small college meant four courses per semester with little release time for my pet projects. At times I despaired of ever finishing the work, which ultimately stretched into a twelve-year effort. But what always moved me to press on was the combination of natural interest in the person I was writing about and a white Birminghamian's almost religious need for redemption. Others call it liberal guilt. So be it. Being a white southerner has fueled my interest in telling this part of a story that engulfed my childhood and has lasted well into my adulthood. More than anything else, being a southerner has shaped what I have studied and why I have studied it.

David Garrow, who himself has spent a good deal of time studying Martin Luther King Jr., has said that without an emotional connection with the subject, little important history gets written. "You have to have an emotional connection, not just an academic interest, in the subject you're writing about," Garrow explained. "And you have to believe there is an untold part of the history which at least for some people will be truly emotionally motivating."[8] What has led a Massachusetts Yankee like Garrow to devote so much of his time to the southern civil rights movement I do not know. But being a white

Birminghamian has made the interaction of race and religion in the South emotionally motivating for me for more than twenty years. Being a *Greek* Birminghamian will spark my next round of research, as I expand my interest in ethnic religious groups in the South. How did being Greek immigrants in the American South reshape the faith of the people who brought me into this world? Now, almost twenty years after my mother's death reconnected me to my ethnic origins, I still do not know many of the answers to that question. After so long, it is time I started finding out.

Notes

1. Martin Luther King Jr., *Why We Can't Wait* (New York: New American Library, 1963), 90–91.

2. James Baldwin, *The Fire Next Time* (1963; rpt., New York: Vintage Books, 1993).

3. Andrew M. Manis, "Silence or Shockwaves: Southern Baptist Responses to the Assassination of Martin Luther King Jr.," *Baptist History and Heritage* 15 (Oct. 1980): 19–27, 35.

4. E. Brooks Holifield, *The Gentlemen Theologians: American Theology in Southern Culture, 1795–1860* (Durham: Duke University Press, 1978).

5. Andrew M. Manis, "Regionalism and a Baptist Perspective on Separation of Church and State," *American Baptist Quarterly* 2 (Sept. 1983): 213–27.

6. The 1984 dissertation was slightly revised and published as Andrew M. Manis, *Southern Civil Religions in Conflict: Black and White Baptists and Civil Rights, 1947–1957* (Athens: University of Georgia Press, 1987).

7. James H. Evans Jr., *We Have Been Believers: An African-American Systematic Theology* (Minneapolis: Fortress Press, 1992), 2; Cornel West, *Prophetic Fragments* (Grand Rapids, Mich.: William B. Eerdmans, 1988), 6; Carlyle Fielding Stewart III, *Soul Survivors: An African American Spirituality* (Louisville: Westminster John Knox Press, 1997), 5. See also Andrew M. Manis, *A Fire You Can't Put Out: The Civil Rights Life of Birmingham's Reverend Fred Shuttlesworth* (Tuscaloosa: University of Alabama Press, 1999); Marjorie White and Andrew M. Manis, eds., *Birmingham Revolutionaries: Reverend Fred Shuttlesworth and the Alabama Christian Movement for Human Rights* (Macon, Ga.: Mercer University Press, 2000).

8. John D. Thomas, "David J. Garrow: Examining Individual Rights," in "Speaking Out," *Emory Magazine* 74 (spring 1998) www.emory.edu/EMORY_MAGAZINE/spring98/scholars.html (19 Aug. 2000).

Gospel of Disunion:
A Spiritual Autobiography

Mitchell Snay

Rabbi Mescheloff spoke in a voice that was stern if forgiving. "One day," he warned, "somebody will ask you about Judaism, and you will not be able to answer their questions." The rabbi was attempting to restore some discipline that had been sorely lacking at Hebrew School that day. A few of us had locked the door from the inside of our classroom and escaped out the back windows. On crisp autumn afternoons, buying candy and playing football were more appealing to grade school children than learning the Hebrew alphabet or reading Old Testament stories. Because our immediate world was so Jewish and because we were so young, the future value of a sound Jewish education was difficult to fathom.

Almost two decades later, Rabbi Mescheloff's words came back to haunt me while I was engaged in dissertation research at the Presbyterian archives in Montreat, North Carolina. As I stood in front of the cash register at the local store, I was greeted with hospitality and some apparent curiosity by the proprietor, who correctly recognized that I was a stranger. When he asked me if I were a student at the nearby Presbyterian college, I explained that I was there for research. A handshake and more formal introduction quickly followed. Almost abruptly, the man asked me if I was Jewish. Startled by the inquiry and honestly thinking that he, too, might be Jewish, I answered "Yes. Are you?" He replied no. After a brief hesitation, he added, "I'm an American." My collective ethnic unconsciousness immediately surfaced with specters of inquisitions, pogroms, and nocturnal visits from local Klansmen. But before my imagination ran totally away from me, he assuaged my fears with the reassuring comment: "I guess you're an American, too." The conversation continued awkwardly as he probed further into my religious background. "What tribe are you from?" he asked. What tribe was I from? What was he talking about? Ignorant both of the Lost Tribes of ancient Israel and what might have been his own understanding of biblical history, I could only associate that word with Apaches, Crows, or Shoshones. It was then that I regretted my lack of discipline at Hebrew School and wished that I did indeed know more about Judaism. Mercifully, our conversation, undoubtedly disappointing to us both, ended soon thereafter.

This story is one of several that arose from the fact that a Jewish historian was writing about southern evangelical Protestantism. I better appreciate now the ironies and perhaps contradictions of this situation and now find them somehow appropriate for a scholarly field dominated by the voices of C. Vann Woodward and Eugene D. Genovese. When I began working on my dissertation in 1979, I was unaware of any significant connection between my own Judaism and my writing of history. Indeed, I think I unconsciously sought out a topic that was far afield from anything I held personally dear. Though I would have explained this then by holding fast to an ideal of professional detachment, there was undoubtedly an ambivalence over my own religious and ethnic identity lurking further beneath the surface. When my high school girlfriend was training to become a psychiatric social worker years later, she once remarked that there had to be *some* reason why I chose to write about what I had. And a talented student of mine at Denison University, who used my book for an essay in her historiography class, suggested along similar lines that religion *was* important to me.

With almost twenty years of hindsight and with the growing importance of Judaism in my current life, I now believe that my own religious background did influence the writing of *Gospel of Disunion*. Yet there were other and equally significant factors in the creation of the book. My dissertation was conceived at a specific point in historiographical time and reflects those current trends in historical writing. The personal influence of my adviser was decisive. Finally, several key books served as inspirations and models. And undoubtedly, there were influences of which even today I remain unaware.

There is reluctance along with pride in being asked to contribute to this collection. I have never considered *Gospel of Disunion* that important or influential a book to deserve an autobiographical accounting. Nor has it generated the kind of controversy or invited the kinds of challenges that would merit a historiographical essay. Yet for several reasons, the narrative of how I came to write my study of religion and the rise of southern separatism might be worth the effort. A dear friend and colleague reminds me that we all have stories worth telling. Postmodernists have been arguing that all history is constructed, and there indeed seems to be a greater willingness among historians to discuss how their personal pasts shaped their history.[1] Moreover, I believe that the story of *Gospel of Disunion* raises some issues in the field of southern religious history and thus might help future students of the subject.

I grew up in a neighborhood in Chicago where being Jewish, Democratic, and a Cubs fan were unchallenged articles of faith that were passed down generationally in an almost genetic-like fashion. It was in this strongly ethnic community on Chicago's north side, where Rabbi Mescheloff's and dozens of other synagogues dotted the landscape, that the seeds of *Gospel of Disunion* might well have been planted. It was an environment that shaped my understanding of the social and cultural dynamics of religion.

The Jews who came to Chicago were part of the larger stream of Eastern European Jewish immigrants who flooded urban America during the late nineteenth and early twentieth centuries. The approximately two million Jews from the *shtetlach* (villages) of Eastern Europe and Russia settled on the west side of the city and there began the transplantation of traditional Judaism to America. The area around Maxwell Street abounded with kosher meat markets, peddlers' stables, and bakeries. A strong institutional network that included Yiddish newspapers and theaters flourished. (Jane Addams's Hull House catered to the Eastern European Jews of Chicago). More than forty synagogues were scattered through the Maxwell Street area. My grandfather attended Anshe Kanesses Israel, also known as the *Russiche Shul* (Russian synagogue). The Eastern European Jews who settled on the west side of Chicago created a vibrant immigrant community whose sons included actor Paul Muni, musician Benny Goodman, Admiral Hyman G. Rickover, and Supreme Court Justice Arthur Goldberg.[2]

After World War I, upwardly mobile Jewish immigrants moved with their institutions to the Douglas Park area of Chicago's west side. It was here where my parents grew up. Like thousands of other first-generation Americans, my parents then moved from the west side to a neighborhood called West Rogers Park. Located on the northern and western fringes of the city, West Rogers Park was the heart of Chicago's Jewish community during my childhood. Most of

the homes were either modest one-family houses or three-floor apartment buildings set close together on shaded streets. Although there was still much vacant
land in 1940, the Jewish population of West Rogers Park grew dramatically in
the post–World War II era. By 1963 there were an estimated 48,000 Jews living
in West Rogers Park, which constituted roughly three-fourths of the total population of the neighborhood. Though the number of Jewish families has declined
during the past three decades, West Rogers Park still claims the greatest concentration of Jews in Chicago. There had been a strong line of continuity in
the movement of immigrants. Many synagogues bear the names of those established in the Maxwell Street area. Today West Rogers Park embraces more than
fifty Jewish institutions. California Avenue, across the alley from my old house,
contains a Zionist center, eight synagogues, two Hebrew elementary schools,
and a home for the Jewish aged. Ultra-Orthodox Jews with their traditional at-
tire of long black coats and black hats fill the sidewalks on Sabbath mornings.
For these reasons, one rabbi characterized West Rogers Park as "the last bastion
of neighborhood Judaism in the city." Or as an observer of Chicago politics
noted, "The preferred fish [here] is gefilte, not catfish or trout."[3]

With some unavoidable doubt and uncertainty, I can discern several ways in
which my Jewish, urban, middle-class background might have influenced my
scholarly study of antebellum southern religion. First, it shaped my understanding of religion. In such an ethnically and religiously homogeneous neighborhood as West Rogers Park (where the local public schools essentially closed for
the Jewish holidays), I instinctively sensed the importance of religion as a cultural and social force. Since my experience of Judaism was deeply imbedded
in a particular social and cultural context, I became inclined to think of religion more in terms of community and identity rather than a personal relationship with God, which perhaps made me more receptive to sociological approaches to religious history. In our home, for example, my mother dutifully lit
the *Shabbat* candles every Friday night, though we did little else as a family to
follow Jewish rituals. I also wonder if my personal inclination toward scholarship was reinforced by the importance traditional Judaism placed on learning.
In the orthodox communities of Eastern Europe, Jewish men read and studied
the Torah at *yeshivas* (schools). While much of the rigid orthodoxy of Judaism
was lost in the transformation of Eastern European Jews into Americans, the
spirit and rigor of Talmudic study survived in the urban colleges and universi-

ties that emerged in response to the Jewish emphasis on education. Though commercial success was the key to the immigrant's upward mobility, education was truly valued. Advanced degrees and academic professors were held in high esteem.[4]

Finally, my religious and ethnic background supported leftist political views current in the late 1960s. The penchant of Jewish immigrants toward labor activism in the early twentieth century has been well documented. In my personal history, my maternal grandfather was a founder of the painters' union in Chicago, whereas my father's father was a reader of the New Republic who flirted with socialism during the 1920s. Whatever "critical" approach to social and economic institutions I acquired from my heritage was strongly reinforced by the radical protest movements of the 1960s. After four years of college in Ann Arbor, Michigan, I was even more disposed toward New Left history and a Marxist interpretation of the slaveholding South.

Perhaps most important, my social upbringing provided me with a profound sense of cultural identity. The peculiar historical circumstances that produced West Rogers Park in the 1960s created in its people a strong sense of belonging to a particular neighborhood, religion, and ethnic group. Gospel of Disunion is a book that was written about identity. It is perhaps not surprising that the intimate relationship between personal and communal identity I experienced growing up would lead to a study of how southerners at a certain time in history developed a sense of self-consciousness and separateness that made secession and Civil War possible.[5]

Growing up in Chicago also taught me about race. The lessons I learned there provided one lens though which I viewed the complexities of southern race relations in the nineteenth century. When I was a child, an African American woman named Alice would come to our house three days a week to help my mother clean. Alice was originally from Hattiesburg, Mississippi. Years before, Alice's mother had hastily put Alice and her brother on a train north to avoid the southern consequences of his "uppity" behavior toward a white woman. I liked Alice for her warmth and kindnesses to me and found her presence in the house inexplicably reassuring. She would always hang her purse in the stairwell to the basement, where I had acquired "customary rights" to go into her purse for chewing gum. One day, Alice accused me of stealing money from her purse. A few days later she no longer worked for my mother. It is still painful to recall feeling why I had been wrongfully accused of stealing and why Alice would no longer speak to me. Years later my mother explained that Alice did not want to work for us anymore and that she had fabricated the story of stealing to avoid the pain of saying goodbye. The hidden structures of subordination and construction of a "true" narrative imbedded in this story are perhaps disturbingly familiar to students of the nineteenth-century South.

Alice personified a practice of domestic service widespread in our neighborhood, where African American women worked for daily wages in Jewish middle-class homes. They had to commute sometimes hours each way from the south side. My perception at the time was that racial relations between housewives and domestics were friendly and benevolent. My outgrown clothing would be given to Alice's children to wear. It was not uncommon to see a few African Americans at bar and bat mitzvahs as our maids became part of the family. Yet the structure of labor and race relations was clearly hierarchical. In conversations, it was "Alice and Mrs. Snay" rather than "Mrs. Merritt and Mrs. Snay" or "Alice and Lillian." Most disturbing was the use of the word *schvartza*, derived from the Yiddish word for black, to describe these women. Despite denials from our parents' generation, the connotations were as racist as the "N-word."

Alice and a few other maids who worked for my mother were one avenue of contact I had with African Americans. There were others as well. Recapturing these memories and understanding their influence on my approach to southern religious history is a difficult and elusive task. For alongside a hatred of prejudice and a genuine commitment to human equality that I learned both at home and school was a fear of black people too often manifested in distrust and enmity.

Important demographic changes help explain Jewish racial attitudes during the post–World War II era. Chicago was then and remains today a largely segregated city where most African Americans live on the south and west sides. In my youth, the west side (not far from Maxwell Street) was beginning its tragic decline into urban poverty and violence and was continually portrayed as a dangerous place. The south side was equally distant in geographical terms but closer in cultural ones. Hyde Park was home not only to the University of Chicago but to the older and wealthier German Jews who arrived in the early and mid-nineteenth century. The South Shore, which included those neighborhoods surrounding 79th Street, had a considerable Jewish population. Beginning in the 1950s, however, African Americans who worked in the steel mills of Gary, Indiana, and South Chicago gradually began to migrate northward into this area. The black population of the South Shore, which had been less than 1 percent in 1950, had grown to 70 percent two decades later. By 1970 most middle-class Jews had migrated with their businesses and families either to West Rogers Park or the northern suburbs of Chicago.[6] My own memories accord with these facts of historical geography. I would occasionally visit friends from summer camp who lived in the South Shore but was told to "be careful" in walking down 79th Street. It was from these friends that I first heard the tales about the feared street gang, the Blackstone Rangers. By my first year of high school in 1967, a growing number of self-styled Jewish exiles from the south side were moving into the neighborhood with an unfortunate bitterness toward blacks, who were blamed for forcing them out of their businesses and homes.

Demographic factors provided one context in which my understanding of race developed. My parents' high personal integrity, the respect shown to individuals in my home, and the civil rights, antiwar, and urban antipoverty programs strongly inclined me toward more radical critiques of American race relations. Perhaps like many budding historians at that time, I saw in the writing and teaching of American history an opportunity for moving people toward an acceptance of racial equality. In fact, abolitionism was my real love as an undergraduate history major. My senior thesis at Michigan was a study of the antislavery thought of Zebina Eastman, an Illinois Republican editor of the 1850s. My first-year paper at Brandeis was a prosopographical study of the founders of the New England Anti-Slavery Society. One of my fellow graduate students jokingly advertised an end-of-the-year excursion to Newburyport, Massachusetts, with the promise of seeing Mitchell Snay at the shrine of William Lloyd Garrison's birthplace. It was Garrison the radical rather than evangelical abolitionists like Theodore Dwight Weld who drew my respect and affection. At least at this stage in my professional development, religion had not yet surfaced in my historical concerns. How a neo-abolitionist eventually wrote a book on proslavery clergymen still defies a suitable explanation.

By providing the earliest setting for developing attitudes toward religion and race, my Jewish upbringing in Chicago during the late 1950s and early 1960s left an important, if often indiscernible, mark on my study of southern religious history. Ultimately, however, the decisions surrounding my dissertation were primarily intellectual ones made in an academic setting. The questions I asked and the methods I used reflected not only my own personal scholarly development at that time but the historiographical trends of the late 1970s. Exploring the intellectual origins of *Gospel of Disunion* is once again an act of construction beset inevitably by lapses of memories and moments of self-conscious creation.

Although my choice of a dissertation topic was a prolonged process with seemingly endless detours and dead ends, it was clear that I would be writing about the "Middle Period" of American history (ca. 1815–77). After a six-month sabbatical working on a political campaign, I returned to Brandeis late in 1978 and began reading some selected monographs on the impact of the Civil War on northern society and culture. (Since community studies were then the rage, my initial thought was to trace a northern community from the 1850s through the end of Reconstruction.) In looking for other examples of state or local studies, I soon encountered J. Mills Thornton III's *Politics and Power in a Slave Society: Alabama, 1800–1860* (1978). That book changed the course of my academic career.[7]

First, it marked my conversion to southern history. Though I had dutifully read the major works on slavery and the antebellum South, I did not consider myself a southern historian. I had read C. Vann Woodward's *Origins of the New South* as one of the proclaimed "classics" in American history yet had little comprehension then of the power of the book or its author's heart and mind. None of the faculty in the Brandeis Ph.D. program really specialized in southern history. Among my contemporary fellow graduate students only Raymond O. Arsenault had written on the South, and he had left Brandeis soon after I arrived. In other words, there was little institutional encouragement to pursue southern history. Nor was there much of a personal incentive. I had grown up in the urban North, and up to that point my only time spent in the South had been visiting my girlfriend of the time, whose parents lived in a suburb of Birmingham. Perhaps more often than any other question I have ever been asked as a historian is how I (as a northerner) came to write about the South. Though it is still a difficult question to answer, I was dimly aware at the time of wanting to write about something far removed from my personal concerns. I simply wanted a strong demarcation between my personal past and my present life as a historian.

Reading Thornton's book triggered other intellectual and practical dynamics. Obviously, the field would allow me to explore my broader interests in the Civil War era. In addition, southern history could give me a niche in the larger field of American history where I could stand apart from my fellow graduate students in the Boston area. But basically, I fell in love with the history of the South, the kind of rare passionate attachment that graces the life of a scholar. I devoured as many books and articles as possible. I could hardly wait to get up and read antebellum southern newspapers on microfilm.

Politics and Power in a Slave Society also suggested the kinds of questions I wanted to pursue in my own dissertation. Thornton argued for the need to see how the Civil War emerged from what we would now term the "context" of mid-nineteenth-century politics. If he were right and if the Civil War could best be explained by Jacksonian political culture, what other contexts could help explain secession? My reading in secondary sources suggested that the relationship between religion and southern sectionalism was worth pursuing. For one thing, religion had played a critical role in the coming of the American Revolution. There was little recent scholarly work on religion and the Civil War, and the books that were beginning to appear, such as Donald G. Mathews's *Religion in the Old South* (1977) and James H. Moorhead's *American Apocalypse: Yankee Protestants and the Civil War, 1860–1869* (1978), were evocative. On the basis of these readings and some sampling of primary sources, I began to formulate questions I thought both significant and answerable: What was the role of religion in the development of southern separatism before the Civil War? What were the possible points of interaction between parallel movements toward sectionalism and religious orthodoxy? How was the sectional controversy over slavery shaped by the religious context of the mid-nineteenth century? These questions provided the essential outline of the dissertation and remained the framework for the book.

Other intellectual influences converged to shape the dissertation. Foremost among these were the historical studies of ideology that had begun to eclipse the study of the nineteenth-century United States by the early 1970s. Ideology became an attractive concept to intellectual historians for several reasons. It was one way to move the history of ideas out of the exclusive realm of intellectuals to capture the attitudes and values of a larger population. Ideology could also show the impact of ideas since by definition it attempted to explain the link between thought and behavior. I was especially influenced by Eric Foner's *Free Soil, Free Labor, Free Men: The Ideology of the Republican Party before the Civil War* (1970). In my more ambitious moments, I had hoped my dissertation would do for the antebellum South what Foner had done for the pre–Civil War North. My inclination toward an ideological approach was also evident in some of my other favorite books in American history, such as Stanley M. Elkins's *Slavery* (1959) and Bernard Bailyn's *Ideological Origins of the American Revolution* (1967). Marvin Meyers, my dissertation adviser, exerted a decisive intellectual influence on *Gospel of Disunion*. His *Jacksonian Persuasion: Politics and Belief* (1957) was one of the seminal studies of ideology in nineteenth-century America written during the post–World War II era. I first read Meyers's book my freshman year in college, though its nuances, subtleties, and paradoxes escaped an untutored mind. Meyers's influence was conveyed in countless discussions of the dissertation and in the scribbled comments that filled the margins of my chapter drafts. Though my affection for him might prejudice my professional evaluation, I believe that Meyers was a excellent historian and that *Jacksonian Persuasion* is a great book. I also consider him brilliant, a word I reserve for only a few people I have met in my life. I would often leave his office or living room perplexed by comments and criticisms that I often understood only years later. Meyers taught me to think of history in terms of questions to be discovered and answered. The entire atmosphere in the Brandeis program in the 1970s encouraged us to go after the *big* questions. Most importantly, Meyers helped me to see that good history grapples with complexity. He pointed out the tensions and paradoxes in the writings of southern clergymen but forced me to look for the resolutions.

Since Marvin Meyers was a student of Richard Hofstadter's at Columbia, I have often fancied myself as the historiographical "grandson" of Hofstadter and believe that my book might be profitably read in this context. Hofstadter is most often considered part of the "consensus" school of American history, a group of historians who played down class conflict in American history and stressed the ideological consensus around the ideals of liberal capitalism. Like other consensus historians, Hofstadter seemed particularly concerned with the problems of a democratic society and polity. Beyond his elegant style, what attracted me to Hofstadter was his ability to identify significant problems in the American past and to apply rigorous thinking to resolving them.

One could make a suggestive case for the influence of Richard Hofstadter on *Gospel of Disunion*. In terms of direct lineage, Meyers might have passed on to me what he learned from writing under Hofstadter. It is not coincidental that the historians I admire most, like Meyers, Foner, Elkins, and Eric L. McKittrick, were also products of Hofstadter at Columbia. Since Hofstadter was interested in American political ideas, it is not surprising that his students pioneered new ways to understand how ideology worked in nineteenth-century American politics. Finally, Hofstadter was drawn to paradox. In *The Age of Reform*, he asked how Progressivism as a reform movement could succeed during a time of prosperity. Meyers's "venturous conservative" was similarly a study in paradox: how Jacksonian rhetoric could appeal to the past while moving toward the future. In my own far more modest way, *Gospel of Disunion* is an extended analysis of the paradox that southern clergymen entered the political realm to justify slavery on scriptural grounds while insisting that religion and politics were separate spheres. I have learned from my mentors that good history often begins with identifying a paradox worth unraveling.[8]

Acknowledging Hofstadter's influence on my historical writing does raise some interesting ironies. Hofstadter the historian was closely tied to Hofstadter the intellectual. That is, he sought in the study of American history those problems that engaged him and other New York intellectuals at the time, such as Lionel Trilling and C. Wright Mills. Hofstadter and I also shared an urban Jewish background, though his East Coast orientation seems more influential, as his critique of the Populists makes clear. As stated earlier, I began my dissertation without any conscious connection between my own personal or political concerns and my writing of history. If I was influenced by Hofstadter as a historical craftsman, I failed to see how he was engaged with the issues and concerns of his time.

During the summer of 1981, I spent a few weeks of dissertation research at the Southern Baptist Convention Library in Nashville. I was looking for the responses of local Baptist churches and state conventions throughout the South to the denominational schism of 1845. Slavery was the manifest cause of this split, which prefigured political secession by dividing the national denomination into northern and southern branches. I was discussing the schism late one afternoon with a fellow researcher, a dean from the Southern Baptist Theological Seminary in Louisville. After a careful review of the details of the schism and some thoughtful considerations, he concluded that the Southern Baptists were constitutionally right but morally wrong. I was struck profoundly at that moment by the fact that *I* did not care whether Southern Baptists were morally wrong or right. Once again, I was the dispassionate historian who sought the truth of the past and who possessed neither the time, understanding, nor wisdom to consider that moral issues from the past could still have meaning to others. My fellow researcher cared that the Southern Baptists had been morally wrong, while it was all history to me. Despite my blinders, I did have some recognition that he had to go back to parishioners, students, and perhaps himself to face the burdens of southern history.

In the spring of 1996 I was at Cambridge University commenting at a session of the annual meeting of the Southern Intellectual History Circle. SIHC, as it is affectionately referred to by its small membership, is a group of about thirty historians and literary scholars devoted to the study of the South. At each SIHC gathering, conversations turn inevitably to the nature and practice of writing southern history. People seem more eager to discuss the complex ways in which southerners "construct" their own identities and pasts. In Cambridge, historian Paul M. Gaston spoke passionately about the intellectual and personal influence on him of C. Vann Woodward. I learned afterward that Gaston had been physically injured in attempting to promote the civil rights movement in Charlottesville in the 1960s. It was then that I realized that perhaps it did make a difference if you were a southerner, something that had escaped me in Nashville in 1981. Fifteen years of both professional and personal maturity since my encounter in Nashville had led me to rethink the value of "dispassionate" history. I have begun to sense that perhaps I have missed something as a nonsouthern historian of the South: southern history, whether of the 1840s or the 1960s, matters very much to some people in ways I have not fully understood.

Writing this intellectual autobiography has led me to face my own uncertainties about the place of personal concerns in the writing of history. In what ways do our own engagements in contemporary issues shape the questions we ask of the past? How do they influence the way we select and read sources? To what extent should a strong personal voice be present in our writing? Listening to the voices of postmodernism, I am more open to the possibility that the personal voice adds an energy and richness often lacking in works of scholarship.

A friend of mine once remarked that all great history in some way addresses the human condition. There are thus advantages to southerners telling their own stories. Perhaps history is more compelling when the rage to explain is more pressing. Southerners who came of age during the civil rights movement would seem to have more of a stake in the history of southern race relations than outsiders. Because of their own personal experience, they might feel the real tension between Christian ideals and segregation. At times, I have even sensed in some of my more thoughtful colleagues a feeling of guilt for their own complicity in poisoned race relations.

My current involvement with Temple Israel in Columbus, Ohio, has given me new insights into the limitations of my approach to southern religious history. I formally joined the synagogue in the fall of 1995. I had gone there in observance of the High Holidays for years and was beginning to feel guilty for not paying dues. I had taken my eighteen-month-old son, Elliott, to their parent-toddler play group and enjoyed the congregants I met there. I also liked Temple Israel for what one rabbi termed "the aesthetics of worship"—it simply looked and felt like the synagogue I attended as a child. Perhaps more than anything else, I joined because I wanted Elliott to grow up with a strong presence of Judaism in his life, and I knew that the world of West Rogers Park could not be replicated.

When my son and I did join in 1995, Temple Israel had a recently troubled past. Membership over the last few decades had dropped precipitously, and bitter factionalism over the previous rabbi was still evident. In his wisdom, the new rabbi insisted that the temple go though a formal healing process with the help of clerical professionals. The term in Hebrew was *beresheit*, or "new beginnings." Any such communal self-reflection was bound to be painful. Many congregants expressed feelings of anger, hurt, and resentment. What struck me more than anything else while listening to those sessions, however, was the depth of the feelings. The expression "temple family" took on a new meaning to me, because the emotional intensity manifested in these meetings suggested that being part of a religious congregation seemed to mean very much to a large number of people. Ever the historian, I began to wonder if congregations in the past had evoked similar feelings among their members. What followed was a growing realization that something was missing in the way I and other scholars had written about the history of religion.

When I began to look into southern religious history in the late 1970s, most of the work seemed to have been written by church historians interested in formal theology and denominational structures. With a few exceptions, the vitality and creativity brought to the study of New England Puritanism was absent in the study of southern religion. In addition, current works at the time, like Paul E. Johnson's *Shopkeeper's Millennium* (1978), which linked the rise of evangelical Protestantism to the processes of capitalistic development and class formation in the antebellum North, had no counterparts for the South. The older denominational histories had tended to compartmentalize religious history, isolating it from the mainstream of American history. The limitations of the "new religious history" were more difficult to see. At the risk of oversimplification and generalization, I feel that much of this new religious history has not attempted to understand religion on its own terms and in its own historical context. There seems to be a tendency to use religion as a vehicle to examine other social or cultural changes. The assumption is that religion is less important than other—implicitly more important—economic, social, or cultural dynamics in history. Interpreting religion as an ideology obscured as much as it illuminated.

I fear this was partially true for *Gospel of Disunion*. Religion was an accessible and revealing way to explore the intellectual origins of southern nationalism. Though I served my time reading through the *Southern Presbyterian Review* and *Methodist Quarterly Review*, I never really gained a command of antebellum southern theology.[9] My initial hope was to deeply immerse myself in the corpus of southern Protestant thought and look at the sectional controversy through the eyes of southern ministers. This goal was never fully realized. Were I to conceive such a study now, I would be more open to the multiple levels on which religion operates.

My dissatisfaction with my own and other books has led me to believe that in many ways the religious history of the American people has yet to be written. My adult experience as an involved Jew has suggested what such a religious history might look like. First, religious congregations merit the kind of close attention colonial New England towns received almost thirty years ago. How did the church as an institution mediate in social relationships? How did congregations function as a community? What did church membership mean to individuals? The records from the antebellum South probably permit a good degree of church reconstruction. Secondly, historians need to devise creative ways to recover the spiritual dimensions of individual religiosity in the past. This line of inquiry poses more difficult obstacles. If it is true that many historians are secular-minded academics, how can we take seriously men and women of the past who felt God as a presence in their lives? Is it possible to avoid a patronizing approach that either looks for "underlying" reasons or reifies the lives of the ordinary?

Like most works of history, *Gospel of Disunion* was a product of its time. It sought to show the role religion played in the development of antebellum southern sectionalism. It was concerned with the intellectual origins of the Civil War. On these levels, I like the book, see its imperfections, but remain proud to be its author. Years of reflection and personal growth, closely tied to my involvement with Judaism and the Jewish community, have made me increasingly aware of the influence that my upbringing had on my writing of the book. I grew up with a strong sense of place, an identification with a closely bounded community, and a deep historical consciousness that goes a bit further back than Appomattox. During all the years of researching and writing *Gospel of Disunion*, I was often reminded of the manifest differences between myself and my subject. Yet my deep attachment to my roots and my recognition of the intimate connection between my personal and collective identity might make it easier to explain why I became a historian of the South.

Notes

1. For instance, Drew Gilpin Faust, *Mothers of Invention: Women of the Slaveholding South in the American Civil War* (Chapel Hill: University of North Carolina Press, 1996), xi–xii.

2. Irving Cutler, *The Jews of Chicago: From Shtetl to Suburb* (Urbana: University of Illinois Press, 1996), 40–102.

3. This description of West Rogers Park was compiled from Cutler, *The Jews of Chicago*, 249–54. A brief discussion of the 50th Ward of Chicago, which closely coincides with West Rogers Park, can be found in David K. Fremon, *Chicago Politics Ward by Ward* (Bloomington: Indiana University Press, 1988), 334–39. The last quote is from Fremon, 335.

4. The impact of immigration upon traditional Judaism is explored by novelist Abraham Cahan in *The Rise of David Levinsky* (1917; rpt., New York: Harper and Row, 1960).

5. Gerda Lerner, in *Why History Matters: Life and Thought* (New York: Oxford University Press, 1997), also discusses the importance of Judaism in her life as a historian, especially 1–55.

6. Cutler, *Jews of Chicago*, 207.

7. Mills and his wife Brenda are now good friends of mine. It was a great pleasure a few years ago to share with him the impact his work had on my budding career as a historian.

8. A good essay on Hofstadter is Daniel Joseph Singal, "Beyond Consensus: Richard Hofstadter and American Historiography," *American Historical Review* 89 (Oct. 1984): 976–1004. See also Gene Wise, *American Historical Explanations: A Strategy for Grounded Inquiry* (Minneapolis: University of Minnesota Press, 1980), especially 241–43.

9. A point made to me by Eugene D. Genovese, who, to his credit, takes the history of southern theology seriously.

Southern Fried Grace

Lynn Lyerly

I first read William Faulkner's *The Sound and the Fury* in tenth grade. The year, 1976, was a momentous one for me, for it was when long-festering racial tensions at my high school erupted in a riot. In that climate, the novel was bound up with not just the southern past that haunted Quentin Compson but the southern present that haunted me. Quentin *became* the South for me, always burdened by the past, unable to envision a future. White women were all like Caddy, forever confined by impossible standards of southern womanhood. Black southerners, like Dilsey, could hope, at best, to endure. The only potential for deliverance lay with Benjy, who loved without regard to color or gender or class. And if the idiot represented the South's only chance, we were, indeed, doomed. The Easter service at the end of the novel was not redemptive but tragic, since the South seemed bent on slaughtering its saviors (the memory of 1968 haunted, too). I filled page after page in my diary, trying to find words to explain what had happened in my high school, and when my words did not explain, I knew why: Faulkner had said it all, and he said it better.

Today (it is twenty-five years later, and I live in the most northern of cities, Boston), I no longer believe Faulkner said everything there was to say about the South, and could not, for I study and write about the South for a living. But I do not laugh at the conclusions I drew in 1976, either, for my formative years were ones in which it was hard to be optimistic about change, and there were always more questions than answers. What follows is my attempt to isolate the past experiences that bear on my scholarship and to examine the ways I interpreted them. As I worked on this essay, though, I realized how my scholarship has allowed me to explore the questions I have been asking all my life in a remote, sometimes alien, South. In some ways, then, this is also the story of how

I came to terms with the all-knowing, honeysuckle-scented, doom-spelling ghost of William Faulkner.

In Hickory, North Carolina, Lutherans were religiously suspended some-where between the evangelical center and the marginalized.[1] The one Jew in my grade had to endure many a supposedly "ecumenical" prayer at school func-tions, prayers that invariably ended with "In the name of the Father, the Son, and the Holy Ghost." If being asked if I was "saved" was tough for me, it must have been truly alienating for him. My friend Cindy, the lone Mennonite in our high school, whose white cap and mid-calf length skirts ("She can't wear shorts, even for gym class!" everyone would whisper) evoked snickers and taunts. When the first Mormon family moved into the neighborhood, they were the center of excited speculation. Were Mormons "really" Christians? Would there soon be clean-cut missionaries at every door? Had the Mormon rank and file finally renounced polygamy in their hearts? Then there were the slightly more numerous Unitarians and Roman Catholics, and I would be hard-pressed to say which group the Protestant majority of the town found more heretical. The Unitarians seemed to be considered traitors from within, Protestants who had fallen away from the Trinitarian truth. The Catholics were seen as misguided, of course, but since they had not rejected the divinity of Jesus, they were toler-ated in most ways. There were two Catholic errors, however, that could not be forgiven by Hickory Protestants. The first, universally condemned, was their "worship" of Mary, who occupied too high a place (so said Protestants) in the Catholic cosmology. I wish I had probed enough to find out whether it was the elevation of a woman that irritated everyone or whether it was, as non-Catholics claimed, a theological dispute over the place of intercessors and a commitment to the priesthood of all believers. The second objection was the province of moderate and liberal Protestant women: if a pregnant Catholic woman were in danger of dying in childbirth, the priest would counsel that the baby be saved. Before the abortion wars, every older woman I knew had a "friend of a friend" tale in which a Protestant was in the hospital about to deliver and in the next bed was a Catholic mother condemned to die by her callous priest. There simply were not enough Catholic women in Hickory for all of these sto-ries to be true.

Being Lutheran, in this context, was not all that difficult.

Yet Lutherans were different. We knew it, and so did all the non-Lutherans.

Most obviously, we were not "born again," and as such we were targets for pros-
elytizing. Some efforts to "save" us were condescending, but many were heartfelt. An earnest friend invited me to a tent revival meeting when I was in junior
high. I loved the music, the clapping, the show, the hot humid air under the
tent, even the preacher's sing-song style of delivery. My friend and her parents
smiled encouragingly at me when the preacher made his altar call. The atmosphere was contagious, and I had been informed my friend would receive some
sort of recognition for any souls she helped lead to the light: I wanted to go. But
I also knew that to volunteer to be prayed for was to acknowledge what the
evangelicals said about Lutherans being deluded.

We were, after all, still too Catholic. Our errors included recital of the liturgy, our use of wine during communion, the different vestments for the different days of the church calendar, and our constant shift between kneeling, standing, sitting. It did not help that the intricacies of Lutheran doctrine could not
easily be explained by a child. I understood why Luther protested the indul-
gences and nailed the ninety-five theses to the church door in Wittenberg. I
knew that we believed every adherent was a "saint" (the lack of capitalization
was stressed by Sunday school teachers and our pastor). All this doctrinal history seemed inconsequential to me at the time, but I suppose we were well armed
to combat the charge that Lutherans were really "Catholics without a pope."
More important, the theological core of Lutheranism (and much effort was
expended in hopes that we would master the doctrine) was the way you got to
Heaven: by grace, through faith. "By grace, through faith" had a nice ring to it,
and those of us in catechism class could say these words in our sleep. But what
did they really mean?

Our parents, Sunday school teachers, and pastor resorted to analogies to help
us understand the crucial doctrine. My favorite, painted by a layman exasper-
ated by our—especially my—incessant questions, involved a pit of grease (God's
ever-present grace surrounding us) with us (or was it our faith?) the object getting fried. I forget the specifics now, but I realized that what Lutherans meant
by "faith" was not an instantaneous knowledge but a steady, abiding sense of
belief. None of this won us battles with the committed born-agains, who were
so certain about *their* salvation. They knew the day they accepted Christ, the
day they stood before the congregation and proclaimed this acceptance, the
day they were baptized. In contrast, we were schooled in our faith on the basis

of our age. After eight weeks of classes directed by the pastor, after you passed the exam, you participated in a liturgical ceremony in which you confirmed the promises your parents made in your stead when you were baptized. It was not nearly as dramatic as our evangelical counterparts. At some point, most of us Lutheran kids just gave up verbal sparring. The eyeball roll and sigh, if delivered with the appropriate flourishes, were our best weapons. There was nothing worse to our enemies than a person seemingly indifferent to these matters.

Because of the family into which I was born, Lutheranism was more than something you did on Sunday: it was our heritage. My paternal grandfather, the Reverend Quincy Oscar Lyerly—who understandably went by "Q.O."—was a Lutheran pastor. Before being cut down prematurely by what his descendants believe were the aftereffects of exposure to mustard gas in the Great War, Q.O. served a series of rural Carolina congregations, helping to found one church. I was in second grade when he died, but I have vivid memories of the memorial service for him, of the condolences offered by his grieving parishioners to his relatives, of the love they expressed for him. He was a member of the family. Besides Q.O., there were my maternal uncles (by marriage), Uncle Jack and Uncle Marion, who became "Rev." when you addressed a card or letter to them. As an extended family, we did not celebrate Christmas *on* the twenty-fifth, since Christmas Day was a working day for preachers. All told, of my parents' generation of relations, only one of nine families was not Lutheran. If you added up my cousins on top of that, you had the makings of a congregation whenever we had a family gathering. Even though I am not a Lutheran by faith today, I still am culturally Lutheran, and Lutheranism informs my moral views at every turn.

Mt. Olive was the church of my childhood. In those days (I was born in 1960 and left for college in 1978), Mt. Olive was lily white, yet it was, by default, ideologically left of Hickory's political center. And in the years 1960–78, the "political" was almost invariably the racial. Our pastor, Walter Hitchcock, was a Yankee who had served in Chile before the coup, and he belied the notion that only evangelicals could preach. Although his style was not demonstrative or physical (and we were silent in the pews), he had a charismatic voice and knew how to use that voice to keep his audience interested. I still recall his sermon on "eros, philos, and agape" and still remember how in the worst of the city's racial turmoil he castigated both those who opposed racial justice and those who were doing nothing to promote it. If they could hear him, the early evangelical preachers I study would undoubtedly say he spoke "too much of morality" in his sermons, but they would probably admire his style, for with his voice alone he could command a room. From him and from my parents, I learned that discrimination was wrong and that our world was impoverished by racism and bigotry.

The people of Mt. Olive could be as ugly as the wider world. When our youth group arranged for an interracial picnic in those troubled years, a threat was phoned in to the pastor. The picnic went on as scheduled. The rumors were that the phone call came from a member of Mt. Olive, and that thought was troubling to me. Weren't the racists out *there?* The members of Mt. Olive could be beautiful, too. There was Brian Anderson, with a football player's build and a salesperson's handshake, the most patient and good-natured soul I have ever had the pleasure to meet. Brian was great with the teenagers, and he made it a point to speak to most of us each Sunday, remembering enough about our interests to connect, understanding enough about our adolescent dislocation to avoid those prickly subjects that would highlight our awkward approach to adulthood. The connections he nurtured were all the more precious because they were born of a simple commitment to make Mt. Olive a home. After he lost all his hair from chemotherapy, he was still his booming self, still hunting us down on the Sundays we came home for the weekend from college. He did not have the sort of head on which one would say bald looks good, but it was wonderful on him because it represented the hope that he would survive. He did not, and all of Mt. Olive mourned him.

We had to drive across town to get to church, and many members lived outside of our neighborhood, but they were part of our community. Every Sunday, Pastor Hitchcock would read the list of members to be prayed for, and as he read the name of someone hospitalized, the adults would turn to each other, whispering a "I hope the cancer hasn't returned" or "She wasn't looking well the last time I saw her." There were the Younts (too many to count and often hard to keep straight if you weren't a Yount), and you could usually depend on a Yount showing up for a funeral or a wedding that took place at Mt. Olive, even if they had not known the folks well. Odell Moose was there every Sunday, often serving as stand-in usher or lay reader (and now he fills in as supervisor of the nursery). And Thelma the organist was a permanent fixture of my childhood Sundays. One rarely spoke with Mrs. Jarvis (she played preludes and postludes, and we were usually in the line to shake the pastor's hand by the time she finished), and I imagined her, because of the thunder and roar of the organ, a formidable woman. Her daughter went on to become a big-city opera soloist, but she would return to Mt. Olive every Christmas Eve for the candlelight service, to sing "O Holy Night" so angelically she always stunned the packed congregation. Becky Psioda and the Arndts, the Seabocks, and the Sigmons were fixtures at Mt. Olive. We constituted a community not by virtue of our common interests or even our doctrinal similarity. We were a community because we worked to make it so.

I have spoken with a number of academics who have only miserable memories of their childhood churches or family faiths. Scholars raised with anti-intellectual creeds, in misogynist traditions, or in dogmatic congregations have understandable grievances. But being Lutheran was not difficult for bookish kids. Take evolution, for example. When we broached the subject in school, a number of my classmates were uneasy or angry, and the angriest were the smart kids who had been taught in their churches that evolution was a humanist lie. Lutherans did not have to choose between our teachers and pastors, between religion and science. Our faith was abundantly liberal and pliant to allow us to draw our own conclusions in almost every controversy, as long as they were grounded in the Lutheran ideals of justice, love, and charity. Nor did our faith lend itself to self-loathing or to shame. As children, we were not given a long list of do's and don'ts; guilt was not emphasized as a social construct but as a matter of individual conscience.

Lutherans, I have often heard, do not know their Bibles. And that is true enough (leave the clergy out, they do). I certainly did not. I learned some Old Testament stories, taught as moral fables, in vacation Bible school, and between Sunday school and sermons, the gospels were familiar. What I did not know, until I had to read the Bible more closely for my dissertation, was how much of it made a poor fit with the temper and character of Lutheran faith. It seemed that if a text did not conform to modern notions of love and justice, Lutherans would simply historicize it and claim that any moral guidelines in that text were only true for a specific time and place. Because the Lutherans I knew were not dogmatic, because of their commitment to justice and charity, my loss of faith was not traumatic, nor did it precipitate a family crisis. I never had to rebel against the religion of my parents, and I retain an abiding respect for their beliefs. It must be far harder for them than for me, for the Lutheran style is not to harangue or to condemn, not even to use guilt as a wedge. They continue to tell me how much they wish I would go to church (and here is a revealingly Lutheran sentiment: any church, they sometimes add), and I try not to slip up and mention I went to the Sunday matinee.

Mt. Olive also remains a good memory for me, in large part because the church has adapted since I was a child. The two ministerial candidates the congregation currently supports at the seminary are women, and Mt. Olive has had a number of women vicars. But back then, I knew, as all girls had to know, that women could not be preachers. Women did not serve as ushers or girls as acolytes. I was in my late teens before women assisted the pastor with the communion service. Few women served on the church council, and only girls and women were tasked with managing the nursery. The gender divisions were not all stark—the choir was mixed and usually directed by a woman, the lay readers were sometimes women, and women taught Sunday school and vacation Bible school classes. Women were ubiquitous in the church bulletin, in the schedules for the many women's groups or the lists of those thanked for the flower arrangements, serving a supper, or sewing a banner. For vacation Bible school, the women's circles made refreshments. For homecoming, they coordinated the potluck that followed the service. Much of their ministry was with food, whether in taking supper to a family in mourning or proudly bringing their favorite dish to a special dinner. Women did the detailed needlework for the communion cushions, and they baked the bread for that service, too. More adult women than men were in the pews each Sunday, but a future historian who looks at the membership roster may not realize that. Members were (and are) listed in family groups, and a number of men who rarely came to church with their wives and children are nonetheless on the roster. Some men worked on Sundays, to be sure, but others were playing golf or sleeping in—I know this because their wives admitted it. Women were everywhere and nowhere, present but invisible. They were the workers, men the leaders—if that was not the intention, it was the unspoken message. I gave the treatment of women in Mt. Olive little thought at the time, because the church only mirrored the wider world.

The women's movement was in full flower, but Hickory seemed to be unaffected by it. Leadership was gendered in almost every segment of the city. Principals were men, even in elementary schools where women were the majority of teachers. The school board had one woman at some point, but otherwise the city government was male. Women worked in sales, men in management, women as secretaries, men as corporate presidents. There were some hints of change, but too few to have confidence that feminism would triumph. We bookish girls read Faulkner, not Virginia Woolf, Eudora Welty, not Marge Piercy. We knew some of the issues. We knew that one feminist critique was of the gendered division of domestic labor, and in our own homes we saw that this was all too well the case. Some vowed never to lose their independence in marriage, and some of us confidently predicted we would find male feminists to marry. Yet while we recognized that the pull between career and home, between self and family, would be central to our later lives, we never discussed in depth why only women seemed to have to choose. Our parents were influenced enough by feminism to encourage our educational and career ambitions, but not influenced enough to alter the gender roles they had adopted. Thus while on the one hand we were told we could be "anything we wanted to be," we tacitly concluded that career ambitions would complicate, if not ruin, our chances for the family life we accepted as a normal aspect of growing up. We had precious few role models to look to for guidance. One high school teacher had been awakened by the movement and had gotten divorced (tellingly, we had no personal knowledge of the order of these two events but assumed feminism had precipitated the divorce), and her example seemed only to confirm the anti-feminists' warning that feminism and families did not mix.

Still, we could talk some of the talk. We wanted, at sixteen, to be called "Ms." We were on the watch for sexist jokes, language, and behavior. We were vocal about our views inside the classroom and out. We declaimed against the way Fitzgerald portrayed women in *Gatsby* and the unabashed machismo in Hemingway. I took the fight home, too. In the innocent arrogance only an adolescent can muster, I took my stand one Thanksgiving holiday when I found my aunts and my mother in the kitchen washing dishes—after they had baked the meal, served their younger children, and set out the dessert. I told the women that they were being oppressed and then marched into the den where the men watched football and debated politics with them. (I did not, however, accuse my father and uncles of being oppressors.) I and several of my friends compared holiday encounters, and we made a pact not to learn to cook, as if that would assure us a happy and liberated future. Putting these glimmerings of nascent feminism together in these paragraphs is deceptive. We were far less conscious of our gender than we were of our race. One of our heroes, Barbara Jordan, served on the Watergate investigative committee with North Carolina's own Sam Ervin Jr., and Carolina voters kept returning Jesse Helms to office. Both Helms and Ervin were what we called "dinosaurs" about women, but they were far more dangerous to blacks than to white girls. The pressing issue of our youth was not feminism but racial justice.

My parents were schoolteachers, and thus school desegregation was a constant subject of our family discussions. My father, a high school coach, was deeply embroiled in the controversies throughout my childhood. For small towns, varsity sports were (and still are) one of the only recreational activities, a rallying point for civic pride, and a source of local chauvinism. Besides latent white fears of blacks' athletic superiority (inextricably bound up with the vintage racist notion that whites were the natural intellectuals and blacks the natural laborers), there was the simple and unavoidable fact that athletic competition involved physical contact. The deep-seated phobias unleashed by this knowledge turned sport into an arena vested with symbolic and real potential for undermining the anti-integrationist rationale. Without claiming that athletes are "above" the prejudices of society, it is still the case that team sport ideally requires that players suspend individual ambitions and animosities for the benefit of the whole. If black and white players actually got along, if in such a meaning-laden environment desegregation worked, then the racists' predictions that civilization would end were wrong. Because Hickory High desegregated before Charlotte schools and because the schools in the surrounding counties were all-white, mixed-race Hickory teams were playing largely all-white teams (there was one all-black Charlotte school they occasionally played) for most of these tense years. There were times when the police had to escort the Hickory players to their bus through hostile crowds, times when the Hickory players suited up in a chemistry lab rather than risk the mob waiting outside the locker room.

Funny how memory works. Some years ago, I finally asked my father about the game in which he earned two consecutive technical fouls. In my mind, he was still embarrassed about it; the game *had* been too close to call before he erupted in anger, handing the victory to the opposing team. In my mind, the incident became confused with a more famous display of coaching temper: I "remembered" my father, in a fit of rage, throwing a folding chair onto the court. No, Dad tells me. That was Bobby Knight. My father earned his two technicals by yelling at the referee, and he was not in the least embarrassed about it. Hickory was playing an away game with an all-white county team. The referees, picked by the county school, had made a collective vow to harass Hickory's black players. They whispered racist remarks in the players' ears, called unmerited fouls on them, and seemed to be waiting for a player to argue back. In the final tense minutes of the game, a ref called a foul on Hickory's best black player. The young man looked at the ref, pointed to his own chest, and mouthed "Me?" That gesture was rewarded with a second foul, this one a technical. Both to prevent his player from being blamed for the defeat and to vent the wrath that had been building through the night, Dad demanded the ref explain the foul. "I didn't like the way he was looking at me," was the answer. My father called the ref an idiot, earning his first technical, which only made my dad angrier and louder, earning him the second. Hickory lost, and some of the fans (unaware of what had happened) blamed my father for being hot-tempered. Although I did not understand this particular incident at the time, the values I had been taught at home were quietly reinforced by the teamwork of the varsity basketball players, by their respect for each other and for my father. I admired those young men, black and white. They were strong, beautiful, and talented, and they had a dignity and grace the racists could never understand and never, ever, possess. These young men sustained my hope for a just and humane world.

Hickory city schools were slow to desegregate, and they desegregated gradually, beginning with the upper grades. Administrators handled the process of desegregation as if they were determined to exact a high cultural cost from African Americans. The two existing high schools were Hickory High (white) and Ridgeview High (black); Ridgeview was closed, and with that move black students lost their mascot, their school colors, their school song, and control of the elective student offices. Rather than school officials compromising or creating new symbols, black students were now Tornadoes (instead of Panthers), their colors were now garnet and "old gold" (instead of purple and gold), and the unofficial school song was now "Dixie." Black students, their community stripped of one of its central sources of racial pride, were made to feel like unwelcome intruders at the "white" school. Some teachers pleaded with school officials to institute programs for fostering interracial understanding. The schools were, after all, being asked to do what the wider society had proved unwilling and unable to accomplish. Neighborhoods, churches, and businesses were still thoroughly segregated. Children were supposed to miraculously divest themselves of their parents', the city's, and their own prejudices for eight hours a day? Perhaps administrators did not *want* desegregation to work. The conclusion sounds paranoid, but it is hard not to believe that there is an element of truth in it.

I first had black classmates in junior high (which was, in Hickory, grades seven to nine), and there were no educational programs to prepare us for the transition. My parents talked to me about racism and about the schools' racial problems, and only through them did I learn that the transition would be far harder for African Americans than for us. Many of my (white) classmates in sixth grade expected nothing but strife, crime, and trouble on entering the seventh grade. We would be held up by black kids in the bathroom. We would be beaten up by them. We would be held back by them academically. They hated us. It was a neat trick, this sort of talk, for it turned those of us with color privilege into victims. I wonder what the black kids were saying about us. Some churches did step into the breach and attempt to foster good will and positive understanding. If Pastor Hitchcock's uncompromising sermons did not end bigotry in the congregation, they at least deprived racism of respectability and shamed it underground.

Racial tensions festered for years before the race riot of 1976, but the specific conflict originated in the unwillingness of many Hickory whites to make desegregation work. Their reaction to the protests against "Dixie" as the school song was paradigmatic. White anti-integrationists rallied at the Community Center to declaim against the effort to do away with "our song" and "our traditions." In fact, "Hail to Thee, O Hickory High" was the official school song, a tune as uninspiring and as unsingable as it was difficult for the band to play. The band director, on his own initiative, had switched to "Dixie" instead. (Can the choice of "Dixie" during the years the city school system was being sued by African Americans have been coincidental?) But these Community Center stalwarts were not to be swayed by historical truth. Black "militance" (African American students had staged a sit-in over this and other issues of parity) had to be suppressed, and it was high time for whites to take a stand about how much they were willing to adapt (which was, for these folks, not much at all.) To African American students and to some whites, "Dixie" was unacceptable as a school song, and the intransigence of the anti-integrationists only heightened our belief that their stand was a protest against *any* change in race relations, a desire to return to the "old times . . . not forgotten," when black and white were separate and all whites had power over all blacks. Parents passed on these views to their children, and for weeks some angry white boys came to school ready for any excuse to fight. And some frustrated and angry black boys were all too happy to oblige them. There had been shouting matches, racist graffiti, and threats passed back and forth, but most of us did not realize a major confrontation was brewing.

It was absurd, the incident that inadvertently started the riot. Some weeks later, the nonrioting majority were finally able to joke about the precipitating event, even though the riot itself was never a laughing matter. Our lunchroom was small, so we had two lunch periods. During "first lunch," a biscuit tossed to a friend by a boy of one color landed on the plate of a boy of a different color, and a scuffle ensued. Nothing overtly racial to it. Boys sometimes fight over silly matters of turf. In 1976 in Hickory, though, when a black boy and a white boy did battle, it was on some level *always* a racial incident. Both young men were taken to the principal's office, where, ironically, they made up. But in the meantime, word began to spread among the frustrated and angry; during "second lunch," the riot began. I, a "first luncher," was in class, oblivious, when the bell rang for changing classes. We poured out onto the balcony of the second floor, which overlooked a large open mall we used for assemblies and pep rallies, and peered down onto a mass of our male peers in a giant confrontation. Some of the rioters had chairs; others ran outside to find weapons, returning with bricks that were set aside for a new "Hickory High" sign that was under construction. And my father was in the middle of it, trying to pull boys apart, commanding them to put down bricks or chairs. Miraculously, many did; such was the authority of the coach. Except for a few girls who clashed on the periphery, the riot was all male. Most girls (and most boys, for that matter) just whispered, shouted, and screamed as they watched. We were not surprised by the racial nature of it, but we were shocked at the intensity with which the boys below us flailed at each other.

The police were called in, three young men were hospitalized, and the riot made the headlines of the *Charlotte Observer* (although they euphemistically termed it a "melee"). We had no school the next day, and for some time afterward we had an abbreviated schedule that ended before lunch. Cops and clergymen patrolled our hallways. The next year, the school board brought in a tough, no-nonsense principal who instituted what we students considered a semifascist regime. No hats, no shorts, no going off-campus for lunch. Worse, the outer doors to the restrooms were removed (to prevent students both from smoking and from making trouble inside them), and we needed a hall pass to use them. Order prevailed and learning went on, but I find it telling that instead of addressing the problems that led to the riot, the official response was to create a physical environment in which another riot could not take place. Some churches made overtures across the racial divide; some drama students put on a play about tolerance. Too few gestures, too late. In the annals of race riots, I realize the one at Hickory High hardly merits serious standing. But it was gravely serious to me and my classmates, and it was the definitive incident of my youth. I was compelled then and still am now by the need to understand how teenagers were ready to wound and kill each other right before my eyes.

College dispelled any wide-eyed notions I might have had that racial harmony would emerge naturally from a well-educated populace. The University of North Carolina was as segregated as Hickory High had been. Separate fraternities and sororities, separate tables at the student center, different bars, different music. The only sign of improvement was the entire student body's worship of the basketball team, which, my senior year, included Sam Perkins, James Worthy, and Michael Jordan, and I likely measured this as progress because of my perception, born of my personal history, that sport was the agent of interracial progress.

College men and women were having their share of problems by 1978. Sex, romance, and love were as much a part of the curriculum as English lit and chemistry, but feminism was in full flower, and everyday life became politicized when one least expected it. My creative writing class seemed to be a major battleground in the gender wars, perhaps because we were urged to write honestly. A short story by a fraternity brother about his efforts to seduce a woman he met at a keg party sent the women of the class into a rage. One feminist called the story a "typical male masturbatory fantasy"; the men, feeling attacked as a group, responded in kind. The women rallied around our spokeswoman, and the yelling got so loud our teacher sent us home early. Self-identified liberals discovered that courtship was suddenly a minefield. If he held the door open for you, was this some indication of a deep-seated desire for masculine dominance? If he paid for dinner, were you betraying your values? Male sympathizers had no easy time of it, either. To compliment a woman's appearance or figure could in one context be a boon to courtship but in another could become a retrograde sexist remark. When males did not share our rage, we accused them of being part of the problem. And they did not understand why we seemed to blame them for things they felt they were not responsible for.

The simplest questions provoked long and heated debates because the answers were bound up with our fury over inequality, our anxieties over how feminism might affect our relationships, homophobia, and the gnawing fear that if we did away with the traditional definitions of manhood and womanhood, we would have to find a new path through the debris of the past. There were absolutists among us, feminists who held that to shave, marry, or have children was to surrender to the patriarchy, but if "the feminist" was simply the antithesis of "the lady," were we not returning to a dogmatism just as pernicious as the one we were fighting? We knew all too well that we were bounded by the very values we sought to change, that our imaginations were limited by the culture in which we had grown up. We met the Southern Lady at every turn, if only to hold her up, in desperate moments, as the epitome of what we did not want to be. We knew what our political agenda was but not how to apply feminism to our daily lives. We were southerners who were not used to imagining structural change, much less revolution. Having grown up in the era of desegregation, we found it difficult to summon easy optimism. We had learned how resistant attitudes were to change, and because feminism wed the personal and the political, attitudes would have to change for feminism to survive. So we marched in support of the Equal Rights Amendment, petitioned to keep abortion safe and legal, and held candlelight vigils for the victims of domestic violence, and although we believed passionately in these causes, we wondered what the future held in store for us.

My immediate future upon graduation was signed away in an army recruiter's office. The job market for Ph.D.s was bleak. Because I spoke Russian and passed the intelligence services test, a four-year stint would net me an educational fund of $27,000 to use for graduate school (after which the market would undoubtedly improve, I hoped). My best friend's father had been a Russian intelligence analyst and had only fond memories of his army years. He served when intelligence units were part of the Army Security Agency, and ASA soldiers did not wear uniforms and would not know which end of a rifle to hold if they had to fire one. That sounded like my kind of army. The more I discussed the option, the more veterans (all served pre-Vietnam) I met who claimed that they had learned priceless "life lessons" in the service. Above all, the military promised excitement and adventure. My folks did not have the money to send me on the "grand tour," but the army did. I could see the world. What I did not know was that the ASA was defunct and that the new army policy was that everyone was a "soldier first" and a "specialist second." Or that my first stop on the grand tour would be Fort Polk, Louisiana, which I deemed a very unlikely place for the Soviets to begin their takeover of the United States.

Basic training was unquestionably the most difficult two months—physically, psychologically, and socially—I have ever survived. The drill sergeants sought to break us down and leave us empty, the void to be filled with discipline and esprit de corps. I did become more disciplined, and we trainees *did* turn to each other. We believed that no one (even those who had been through basic before us) could understand what we were being asked to endure. I was lucky that one of my drill sergeants, a giant Vietnam veteran, took me under his wing. He nicknamed me "But Sergeant" because of my habit of asking "But Sergeant, why?" about army policies and procedures that did not lend themselves to rational analysis. I was incapable of doing a single proper push-up when I first arrived at Fort Leonard Wood, was (and still am) a slob by nature, and have never been good at following orders without question. On graduation day, I asked why he had bothered with me. He smiled and told me his story. When he enlisted, he was an Alabama kid of seventeen without much muscle, without a high school diploma, and with a burning hatred for "the Man." A black six-foot-two teenage rural Alabamian with "attitude" was safer, his parents said, in Vietnam than at home. And, he added, he had learned in Vietnam that the army needed more soldiers who asked questions, just like it needed more soldiers with "attitude."

The lesson I learned in basic training was that under enough pressure and stress, the divisions of race, gender, sexuality, class, and education can become irrelevant, especially when there is a common enemy. The sergeant we feared the most was the aptly named Sergeant Cruell, who, though a black woman, had no sense of sisterhood with any female trainees, even the black ones. Another drill sergeant, a lesbian, drove the lesbians in our unit harder than the rest of us. The company commander (the most educated in our chain of command) verbally berated me when I was running or doing push-ups. ("Whatcha gonna do, Lyerly? Wave your diploma at the enemy? Give me twenty more!") We were the lowest of the low, but we were united in our mutual hatred and our shared misery. The practice of punishing all of us for the sins of one worked miracles. Because a woman was caught smoking in the bathroom, our entire platoon was rousted out of bed in the middle of the few precious hours they let us sleep and forced to do midnight runs three nights in a row. Night three, as we were running in a downpour, our drill sergeants shouting the surreal, "Soldiers, don't get wet!" we decided to take corrective action of our own. We instituted a warning system so that whoever was breaking a rule (and there were rules for every trivial thing) would know the moment a drill sergeant started up the stairs to the floor we bunked on. An athlete became my personal push-up trainer, I tutored the trainees who had trouble with the classroom portion of basic, and we took turns helping a woman who had grown up without indoor plumbing and electricity with her ironing, washing, and personal hygiene. We transcended our differences for those months and became a team.

But the army was then, and still seems to be, obsessed with sex, and in the military I first learned how gender was socially constructed. In intelligence units, where everyone had security clearances, the chain of command was obsessed with homosexuality. The policy of discharging gays and lesbians affected all soldiers, but especially all women. Good soldiers who also happen to be women are tough and fit and, when need be, mean. Consider, too, the fact that the army officially discourages "feminine" vanity by strictly regulating makeup, hair, and clothing. The most damning insult one can make to an infantryman is that "a woman" can run faster, shoot better, or do more push-ups than he, an insult that implies "a woman" is by nature a poor soldier. Women who wanted to succeed had to be "one of the guys." And when the witch hunts began, it was precisely these women who were accused of lesbianism. The slacker who always complained that changing the oil in her Deuce-and-a-half (a two-and-a-half-ton truck) made her nails dirty and who was despised by her peers and commanders alike was never swept up in the hysteria. Women who met the highest standards were thus considered "masculine" and in danger of being persecuted as lesbians, while the worst female soldiers were "feminine" and proved that "real" women did not belong in the military. Ambitious and tough straight women worriedly paraded their boyfriends or dates at the barracks. Tellingly, one of the compliments a skilled female soldier often received then (that she had a "big pair") conferred upon her male genitalia. For army women, homophobia and misogyny were inextricably linked.

In intelligence units, the ratio of women to men sometimes approached one to one. In the army at large, of course, women were a decided minority. I served a year at Fort Polk, Louisiana, where there were at least a thousand men to every woman. My platoon and company were not sexist-free zones, but they were a refuge from the casual misogyny of the rest of the post. Most of the examples I could give would necessitate using language that makes civilians cringe, but one I can mention is the commander's policy on swimwear. On Fort Polk, female soldiers were forbidden to wear swimming suits when they laid out in the sun. The post commander, in his memorandum about the new regulation, explained that he was trying to prevent rape. It was true that misogyny too easily shaded into violence, and that there were an astounding number of rapes, both reported and unreported, on that post. But how a general who believed that he could stop rape by banning bikinis wound up in charge of the equivalent of a small city (where all the inhabitants were well armed and trained) is beyond my comprehension. Despite such an official atmosphere, I served with many men who did not care that I was a woman as long as I did my job well. Most of my commanders and platoon sergeants were decent and equitable. My fellow soldiers could be coarse and used sexist language so often that it lost its power to wound, but they, too, were more concerned that I did my job than that I was a woman. As in basic training, we were a unit first, individuals second. And should someone outside the unit attempt to make a sexist remark, my male colleagues were as quick with the reproof as I was. Institutional cultures do not necessarily determine the day-to-day interactions within that institution.

Outside the relative haven of my units, I became acutely conscious of being a woman. I did not walk around, in high school or college, thinking that my gender was the central aspect of my being. It was hard not to come to that conclusion in the military. I now try to remember, in my teaching and scholarship, the way people emphasize different aspects of their identity in different contexts. One of my black army supervisors was a fundamentalist Christian, and the first day I was assigned to him, he announced that a woman's place was in the home, adding that he also believed in following orders, however wrongheaded they were. All women in his unit were treated with equal condescension. During my tour in West Berlin, there were moments when I was no longer the unwelcome gender, but an American, moments when it did not matter that I came from a family of modest income, or was a southerner, or even that I was white. To some Germans, as well as to the terrorists who bombed a disco in which soldiers from my unit were dancing, we in uniform were representatives of our government. Whether tourists or soldiers, any American could become a symbol of corporate greed, of militarism, of nuclear proliferation, or of a threat to German culture.

After eight years in the army (I reenlisted to extend my time overseas), graduate school was a delight. Because I had been obsessed with gender for so long, I resolved, at first, not to study women. But my mentor at Rice University, John Boles (who has requested I not discuss him but whose influence on me was and is profound), infected me with his enthusiasm for southern religious history. Here, indeed, were problems of race, class, values, identity, and, inescapably, gender. As I worked on my first seminar paper for him—an analysis of sermon texts by early Methodist preachers—I found women everywhere. I was stunned by how active these women were in the church, at how assertive they were about their faith. They were not hidden, not even peripheral; they were not southern ladies and were not like the church women of my childhood.

Part of what intrigued me about the early Methodists was the fact that they were so different from the twentieth-century Lutherans I knew. But I still brought Lutheran sensibilities to my work. Boles, with his extensive knowledge of southern religious history, kept me grounded. I recall a chapter draft of my dissertation in which I was analyzing the importance of Methodist wives' conversions of their erstwhile scoffing husbands. My points were good ones. Because the ethos of the church was vastly at odds with the southern male culture of honor, a wife turned family evangelist could expect significant behavioral changes in her husband after his conversion, changes the culture of the time deemed feminine. I pondered the significance of the wife as moral leader, emphasizing how often Methodists told the stories of their conversions, how the wife's leadership would be reasserted in each telling. Boles did not disagree with these and other conclusions. But in the margin of the text, he asked a simple, and wry, question: "Perhaps they wanted to save their husbands' souls, too?" It was an embarrassing omission, especially since I had stressed, in a previous chapter, the centrality of the Methodists' belief in free will to their conversion-oriented faith, yet it was an error in keeping with a Lutheran orientation to religion.

Early Methodists were acutely conscious of their sectarian identity, and this identity profoundly shaped their lives and perceptions in direct and immediate ways. What Lutheranism had meant to me was far more abstract, far more diffuse. I was reared in the family faith; most early Methodists converted as adolescents or adults, and many broke with their family faiths in the process. I was raised in an era in which identities were less fixed, when gender and race were being redefined and reexamined. Early Methodists, however, experienced race and gender as immutable facts that permanently defined a person. Religion was one of the only aspects of their identity that they could control. Methodism enabled them to create a part of the self that was not solely predetermined by the South in which they lived.[2]

Small wonder that they were sometimes able to transcend their differences and band together—as Methodists. They had a strong theological basis for their unity; the church taught its members to be separate from the world and, through rituals and values, nurtured communal solidarity. And the "enemies" Methodists faced were legion: people and pleasures of the world, those in their families and communities who persecuted them, and the religious of different doctrine who scorned them. Yet Methodists were not extricated from the familiar and placed in a controlled environment, as we were in basic training. What rendered Methodist unity fragile was the fact that they could not *be* completely separate. After services and love feasts, classes and camp meetings, Methodists returned to homes, neighborhoods, and plantations where their worldview was rarely dominant. Ultimately, the values of the wider southern world crept into the church, especially into its white members. Still, early Methodists could (and did) transcend southern culture and convention. Some of them dared to hope, just as I had in my youth, that the future was open to change, even radical change. Considering how rigid the boundaries of race and class must have seemed in the late eighteenth century, I now appreciate the power of religion to expand imaginative universes. And although many of even the most radical dreamers fatalistically surrendered to an intransigent South, elements of Methodism seeped into southern culture, too.

As life influences scholarship, so scholarship influences life. The more I study southern religious women, the more I question my teenage interpretation of the women of Mt. Olive. I never considered how deep their influence was in the congregation or how profoundly the experience of worship was shaped by their gifts and service. From the organ music to the handstitched communion cushions, their gifts brought dignity and beauty to the services. Their roles were pastoral, too, whether in taking food to a grieving family or visiting shut-ins. I always knew my mother was a craftswoman and artist who, had she had the resources, could have made a career of her hobby. Now that she has retired from teaching elementary school, she dedicates much of her artistic talent to the church. The tablecloths she made for the fellowship hall and the banner she designed and crafted for the capital campaign bear witness to her love for the church community and her dedication to her faith. She served on the last pastoral search committee and has given (because of her expertise with youth) many a children's sermon at Mt. Olive over the years. Because I matured in the era of feminism, it was difficult for me to uncouple my loathing of institutional sexism from my interpretation of women's church work. We scholars sometimes write as if the pastor and male administrators define a congregation's religious experience. But that was not the case for early Methodists, and it was not the case, I subsequently realized, for Mt. Olive Lutheran Church. The lived religion of the congregation bore the unmistakable imprint of the women in the pews. And because the wider world has changed, women of a different generation will bring other talents to the church, as does the current associate pastor.

My new project continues my quest to understand how race and gender intersected with and were shaped by religion in the southern past. While writing my first book I was constantly struck by the fact (as were many historians before me) that in those years the rational-leaning and high-church denominations were the least tolerant and the most committed to dominant southern mores, almost the inverse of what I experienced in the 1970s. Growing up, I had assumed there was a connection between rationalism and social justice, but the early Methodists, who were certainly not rationalists, were more committed to social justice than their high church contemporaries. I also observed, in researching that first book, the way defenders of rational religion quickly moved from denunciations of enthusiastic and revelatory religiosity to disparaging generalizations about the "natures" of women and African Americans. By exploring the debates over reason and revelation in the eighteenth-century South, I now hope to trace and analyze how the religious controversies of the era shaped the discourses of both race and gender. Even early in the project, I can see how dialectical the process was; the discourses of race and gender also influenced the debates over reason and revelation. I can glimpse the roots of the belief that religion is "woman's work" even in the decades when women were not assumed to be naturally more pious than men. What I have to struggle to remember is that, in the early eighteenth century, reason was not yet associated with a progressive social agenda or even a vague humanitarianism. The "rational religion" of my family and upbringing bears only liturgical and stylistic resemblance to the "rational religion" of the early South.

I am awed by (and a little envious of) scholars who have for their work a passion that is purely intellectual. For me, my work is bound up with my life experiences, and the questions I ask in my scholarship are versions of ones that I have been asking for years. I do not find, in the 1700s, answers to questions I posed in my youth. The South of my work is too distant for that, the people I study too unfamiliar. But I often see their southernness, even if it is not the same as my own, even if it is not the same as Faulkner's.

Perhaps it is typical of liberals of my generation, but I don't know whether to lament how far we have yet to go or to celebrate how far we have come. We could all use a little more of the early Methodists' perfectionism. For them, the self and, by extension, the South and the world were always a work-in-progress. To be sure, they could get discouraged. But they did not abandon the effort to improve, to be pure, to be perfect. I am told that there is a plaque on a Charles River footbridge that identifies it as the one from which Quentin Compson jumped to his death. Some day, for nostalgia's sake, I will try to find it. I now realize that Quentin gave up his quest to understand the South too soon, and I no longer feel haunted by William Faulkner or his characters. Through my scholarship, I finally have a sense of southern grace.

Notes

1. I should note that we were Lutheran Church in America (LCA) Lutherans (now the Evangelical Lutheran Church in America) and not Missouri Synod Lutherans. Every adult in my extended family followed the words "Missouri Synod Lutherans" with some pursed-lip remark about how they were "like the fundamentalists," "like the Baptists," or "extremely conservative."

2. My revised dissertation was published as *Methodism and the Southern Mind, 1770–1810* (New York: Oxford University Press, 1998). I also published several articles in connection with my first research project: "Passion, Desire, and Ecstasy: The Experiential Religion of Southern Methodist Women, 1770–1810," in Catherine Clinton and Michele Gillespie, eds., *The Devil's Lane: Sex and Race in the Early South* (New York: Oxford University Press, 1997); "Religion, Gender, and Identity: Black Methodist Women in a Slave Society, 1770–1810," in Patricia Morton, ed., *Discovering the Women in Slavery: Emancipating Perspectives on the American South* (Athens: University of Georgia Press, 1996); "Enthusiasm, Possession, and Madness: Gender and the Opposition to Methodism in the South, 1770–1810," in Janet Coryell, Martha H. Swain, Sandra Gioia Treadway, and Elizabeth Hayes Turner, eds., *Beyond Image and Convention: Explorations in Southern Women's History*, Southern Women series, vol. 3 (Columbia: University of Missouri Press, 1998).

Contributors

FREDERICK A. BODE (Ph.D., Yale University, 1969) is a professor of history at Concordia University, Montreal, Quebec, Canada.

JOHN B. BOLES (Ph.D., University of Virginia, 1969) is William Pettus Hobby Professor of History at Rice University and Managing Editor, *Journal of Southern History*.

THOMAS E. BUCKLEY, S.J. (Ph.D., University of California at Santa Barbara, 1973) is a professor of history and convenor, Graduate Theological Seminary, Berkeley, California.

ROBERT M. CALHOON (Ph.D., Case Western University, 1964) is a professor of history at the University of North Carolina at Greensboro.

WAYNE FLYNT (Ph.D., Florida State University, 1965) is University Professor at Auburn University.

JEAN E. FRIEDMAN (Ph.D., Lehigh University, 1976) is an associate professor of history, emeritus, at the University of Georgia.

DAVID EDWIN HARRELL JR. (Ph.D., Vanderbilt University, 1962) is Breeden Eminent Scholar and professor of history at Auburn University.

SAMUEL S. HILL (Ph.D., Duke University, 1960) is professor emeritus of religious studies at the University of Florida.

E. BROOKS HOLIFIELD (Ph.D., Yale University, 1970) is a professor of American Church History at Candler School of Theology, Emory University.

LYNN LYERLY (Ph.D., Rice University, 1995) is an associate professor of history at Boston College.

ANDREW M. MANIS (Ph.D., Southern Baptist Theological Seminary, Louisville, Kentucky, 1984) is a lecturer in American history at Macon State College.

DONALD G. MATHEWS (Ph.D., Duke University, 1962) is a professor of history and American Studies at the University of North Carolina.

ALBERT J. RABOTEAU (Ph.D., Yale University, 1976) is Putnam Professor of Religion at Princeton University.

JOHN SHELTON REED (Ph.D., Columbia University, 1971) is William Rand Kenan Jr. Professor of Sociology at the University of North Carolina and director of the Howard W. Odum Institute for Research in Social Science.

MITCHELL SNAY (Ph.D., Brandeis University, 1985) is an associate professor of history at Denison University.

CHARLES REAGAN WILSON (Ph.D., University of Texas, 1977) is a professor of history and director of the Center for the Study of Southern Culture at the University of Mississippi.